Fly Fishing FOR BONEFISH

Fly Fishing FOR

BONEFISH

DICK BROWN

L&B

LYONS & BURFORD, PUBLISHERS
NEW YORK

Design by Ruth Kolbert

Printed in the United States of America

10 9 8 7 6 5 4 3

Library of Congress Cataloging–in–Publication Data

Brown, Dick, 1942–
    Fly fishing for bonefish/Dick Brown.
            p.   cm.
    Includes bibliographical references and index.
    ISBN 1–55821–203–5
    1. Bonefishing.   2. Bonefish.   3. Fly fishing.   I. Title.
    SH691. B6B76   1993   93–4223
    799. 1'751 — dc20   CIP

Photographs by Carol Wright
Illustrations by Bob White

For Joe and for Carol
No man ever had a truer guide
or a surer partner

CONTENTS

Acknowledgments

Since I have never written a book before, I had no idea how much a writer depends on other people to produce one. The effort and time spent by others on this little volume astounded me. Even more surprising was the willingness of contributors and advisors to give freely of their knowledge and insight to a work that would have someone else's name on it. I am humbled by their generosity and grateful for it.

I wish to express my deepest gratitude to three men who gave me the courage to begin the book in the first place: Frank Woolner for being the grandest mentor and the kindest snag-catcher ever. Bill Tapply for believing in me — even before I did myself — and for always being there throughout the toughest days; his clear eye and steady hand were not afraid to give the rarest gift of all — honesty. And Nick Lyons. How does one acknowledge this quiet, unpretentious man who, at a time and place in life when other men find nothing left to prove, still bets on dark horses — simply because he believes in them? How, indeed.

For help on bonefish behavior and habits, I owe much to Dr. Douglas Colton. He gave me access to published and unpublished research, advised me on my conclusions, and took time from his very busy career to comment on the bonefish and prey chapters of the manuscript. I thank Donald Erdman for his unpublished research on feeding behavior and for his conversations and advice on feeding in windward reef areas. I am grateful to David Camp for help with the chapter on what bonefish eat, and to Gerard Bruger for his research and correspondence on their growth rates and feeding habits in the Florida Keys.

I want to thank all the anglers and guides I have fished with, talked with, and learned from over the years — especially those in the Bahamas and Keys. I appreciate also the fishermen, guides, professional tiers, and other fly designers who found time to tie and send me samples of their creations for the pattern section of the book. I am obliged to A.K. Best, Tim Borski, George Hommell, Jim McVay, Pete Perinchief, Carl Richards, Kate and Bill Howe, Phil Taylor, Bill Hunter, Jeffrey Cardenas, Ben Estes, Jack Gartside, Lefty Kreh, Craig Mathews, Bob Nauheim, and Jim Orthwein. The latter seven also agreed to appear in the book's "experienced angler" section in Chapter 14 along with four other flats veterans: Vic Gaspeny, Joe Cleare, Jim O'Neill, and Charlie Neymour — I am greatly indebted to them all.

For information on travel and destinations, I thank Chip Bates, Doug Schlink, Bob Nauheim, Bill Goehring, and Mike and Susie Fitzgerald. I am grateful to Nick Wilder, Dave Beshara, Al Bovyn, and Bill Sullivan for help with equipment. I also want to thank Steve Abel for his insight in determining reel rpm rates, his thoughts on reel drag dynamics, and his wonderful stories about Christmas Island. Additional help with equipment and product specifications came from John Harder at Lamson, Larry Valentine of Valentine Reels, Bruce Richards of Scientific Anglers, Andy Sonnek at Cortland, Joe Fisher of Fisher Rods, Frank Gasparach of G. Loomis, Alan Bramley of Partridge Hooks, Klaus Kjelstrup of Mustad, Bill Munro of Ande, and Bill Wohl of Dupont.

I thank Bob O'Shaughnessy, Val Atkinson, Andy Anderson, and Nick Wilder for advice on photography. Thanks also to Jeff Fox and Jay Morgan for underwater work. And a very special thanks goes to David Mishkin, Joe Kolko, and Tracey Mosseau at Just Black and White for their excellent work and for delivering all the black-and-white prints on time.

For helping me track down endless reports, research papers, records, and other data, I am grateful for the help of the late Elwood Harry and of Michael Leech of the International Game Fish Association, Rosalie Schaffer of the National Marine Fisheries Service Library in Panama City, Dr. Roy Crabtree of the Florida Marine Research Institute, Dr. C. Richard Robins of the Rosensteil School of Marine and Atmospheric Sciences, L. Wayne Landrum at Biscayne National Park, Fritz Stoppelbein of the Florida League of Anglers, Carl Minns of the Bahamas Tourist Office, Dorothy Rosenthal of the University of Miami Library, Linda MacIver of the Boston Public Library, and the librarians at Harvard University's Museum of Comparative Zoology and the Wood's Hole Marine Biological Laboratory.

I am also grateful to a number of people for helping me track down fly patterns and tiers including Mike Fong, Philip Hanyok, Eric Leiser, Ken

Menard, Bruce Olson, John Randolph, Dick Stewart, Dick Talleur, and Randy Towe. I especially want to thank Lefty Kreh and Mike Michalak, who went to great lengths to help me locate several key tiers.

For his wonderful anecdotes and help in tracing the early days in bonefishing, I thank George Reiger.

For his insightful and clear illustrations, I am grateful to Bob White. And I thank Jim Butler for his crisp copy editing and Bayard Stern for all his help guiding the manuscript through editing and production.

I wish to acknowledge several friends who graciously served as sounding boards along the way: Phil Taylor, Dick Edson, George Board, Dana De Blois, and Dick Conroy, who took the time to read, question, and suggest.

I also wish to thank a couple of close family members — my mother for her encouragement when I first began exploring the mysteries of Sawmill Pond with a fly rod thirty-five years ago, and my son Jake, for spending two weeks of his hectic life taking care of things at home while my wife and I were in the Bahamas doing the final photo session for the book.

And I must also mention Soren — my faithful shepherd-collie companion and best fishing friend on rivers from the Madison and Deschutes to the Cains and the Margaree. She spent the last year of her life lying at my feet as I worked on this manuscript, and I will never forget the companionship she gave to me every day for fourteen years.

But most of all I want to thank my wife, Carol. I fear this will appear to be just another of those gratuitous thanks-for-all-the-wifely-support recognitions writers make. But that would be a great injustice. Carol has been at the core of this book from the beginning. She was instrumental in helping me locate and examine much of the research and destination information. She took the book's photographs. She read, questioned, and advised — then read again. Most of all she lived the experience underpinning the book, fishing side by side with me on the flats. A man never had a better partner — in fishing or in life. I am forever grateful.

Finally, I want to thank "Bonefish" Joe Cleare of Harbour Island. Without his knowledge, insight, and love all these years, none of this ever would have happened.

Introduction

The sleek silver shadow streaks across the pale sand, slicing a path through the thin water as the bonefish tries to escape toward the open sea. Fly line spurts out through the rod guides and rips a jagged, turquoise scar across the placid face of the tropical flat. You raise your rod as high as you can. Your arms stretch upward to hold the line clear of the coral heads, and you bear down hard on the rod grip. You think that if you can only tighten your fingers around the cork a little more, it will slow the fish. You squeeze harder, and it is then that you sense the vibrations from the tail pulses of the frenzied fish. They hammer down through the line into your fingers — they feel like tiny heartbeats in your hand.

The fast-swimming fish is a football field away. It shows no sign of slowing. It bucks sideways, arcing to the right. Then it breeches, and you sense that it is coming back around. But just as you start to think the fish has quit, it turns back out and sprints another fifty yards. All you can do is hold on and watch the vicious pumping of your rod against the sapphire horizon.

It doesn't take many experiences like this to understand why the bonefish has become one of the most exciting and rewarding pursuits in fly fishing today. But the silver phantom has also humbled many anglers — both veterans and novices alike. I have not forgotten my own unnerving introduction to *Albula vulpes* more than fifteen years ago. Even though I had been fly fishing since I was a boy, I was totally unprepared for this unique saltwater quarry.

I had never cast to a moving fish before, and the prospect of aiming flies at

Bonefish are well-disguised predators that roam tropical inshore saltwater flats in search of bottom-dwelling prey. (Photograph by Jay Morgan.)

fast-swimming targets excited me. But my enthusiasm didn't last long. I soon found that I couldn't see a single fish — I might as well have been fishing at midnight. And even if I *had* been able to spot one of these invisible phantoms, I would not have known what to do next. I had no idea how to get a fly to the fish's level, or what action to give it, or how to play a fish that could streak through coral and mangrove shoots at twenty-five miles an hour!

I did eventually catch a fish on that first trip, in spite of all my frustrated and fumbling efforts. It was an undeserved gift from a tenacious, hardworking guide and one that I never forgot. The feel of that little fish as it screamed one hundred and fifty yards over the turtle grass began a lifelong love affair with this phantom of the flats — one that became an obsession and drove me to learn everything I could about the bonefish and its world.

I began by devouring every book and magazine article on bonefishing I could find. But I soon found myself searching for knowledge that did not exist in angling literature. I wanted to learn about bonefish anatomy, sensory abilities, and behavior. How did these spooky fish see, hear, and smell? How fast could they swim? What temperatures did they prefer? What did they eat? And how did they camouflage themselves?

Could you, I wondered, predict how they would appear in different

Stalking bonefish together creates a closer relationship between angler and guide than any other kind of fishing.

habitats and circumstances? Could you learn how to see bonefish on your own, how to read a tropical flat, how to evaluate different locations for food potential, and how to track fish by following feeding signs?

But learning about the behavior characteristics of bonefish was not enough. I also wanted to learn which angling techniques were most effective on them. Which drag-setting strategy was best? Which casting techniques should you use in a twenty-knot wind? Why did a strip-strip-and-stop retrieve pattern often work better than a continuous strip-strip-strip? Where was the best place to aim your fly to a tailing fish? Or a cruising fish? And why did a few fly patterns seem to work so much better than all the others?

The answers to many of these questions eventually came from spending a great deal of time on the flats and from the fish itself. Sometimes you learn the most in fishing if you put your rod down for a while, open your eyes, and just watch the fish.

Other answers, however, required trips to marine research libraries and conversations with ichthyologists and marine biologists who had studied bonefish, their prey, and their habitats. Still other insights — those about techniques and strategy — came from guides, other fishermen, and friends I met on the flats. Ultimately, thanks to the generosity, patience, and kindness of a great many such people, I have been able to learn most of what I set out to find.

Just when and how this personal quest for learning turned into an idea for writing a book, I do not know. But once it did, the concept took on a life of its own. It was suddenly clear that there was no single source that told anglers what they needed to know about both bonefish behavior and about bonefish angling techniques. That is what I have tried to make this book do.

If I have done my job as I intended, *Fly Fishing for Bonefish* will serve both beginning and experienced anglers alike. I tried to make it, in effect, the book that I wish I had been able to find when I began: one that is basic enough to cover the sport's fundamentals for a newcomer and one that has the depth, breadth, and richness of detail to grow with the needs of an advanced flats angler.

I have also included a fair amount of diversity in the book. For the most part, the main chapters offer my own point of view — the methods and techniques that I have found effective in bonefishing. But as I have learned more and more, I have also found there are many other valid approaches to this complex sport — some that do not always coincide with my own. So in the final chapter, I have included a number of different (and sometimes even contradictory) views on flats strategies from eleven of the most successful bonefishing veterans in the world.

You will find in this chapter that there is no single way to set your drag or to give action to your fly that is agreed to by all experienced flats anglers. But by seeing the different approaches that are used by a variety of veteran fishermen and guides, you can better decide which of them fit your own fishing strategy and style. I trust both new and older flats anglers will find this chapter useful and that it will stimulate more thinking and fresh approaches in the sport.

I hope that this book will also repay some debts to many friends — anglers, guides, and others — who have walked the flats before me. There is a special sense of fraternity among the men and women who stalk silver shadows across the saltwater flats of the world. They share an uncommon willingness to pass on to others the knowledge they have gained, and I thank all those who have helped me along the way.

Most of all, I hope this book deepens angler understanding of the bonefish and effects more protection for the fish and its environment. The bonefish's stark, prehistoric world — a place of breathtaking primal beauty — is on fragile ground today. And if we lose these mangrove and sea-grass habitats at the edge of the ocean, we lose everything. The saltwater flats, like the rain forests, are the sentinels of our future. We should heed them. And we should save them while there is still time.

— DICK BROWN
Harvard, Massachusetts
May 1993

Fly
Fishing
FOR
BONEFISH

1

Fly Fishing for Bonefish: The Ultimate Challenge in Angling

Fly fishing for bonefish is unique. Whether you wade on sandy bottoms or drift downwind on the deck of a skiff, you become a predator. Your eyes strain to pierce the water's surface. Your hands tremble as you see silver shadows zigzag against the mottled bottom. Then you connect. Suddenly, you feel the raw survival instinct of one of the earth's oldest creatures. It scorches across the flat, streaking for the safety of deep water. Nothing else you do in fly fishing will ever come close to what you feel at this moment.

THE ULTIMATE QUARRY IN FLY FISHING

The bonefish is the nearest thing there is to a perfect game fish for fly fishing. A voracious predator, it readily (but warily) takes flies. It accelerates faster and sprints farther than any other fish you take on light tackle. It fights more doggedly than most fish twice its size.

This performance alone would qualify the bonefish as one of the world's top fly-fishing targets. But what makes it the ultimate quarry in the sport is that you must see it — sometimes from eighty feet away — before you can cast to it. You stalk it like a predator. You track it down, take your aim, and cast with precision. You must make no mistakes. The ruthless, primitive instincts of this skittish creature leave no room for error.

Many other light-tackle game fish test anglers. No fly fisherman can deny

1

The bonefish's primitive survival instincts and its twenty-five-mile-an-hour burst speed make it the ultimate quarry for fly-fishing anglers.

the challenge of hooking a sipping spring-creek rainbow, or subduing a giant leaping tarpon, or enticing a shy, reclusive permit. But in all of fly fishing, there is nothing quite like the liquid-lightning rush of a bonefish as it streaks for the blue horizon.

The raw power, speed, and intensity of an average adult bonefish forgive no mistakes, marginal tackle, or casual angling. While a trout runs at five miles per hour and a salmon sprints at twelve, a bonefish rips across the flats at twenty-five. The length — sometimes five hundred feet — and intensity of its runs — will test an angler's tackle and fish-playing skills to their limits.

THE ULTIMATE TECHNIQUE FOR THE ULTIMATE FISH

Until ten or fifteen years ago, most anglers pursuing bonefish used a spinning rod. At least, they began their bonefishing with one. Anglers can master spinning gear easily and quickly. It casts farther and cuts through the wind better than fly tackle — not many anglers can double haul as far as they can throw a quarter-ounce jig. By starting with spinning gear, an angler could concentrate

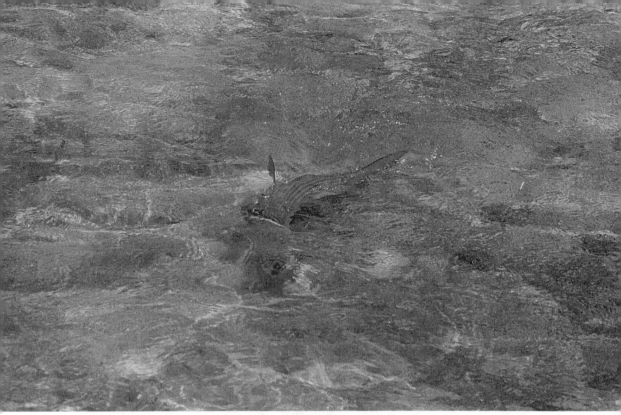

While the high-speed run of a bonefish will test your fish-playing skills, its phantom-like invisibility will challenge your fish-spotting *abilities even more.*

on mastering skills like hunting, spotting, hooking, and playing fish right from the beginning. Later he could switch over to fly fishing in order to experience the added stealth, control, and thrill it gives an angler. But today, fly fishing has come to dominate the sport. Most bonefish anglers know the advantages of it over spinning, and they want to start with the fly rod right from the beginning.

Fly casting does have advantages over spinning. Quieter presentations are possible because it doesn't require heavy jigs that smack the surface and spook fish. Fly casting also allows you to change direction quickly and recast fast. With a spinning rod, you have to retrieve your jig all the way to the end of your rod before you can cast again. Fly casting also lets you vary the sink rate. You can cast flies of different densities to accommodate different water depths.

But aside from practical advantages over spinning, fly fishing and bonefish just seem to have been made for each other. The intimacy of the strike and the sensitivity to the fish's streaking runs connect you to the fish as if you had your hand on its soul. If fly fishing had not existed already, a bonefisherman would have invented it. But this love affair between bonefish and flies did not always exist.

No other angling technique lets you achieve the stealth and delicacy you attain in fly fishing —
qualities that are critical in pursuing the wary silver phantom of the flats.

THE IGNOBLE HISTORY OF BONEFISHING

In the short and checkered history of fly fishing for bonefish, this game fish we so highly prize today was the target of anglers' slurs far more often than it was the object of their admiration. In fact, the very first man we can identify as taking a bonefish on a fly showed no appreciation for it. He considered it a nuisance.

Saltwater Suckers and Marlin Bait

One morning in 1924, a retired Washington lobbyist named Holmes Allen became the first man to hook a bonefish on a fly. The encounter was accidental, as he was casting for snook. Puzzled by the brisk run of the fish that took his fly, Allen waited for it to jump. It never did. "I thought it was a saltwater sucker," was all he said at the time. Allen went on to become an avid bonefisherman and an eager proponent of the sport. But his initial reaction set a second-class tone that would stay with the bonefish for many years.

Novelist, *Saturday Evening Post* writer, and angler Philip Wylie angered Miami sportswriters by challenging their claims of the bonefish's sizzling runs. Wylie said the bonefish was grossly overrated and alleged it could not even break a six-pound tippet unless it reached its maximum running speed.

Expert blue-water anglers Ernest Hemingway and Kip Farrington, who pioneered big-game fishing for marlin and tuna on the west end of the Bahamas, showed even more disrespect. According to angling historian and writer George Reiger, "While millions of Americans went to MGM musicals to forget hard times, Hemingway and a handful of others simply ignored the Depression and went fishing. And certainly Bimini was the kind of place where the only thing you had to fear was not fear itself, but whether you would be able to get a supply of fresh bonefish for the next day's trolling."

But not all attitudes toward bonefish were so denigrating. The fish was, after all, included among the big three at Florida's Long Key Club, where noted celebrities and fishermen such as Zane Grey, Herbert Hoover, Edward Vom Hofe, and Andrew Mellon set the standards for saltwater angling for two decades. Only three species — permit, tarpon, and the bonefish — qualified for Long Key's highest diamond and gold award pins.

Prodigious young writer and respected saltwater angler Van Campen Heilner avidly championed the bonefish in these early years. Perhaps because of his love for bird shooting, Heilner was one of the first men to explore the thrills of stalking and sight-casting for bonefish. His descriptions of wading on the flats on the south side of Bimini with his guide, Benjie, are still some of the most insightful and moving passages about bonefishing ever written.

For the most part, however, offshore fishing and big-game fish dominated the period before World War II. With one exception, bonefishing, and especially bonefishing with flies, would wait until after the war for its celebrity.

The First Real "First" — and Without The Pig

The exception occurred at the end of the 1930s, just before the world was plunged into war. Several other events like Holmes Allen's "saltwater sucker" experience took place during this period. One fly fisherman after another caught bonefish by accident while fishing for other species. But no record exists of anyone taking bonefish by flies *on purpose* until a decade and a half later. It was then that an aging George LaBranche, the innovative father of American fast-water dry-fly fishing, succeeded in goading a Florida guide named Bill Smith to stop putting pork rind tails on his flies.

Smith, who eventually became one of the legends of the Florida Keys bonefishing guide community, had been successfully taking bonefish on bait for some time. Not surprisingly, he added a little "tail" of pork rind on his first

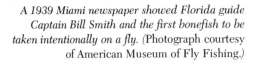

A 1939 Miami newspaper showed Florida guide Captain Bill Smith and the first bonefish to be taken intentionally on a fly. (Photograph courtesy of American Museum of Fly Fishing.)

fly patterns to spice them up a bit. Unfortunately for Smith, his first success with the method turned into a disaster. He hurried his catch off to a local grocery store to weigh it at the meat counter and ran into LaBranche, who was buying groceries. Smith told LaBranche he had just caught a bonefish on a fly, and the short, peppery LaBranche, seldom a word-mincer, looked at the pork rind tail and asked Smith why he hadn't just gone all the way and tied the pig's four feet onto the hook too!

Angered, Smith went home and brooded. But he got over it and tied several new flies using only white chicken feathers. He took his fluffy flies back to the flats and poled himself to a large shoal off Islamorada where bonefish often fed. There, on an afternoon in 1939, he hooked and boated an eight-pound fish that was witnessed as properly caught by an angler named Norfleet and his guide Bert Pinder. A photo of Smith holding his bonefish and fly rod appeared in the Miami papers and the world finally had its first legitimate (and intentional) bonefish on a fly.

Pioneering saltwater fly-fishing angler Joe Brooks (left) often fished with guide Captain Jimmie Albright (right). The two men are shown here in the late 1940s in the Florida Keys with three of the earliest bonefish taken on flies. (Photograph courtesy of Ben Estes.)

For the next decade bonefishing, along with just about everything else, took a back seat to World War II. One other event occurred during this period, however, that would influence bonefishing after the war and for many years to come. When Bill Smith went off to war, his wife Bonnie took over his business and became one of the most adept flats guides in the Keys. In 1942, Bonnie guided a young soldier named Jimmie Albright to his first bonefish and also introduced him to her sister Frankee. Albright, clearly affected by both encounters, married Frankee and became one of the greatest bonefishing guides of all time. He and his wife later befriended Joe and Mary Brooks. It was Albright who guided Brooks on what was probably the most important morning in bonefishing history.

The Laidlaw sisters frequently guided such fly-fishing celebrities as Joe and Mary Brooks and George LaBranche on early attempts to take bonefish on flies. The sisters were married to three of the best known bonefishing personalities in the Keys. Left to right: Beulah was the wife of guide John Cass; Bonnie wedded guide Bill Smith; and Frankee was Mrs. Jimmie Albright. (Photograph courtesy of Ben Estes.)

The Second First Is Greater Than the First First

It was June, 1947. The war was over. Jimmie Albright was now Captain Jimmie Albright. At 8:00 A.M. on a bright calm morning in Islamorada, Florida, Joe Brooks climbed aboard Albright's boat, the *Rebel*, and the two headed off toward the Peterson Key area. Lowering a small skiff, they poled quietly across the flats. Brooks began casting to a school of visibly tailing bonefish. Using a grizzly-winged fly with a white chenille body tied for him by a Miami barber and avid saltwater angler named Red Greb, Brooks took an eight-pound bonefish. Then, with the same fly, he took a second fish that was eight-and-one-half pounds.

For several years it was thought that this catch by Brooks was the first bonefish that had been intentionally taken on a fly. But we now know that this "first" honor already belonged to Bill Smith and his 1939 catch. (Later accounts of Brooks' catch point out accurately that his was in fact the first recorded case of taking a *tailing* bonefish on a fly.) Brooks' catch, however, was far more important to the sport. Because of his growing stature as an angler and writer, Brooks' two fish influenced fly fishing more than Smith's earlier record ever could. In a real sense, fly fishing for bonefish was born on that June morning in 1947. On that day it became both a reality and one of angling's highest pursuits.

For the next two decades, Brooks led the way in bonefishing with flies. Soon other pioneers such as Stanley Babson, baseball's Ted Williams, A.J. McClane, and Bermuda's Pete Perinchief joined him. Later, other disciples followed. Lefty Kreh, Chico Fernandez, Jack Samson, and many other anglers popularized the sport. Business-oriented anglers such as Leigh Perkins, George Hommell, and Bob Nauheim expanded the sport and helped organize it and develop new fishing locations.

Perhaps most important of all, a cadre of highly experienced guides grew up with the sport, including Sandy Moret, Steve Huff, Rick Ruoff, Stu Apte, Harry Spear, Vic Gaspeny, Al Polofsky, Eddie Wightman, Bill Curtis, Dick Williams, Tim Borski, Randy Towe, Jeffrey Cardenas, and many others. Without these men and their counterparts in the Bahamas such as Joe Cleare, Charlie Smith, and Rudy Dames, bonefishing would never have gotten underway and become what it is today — saltwater fly fishing's Holy Grail.

BONEFISHING TODAY — CELEBRITIES AND THE SECRET SERVICE

Today everyone in America who fishes with a fly rod wants to catch a bonefish. ESPN does features on bonefishing. Tom McGuane wrote a novel about it. Articles appear in *Town and Country*, the *Smithsonian*, *Fortune*, the *New York Times*, and even on the front page of the *Wall Street Journal*. America's aristocracy — its sports, entertainment, and political celebrities — adopted bonefishing. For the last few decades names like Jack Nicklaus, Ted Williams, Larry Hagman, and Carl Navarre have regularly found their way into the rosters of flats guides or bonefishing clubs. Even two of the last four

Fly-fishing anglers stalk bonefish on the shallow rims of the ocean, some of the most primitively beautiful places on earth.

American presidents became bonefishermen — a fact that is hard to ignore once you've seen country leaders like George Bush on the national news in hot pursuit of *Albula vulpes* on the Florida flats with a flotilla of national press corps and Secret Service men being poled behind him.

In some ways, this celebrity is good. The more men and women who bonefish, the more developers, investors, and outfitters will venture to open new bonefish waters in places like South Andros, Cuba, East Africa, the South Pacific and the Far East. Even more important, this increasing popularity will encourage support for research and conservation to protect bonefish waters and fisheries. As the world's oceans become more crowded, marine research and environmental protection policies will become more critical. Florida's Department of Natural Resources recently launched a new study on bonefish eating, spawning, maturation, and migration habits. Undertaken to investigate the decreasing quality of bonefishing in the Keys over the last decade, the research will determine the extent to which commercial netting of the flats, habitat degradation, and recreational fishing pressure have affected *Albula vulpes* in the very birthplace of the sport.

This knowledge is crucial for the long-term protection of the bonefish and its habitat. The Florida study, under Dr. Roy Crabtree, will expand our knowledge of the bonefish and build upon the work of earlier research pioneers like Donald Erdman, Gerard Bruger, and Dr. Douglas Colton. It will give us more tools to shape the future.

All who love this fish and its habitat must do all we can to ensure that such knowledge results in protective policies that eliminate pollution, reduce commercial netting, and hold back the development of shoreline areas and mangrove habitats on which the bonefish's survival depends.

Two decades ago, the provinces of eastern Canada discovered that an Atlantic salmon was worth a lot more on the end of a fly line than in the nets of commercial fishermen. Countries with saltwater habitats are now discovering the economic value of bonefishing tourism. This and the protection of certain areas like Los Roques, Ascension Bay, and the Everglades hold some promise for the future. But like all fish conservation, only the vigilance and effort of all who care will keep these habitats healthy. Only then will bonefishing continue to entice newcomers, reward veterans, and exhilarate all for whom it has become a passion.

2

Understanding the Bonefish

Nothing in bonefishing is more difficult to understand than the fish itself. Even experienced anglers find *Albula vulpes* as hard to read as the dark blue holes that lie at the edge of a tidal flat. But today we know much more about this elusive silver phantom of the flats than many anglers realize. Marine biologists, zoologists, ichthyologists, and other researchers have studied the bonefish for over a hundred years. They have dissected its anatomy, probed its sensory capabilities, and cataloged its eating habits.

Their findings answer many of the questions flats anglers have asked for years: how well can bonefish see; how much do they hear; how fast can they swim; how are they camouflaged; how do they react to water temperature; what prey do they eat most; which prey do they prefer; when and where do they eat; and which habitats do they prefer.

Research even answers some of the obscure riddles that nag at you when you drift a flat with the sun beating down on your neck. Can bonefish see a fly in muddy water? Do they really hear the noises you make in the boat? Do they talk? The answer to all three is *yes*.

Not all anglers will be interested in this research. Many men and women who fish the flats prefer to learn things on their own. Sometimes I have the same tendency — especially when I am impatient to get on the flats and go fishing. And I have been lucky enough to catch several hundred bonefish over the years, many without the benefit of a lot of scientific studies. But while research is no substitute for angling experience, fishermen shouldn't ignore it either. Knowing your quarry is a big part of fishing. And while research often confirms what you know, sometimes it reveals new insight.

THE BONEFISH

Bonefish are well-disguised predators. They roam warm, inshore saltwater flats in search of bottom-dwelling prey. They feed on the tides day and night, filling their oversized stomachs. Voracious grazing machines, they are uniquely equipped to harvest the prey-rich inshore flats. Their efficient predatory mouths contain shell-shattering jaws, a ceramic-hard tongue, and powerful grinding plates. Goggle-sheathed eyes help them see prey in muddy water —even when moving at top speed. Acute eyesight, keen hearing, mirrored camouflage, and lightning speed protect them from capture by enemies. Indeed, they are the perfect inshore flats hunter: sleek and powerful enough to plunder the thinnest water; fast and wary enough to escape just about every other predator on the flat.

As an angler, you will find no other game fish more challenging to stalk, hook, play, and release than *Albula vulpes*. The species is a unique combination of traits that has survived 125 million years of predation—an evolution that has made the bonefish a consummate survivor and the ultimate fly-fishing game fish today.

Classification

The bonefish belongs to the very large "bony" fish class called Osteichthyes, which excludes the small class of sharks and rays, or Chondrichthyes, and the even smaller group of primitive jawless fish, Agnatha.

Within the Osteichthyes class, bonefish are members of the Elopiformes order, which also includes the ladyfish family and the tarpon family. All of the fish in this order are considered "primitive." But this scientific use of the term does not mean that bonefish are somehow limited or underdeveloped. On the contrary, being primitive in this sense ranks as one of Nature's highest compliments. It suggests that the species has hardly changed at all over time. Any creature that exists today in the same form it did a hundred million years ago must have had a pretty successful design in the first place. It is perhaps no coincidence that two of the greatest game fish in the world today, tarpon and bonefish, are both from this "primitive" group.

Ichthyologists recognize three species of bonefish. But fly anglers pursue only one of them, *Albula vulpes*. This species inhabits warm, shallow, coastal waters worldwide. *Albula nemoptera*, the longfin bonefish, lives in thin water

TABLE 2.1
BONEFISH TAXONOMY

Family Megalopidae (tarpon)	Class Osteichthyes (bony fish)	
	Order Elopiformes (eel-like fish)	
Family Megalopidae (tarpon)	Family Albulidae (bonefish)	Family Elopidae (ladyfish)
	Albula vulpes (common bonefish)	
	Albula nemoptera (longfin bonefish)	
	Pterothrissus belloci (deep-water bonefish)	

near river outlets around high islands in the western Atlantic and eastern Pacific. A longer conical snout, a considerably smaller body, and a long last ray on both its dorsal and anal fins distinguish *Albula nemoptera* from *Albula vulpes*. *Pterothrissus belloci* resides in only deep water and anglers never really encounter it.

In 1982 researchers reported two other bonefish species, *Albula glossodonta* and *Albula neoguinaica*, in Hawaiian and Indo-west Pacific waters. These may prove to be distinct species, but many ichthyologists currently dispute them.

Distribution and Size

Bonefish appear on both coasts in the Americas. In the East, they range north to New Brunswick's Bay of Fundy and south to Rio de Janeiro. In the West, their territory edges north to San Francisco Bay and south to Talara, Peru. They also inhabit both the central and south Pacific Ocean, the Indian Ocean, and the waters off both coasts of Africa.

Most of these waters are too cold to hold large concentrations of bonefish and too deep for light-tackle anglers to wade or drift-fish in skiffs. For flats anglers, the best places to fish are the Bahamas, the Florida Keys, Mexico's Yucatan Peninsula, Belize, the Los Roques area of Venezuela, and the Pacific's Christmas Island. The east coast of Africa, the Republic of Tonga in the South

Bonefish inhabit most of the world's tropical waters. But only a few areas contain enough shallow waters for light-tackle anglers to wade or skiff-fish. The most popular are the Bahamas, Florida, Mexico, Belize, and Venezuela in the Atlantic Ocean and Christmas Island in the Pacific.

Pacific, and parts of the Indian Ocean may also hold good angling for the future. The Isle of Pines area in Cuba had good shallow-water bonefishing as well, before the poverty of Castro's economic policies forced hungry local fishermen to all but eliminate the species from Cuban waters. Puerto Rico, Bermuda, and the Cayman Islands also have a few flats, and they offer some limited bonefishing for small fish. (For a comprehensive look at flats fishing destinations, see Chapter 13, "Bonefishing Destinations.")

Anglers often think of fish in three size categories: trout and bass in the lightest class; salmon and steelhead in the middle range; and bigger game like tarpon, striped bass, and sailfish in the heaviest group. Bonefish fit not quite midway on this scale. Slightly smaller than salmon and steelhead, they fight as hard. They pack about twenty pounds of fight into a ten-pound fish.

Bonefish grow rapidly in their first years, then slow to about two or three inches per year from age two to six. After that, growth declines to less than an inch a year. Maximum life expectancy reaches over twelve years and maximum size edges up to about twenty pounds.

TABLE 2.2
FLY-ROD WORLD RECORDS FOR BONEFISH

TIPPET CLASS	WEIGHT	PLACE	DATE	ANGLER
2lb	12lb	Bimini, Bahamas	Nov 12, 1989	James B. Orthwein
4lb	15lb	Bimini, Bahamas	Mar 17, 1983	James B. Orthwein
8lb	13lb 4oz	Islamorada, FL	Nov 6, 1973	Jim Lopez
12lb	14lb 6oz	Islamorada, FL	Sep 22, 1985	Vic Gaspeny
16lb	13lb	Bimini, Bahamas	Mar 4, 1986	James B. Orthwein

SOURCE: *International Game Fish Association, 1992*

The International Game Fish Association, which keeps sport-fishing records, reports that the two largest bonefish ever caught by anglers were a seventeen-pounder caught in 1976 and a nineteen-pounder caught in 1962. Both fish were caught from the beach in Zululand, South Africa, on heavy tackle by anglers using prawns for bait. IGFA world records also show the largest fish caught on flies were taken in Florida and the Bahamas.

Gerard Bruger of the Florida Marine Research Institute studied bonefish weight, length, and age extensively in the Florida Keys. Table 2.3 shows average weight data, which anglers can use to approximate the size of fish caught and released by taking a simple length measurement. Fork length is the distance from the snout to the V or crotch of the tail, not to the tip of the tail.

TABLE 2.3
AVERAGE WEIGHT OF BONEFISH VERSUS FORK LENGTH

FORK LENGTH (INCHES)	WEIGHT (POUNDS/OUNCES)	FORK LENGTH (INCHES)	WEIGHT (POUNDS/OUNCES)
9.0 inches	6oz	22.0 inches	5lb 12oz
10.0	8oz	23.0	6lb 10oz
11.0	11oz	24.0	7lb 9oz
12.0	14oz	25.0	8lb 10oz
13.0	1lb 2oz	26.0	9lb 11oz
14.0	1lb 7oz	27.0	10lb 15oz
15.0	1lb 12oz	28.0	12lb 4oz
16.0	2lb 2oz	29.0	13lb 10oz
17.0	2lb 9oz	30.0	15lb 2oz
18.0	3lb 2oz	31.0	16lb 12oz
19.0	3lb 11oz	32.0	18lb 8oz
20.0	4lb 5oz	33.0	20lb 6oz
21.0	5lb		

SOURCE: *Bruger, 1974; personal communication, 1992*

Anglers can estimate bonefish weight prior to release by measuring from the nose to the fork in the tail. This twenty-six-inch female weighed just over nine pounds.

Bruger also estimated ages of bonefish. Table 2.4 shows the average age for bonefish of different lengths. Bonefish grow considerably older than the nine years shown in the table—Bruger himself examined a 24.4-inch female of twelve years—but larger fish were excluded from these age/length studies, since the methods of estimating age required destroying the fish.

TABLE 2.4
AVERAGE BONEFISH AGE VERSUS FORK LENGTH

AGE (YEARS)*	MEAN FORK LENGTH (INCHES)	LOW (INCHES)	HIGH (INCHES)
1	9.4 inches	7.2 inches	11.8 inches
2	12.8	10.4	15.3
3	15.8	13.3	18.6
4	18.7	15.8	21.7
5	20.9	18.5	23.4
6	22.3	20.2	24.8
7	23.5	20.9	26.2
8	24.3	21.7	26.8
9	24.7	21.1	28.4

SOURCE: *Bruger, 1974; personal communication, 1992*
* *Ages may be understated, especially at the low end, since scales were used as the basis of determination rather than more accurate inner-ear otoliths.*

A FISHERMAN'S ANATOMY OF THE BONEFISH

Bonefish evolved with a different anatomy from most other major game fish. As an angler, you will find many of the keys to understanding the fish's unique and vexing abilities in its anatomical traits: body color and scales that give it perfect camouflage; a tall, slender tail that generates its incredible acceleration; a mouth structure that both senses and excavates food; keen eyes and hearing that detect prey and predators; and a sense of smell that can sniff out prey, men, and boats from across a flat.

Shape, Color, and Scale Pattern

The bonefish propels its streamlined, spindle-shaped body with a large, deeply forked tail. Its prominent snout projects slightly in front of its lower jaw to help it capture bottom dwellers. Hundreds of small shiny scales cover its exterior. One twenty-one-inch specimen I caught in the Bahamas in 1984 had 897 of them. With a slightly bluish-silver cast, this skin of mirrors reflects

Dense, closely overlapping scales scatter light and reflections, making the bonefish one of the most difficult flats fish to see.

the colors and patterns around bonefish and makes them almost invisible.

Barracuda and tarpon also grow rows of shiny scales and use reflectivity to disguise themselves. But the bonefish's scales are dense and overlap closely; they expose only very narrow, crescent-shaped slivers that break up reflections and scatter light. This makes bonefish far more difficult to see than any of their broader-scaled flats neighbors and has elevated their camouflage to a legendary status among anglers.

Tail Structure and Speed

A heavily forked tail and torpedo-shaped body give the bonefish its speed. In fish physics, forked and crescent-shaped tails are extremely efficient. They propel some of the fastest fish in the ocean, including the barracuda, sailfish, marlin, wahoo, and tuna.

Bonefish burst speed has been estimated by researchers at about twenty-two miles per hour, which puts its speed closer to that of trout than sailfish. My own calculations, using a stop watch and measured line segments, place their speed slightly higher, at about twenty-six miles per hour, or just

A forked-shaped tail propels medium-sized bonefish to burst speeds of about twenty-five miles an hour. Larger fish swim even faster.

TABLE 2.5
BURST SPEEDS FOR AVERAGE-SIZE FISH OF SEVERAL SPECIES

SPECIES	BURST SPEED (MPH)
Sockeye Salmon (*Oncorhynchus nerka*)	4.0 mph
Rainbow Trout (*Salmo gairdneri*)	4.6
Brown Trout (*Salmo trutta*)	4.9
Northern Pike (*Esox lucius*)	9.1
Atlantic Salmon (*Salmo salar*)	11.5
Bonefish (*Albula vulpes*)	22.4
Great Barracuda (*Sphyraena barracuda*)	27.3
Yellowfin Tuna (*Thunnus albacares*)	29.0
Wahoo (*Acanthocybium solanderi*)	37.4
Sailfish	67.1

SOURCE: *Hoar and Randall, 1971*

under the top speed of a barracuda. Either way, the bonefish runs much faster than most game fish sought by fly fishermen. But while this clinical raw speed is impressive, what makes anglers rank bonefish so highly as a game fish is that they run at these speeds for several hundred feet in only six inches of water.

Mouth, Tongue, and Sensory Canals

The bonefish mouth is located on the underside of the head, slightly behind a long, conical snout. While similar in shape and location to the oral cavities of other bottom-feeding predatory fish, it appears much smaller in proportion. Rows of tiny, sharp teeth rim the inside and angle toward the back. Large plates containing dozens of closely fitted round teeth line the rest of the mouth. These blunt pearl-shaped molars form a ceramic-hard mosaic layer that crushes the shells of the mollusks and crustaceans the bonefish eats.

This oral structure has several implications for anglers. Built for crushing, the mouth does not easily sense the feel of a hook. Its hard plates resist penetration. You should strike fish firmly, sharpen hooks often, crimp your barbs, and even restrike a fish to make sure the hook penetrates. Once hooked, however, the strong mouth structure holds well, so hooks seldom tear out unless they did not penetrate well in the first place.

Bonefish also have a tendency to rub the underside of their snouts on the bottom when hooked. This reflex action probably stems from grubbing

The area around the bonefish's head and lips is laced with sensory canals that detect minute movements of prey in cloudy water and under the sand.

behavior. It will abrade your tippet unless you keep enough pressure on the fish, turn it fast, and keep it coming back to you.

The mouth area contains another sensory organ that anglers should understand — the bonefish's lateral-line sensory system. This canal network of water-filled pathways laces its way throughout the bonefish's head and lips. With skin tightly stretched across them, these drum-like cavities telegraph vibrations like tiny tom-toms. Bonefish use this sense to detect minute movements of prey hidden in cloudy water and even under the sand. This sensitivity suggests that vibration-generating fly patterns like those with Muddler-type heads or with rattling bead-chain eyes may sometimes be effective, even if they are not seen.

Eye Structure and Vision

Like many fish, the bonefish's eye lenses bulge out from the body surface. They give the fish a wide field of vision to spot distant prey and predators, even those to the rear. Donald Erdman, a fisheries biologist who has studied hundreds of bonefish, believes that the eye is set into the head at an angle to favor upward vision, both to sense threats from above when the fish swims, and to spot prey and predators in the bottom of the water column as it feeds up-ended in the tailing position. The bonefish also has acute color vision, and can discern twenty-four different colors and a wide spectrum of shades of gray.

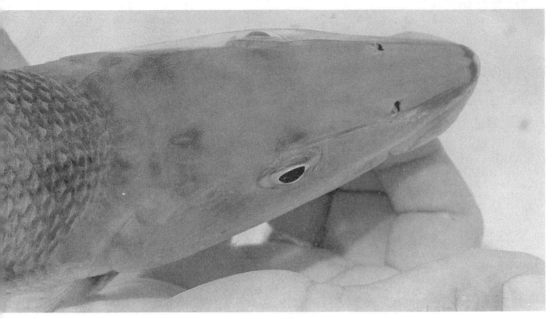

Adipose eyelids, a pair of streamlined goggle-like sheathes, cover the bonefish's eyes and allow vision even in cloudy water.

One unusual aspect of the bonefish eye accounts for its ability to see in cloudy water. A hard, transparent adipose eyelid covers the eye. This very long, streamlined goggle-like sheath protects the eye and permits vision even in debris-strewn, muddy water. It also reduces water turbulence around the eye and allows bonefish to see clearly even when swimming at maximum speed.

For anglers, this total eye structure suggests that bonefish see well under just about all conditions. They see shapes. They see colors. They see in daylight and low light. They see in muddy water and in clear water. They even see well when swimming at top speed. Bright clothing, unnecessary movements, and tall profiles can all be major liabilities for anglers. I have found over the years that wearing pale, neutral colors like khaki and light blue lets me get closer to fish. I also find that crouching when getting in close reduces spooking.

Ear Structure and Hearing

Bonefish hear through two organs: an inner ear and a gas bladder, both of which are common in bony fish. The inner ear senses deep thumps and nearby sounds while the gas bladder picks up and amplifies higher-frequency and distant sounds. The fish is well-equipped to detect all but the stealthiest anglers.

Bonefish are particularly sensitive to lower frequencies. While they cannot hear beyond the narrow frequency range from fifty to 1000 Hz, or cycles per second, they sense noises in the vicinity of 300 Hz especially well. This range includes sounds such as the scraping of a boat hull, the plip of a weighted fly dropping into the water, and the slow-moving drum of an outboard motor. Worse for anglers, unlike deep-water environments that mask sounds, the stark silence of the flats seems to amplify disturbances, making them stand out like a bullhorn at an afternoon tea.

Nose Cavities and Sense of Smell

The bonefish organ for smell opens to the water through a pair of nostrils in front of the eyes called the nares. Sensing devices line a single large nasal sac and connect to the brain through the olfactory nerve. By alternately opening and closing its mouth, the fish moves tiny bones in its head. This pumps water in and out across the sensing devices, giving bonefish a powerful ability to detect scents.

This acute sense of smell should not surprise anglers. When bonefish feed, they do not excavate prey randomly. They target where they dig, even when they cannot see the prey. They sniff out clams, shrimp, crabs, and worms in their lairs. They also detect odors like insect repellent, sunblock, and gasoline. Flies that pick up these scents will put fish on notice. Once in the Keys I had fish spook mysteriously every time I put a fly in front of them. At first I thought lead eyes had caused the problem, but the fish still spooked when I used eyeless patterns. Then I noticed as I was tying on the next fly that it smelled like DEET. My insect repellent had leaked all over my bag and ruined my flies!

Respiration and Expulsion

The bonefish's respiratory system appears similar to that of many other fish. Using both pressure and suction, it forces water through the gills. At the beginning of inhalation, the gill covers close, the mouth opens, and the fish sucks water through its gills. Then the mouth closes, and its cavity functions as a pressure pump, forcing water out through the gill covers.

While most fish breathe this way, the bonefish's respiration has one unusual twist. The fish can reverse its exhalation and expel water out of its mouth in a high-pressure stream. It directs this stream of water down into the sand and mud to blow sediment away from hidden prey. This "sandblasting" spreads bottom particles and debris and makes the underwater clouds fishermen call "muds."

Stomach Size

The bonefish possesses a large stomach; when full, it occupies two-thirds of the abdominal cavity, which accounts for the fish's constant prowling and eating. This also explains why bonefish feed throughout all phases of tides as long as they can find food and avoid danger and discomfort. While anglers often pursue bonefish when water depth is favorable for wading or drifting, they should consider that the fish — driven by the need to fill its belly — also feeds at many other times.

Lateral Line

Each side of the bonefish's body contains a horizontal row of neuromasts — receptors that give fish a "distant-touch" sense. Bonefish use this ability to detect prey and predators and to avoid collisions in schools at high speed. This sense lets them streak across shallows without mishap. It also allows them to feel the push of a poled boat in the water.

BONEFISH FEEDING BEHAVIOR

Bonefish feed like hungry wolves. They scour flat after flat, hunting down shrimp, crabs, clams, and worms in their burrows. They push farther and farther inshore, riding the rising tides that give them access to the inner reaches of the tidal zone. They gorge themselves on the densest concentrations of mollusks, crustaceans, and other prey they can find in turtle grass, sand flats, mangrove stands, and tidal pools.

When you are trying to decide what fly to use or where to search for fish, you can greatly improve your chances of success by knowing what, when, and where bonefish eat. Fortunately for anglers, researchers have examined this area of bonefish behavior more than any other. One investigator, Dr. Douglas Colton, even implanted bonefish with small ultrasonic transmitters and tracked their daily movements with receivers as they fed during tidal changes. This study and three others — two by Donald Erdman in 1960 and 1975 and one by Gerard Bruger in 1974 — conclusively documented the close relationship between tide cycles and bonefish feeding patterns. They also produced

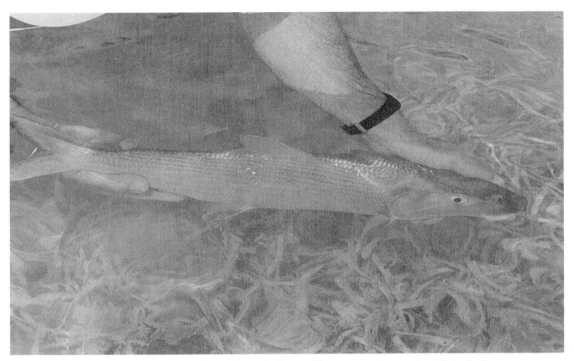

Bonefish feeding on prey-rich sea-grass beds are far more selective than fish feeding on bare sand.

some interesting observations on the effects of water depth, sunlight, temperature, and wind on feeding.

Effect of Tides and Water Depth on Feeding

Bonefish come onto the flats on rising tides. They feed in shallow habitats between the reefline and the shoreline, grazing on progressively shallower feeding areas as the tide rises. As the tide begins to fall, they sometimes hold up in deep holes and sanctuaries on the flats. Other times they head back to deep water off the flats to wait for the tide to rise again.

Research on bonefish grazing behavior shows they often feed throughout a tide cycle as long as food and protective cover are available. They will, for example, continue to feed in a deep on-flat basin rich in food, clouding the area with large underwater muds. They will also feed in off-flat holding areas along shoulders of flats and reefs, unless they are too deep and too barren to contain prey.

When bonefish find no sanctuaries that hold food, they will simply wait out the tide cycle until they can return to the flats to feed. Scuba divers frequently report seeing large schools of bonefish drifting at depths of fifty feet along the edge of steep drop-offs in places like the Tongue-of-the-Ocean in the mid-Bahamas.

Dr. Colton's research on movement and feeding at Deep Water Cay in 1983 graphically documented how bonefish feed in deep on-flat holes, even after falling tides eliminate escape routes. One transmitter-rigged fish returned to the same one hundred and fifty-yard-diameter hole repeatedly as the tide fell. It would wait inside this large bowl for about five hours for the tide to change. Then, as the tide rose, it would resume its rounds on the shallower inland part of the flat.

Anglers should not always be too quick to leave food-rich flats on falling tides. Better to check first in deep holes and channels where fish may continue to feed throughout the tide cycle. This may be nothing new for experienced guides who frequently cherry-pick these "honey holes," but less experienced flats anglers may benefit from exploring them.

Common angler theory holds that the best time to take bonefish is on the first half of a rising tide and the last half of a falling tide. Feeding studies, however, do not fully support this. Unless they are spooked or otherwise traumatically affected, bonefish eat throughout a tide cycle. In fact, during

Bonefish that feed on stark sand flats must forage indiscriminately and work hard for food. They have to process large amounts of substrate to extract clams and other buried prey.

weak tides, which cause little change between high and low tide levels, bonefish will often feed on any flat that holds food during both high and low tide. But on strong spring tides fish feeding will follow tide cycles much more closely. The fish will swim in with rising tides and hunt farther and farther back into the shore, along mangrove stands, and in tidal pools. As the tide reverses, they will start working back out of the mangroves and shore areas across the sand and grass flats, to eventually wait out the lowest tide in channels along the edge of the flats or in deep-water holes on the flats. Anglers often see bonefish crossing the open flats on the beginning of rising tides and the last half of outgoing tides, but this does not mean that these are the only times or places to fish for them.

Effect of Sunlight on Feeding

Bonefish feed as actively at night as during the day. Tide cycles appear to be a much greater factor in determining feeding time than the amount of daylight. Researchers have repeatedly observed bonefish feeding at night in Bermuda. Donald Erdman, who studied hundreds of bonefish in Puerto Rico, took the single largest fish of his investigation at sunset and said feeding significantly increased at the end of the day. Dr. Douglas Colton, whose Bahamas research station and living quarters were along the water, said he often heard bonefish feeding at night. He also saw them feeding on the flats in moonlight when he was taking measurements. He attributes their night-feeding abilities to their acute sense of smell and vibration-sensing lateral line capabilities. Experienced Christmas Island guide Moanafua T. Kofe says bonefish often feed under a full moon on the white sands of the Pacific — sometimes so ravenously that they will not take a fly until the afternoon of the following day.

Anglers also confirm fish feeding at night. Jack Gartside has mentioned seeing bonefish and tarpon feeding with abandon at night in the Florida Keys. I have often noticed increased bonefish activity at first light, sunset, and on cloudy days, three of my favorite times on the flats.

Effect of Temperature and Seasonality on Feeding

Osteichthyes or bony class fish such as bonefish detect temperature through finely branched nerve endings in their outer layer of skin. Some bony fish discriminate temperature changes as small as 0.05 degrees Fahrenheit. We do not know exactly how sensitive *Albula vulpes* is to temperature, but we do know they are cold- blooded. They have no internal temperature regulation, so they constantly move from water at one temperature to water at another temperature to maintain comfort.

This is one reason why bonefish feeding presence changes with the seasons. In the Northern Hemisphere, bonefish appear on the flats in the greatest numbers during March, April, and May and again in October and November, when water temperatures moderate. Bonefish presence on the flats falls to its lowest when temperatures reach their highest, in August, or their lowest, in January. (See Table 2.6.)

Bahamas-, Florida-, and Puerto Rico-based research show a few small variations on this pattern, but all generally confirm it. In Florida, Gerard Bruger found the largest concentrations of bonefish on the flats in April/May and October. In the Bahamas, Dr. Colton found the highest densities in March and November/December. In Puerto Rico, Donald Erdman found the fish were most abundant in May and November. Areas nearest the equator, like Christmas Island, have little seasonal variation.

The International Game Fish Association record book underscores this seasonality in bonefish presence. Most of the largest fish have been taken in November and March (Table 2.2). Jim Orthwein, who holds three of those records, has an interesting theory on this. He believes that a cold day during these high-density periods actually drives the smaller, less desirable fish off the flats, improving an angler's odds of hooking bigger fish more tolerant of low temperatures.

While larger bonefish can withstand cold a bit longer than small bonefish, they have less tolerance than smaller fish for high temperatures. In Dr. Colton's study off Deep Water Cay, larger fish (over twenty-two inches or about five pounds) left the flats in warmer months when water temperatures rose above ninety-three degrees, while smaller fish remained on the flats. During the fall, when temperatures moderate, larger bonefish returned. Their density reached its highest—nearly fifty percent of those present—at about seventy-three degrees, in March. (See Table 2.7.)

Observations by fishermen further confirm this research. Florida Keys guide Vic Gaspeny says he has caught bonefish in water temperatures as high as ninety-four degrees Fahrenheit and as low as 61.5 degrees, but the fish start getting scarce above ninety degrees and below sixty-eight. The late A.J. McClane, who probably collected more data on bonefish for anglers than anyone else in the world, noted that the species generally feeds in the sixty-eight-to-eighty-eight-degree range, with the most active feeding between seventy-five to eighty-five.

Anglers who understand how critically temperatures affect bonefish never go to the flats without a thermometer. Once they start using one regularly they find that temperature varies from day to day, flat to flat, and sometimes even between different places on the same flat, far more than they might have guessed. It's an essential fish-finding tool.

Effect of Prevailing Winds on Feeding

In two research studies off Puerto Rico, one in 1960 and a second in 1975, Donald Erdman concluded that the preferred habitat of bonefish was the shallow sandy bottom on the protected inshore side of windward reefs (those farthest from shore that received the brunt of prevailing trade winds). He further found that the greatest numbers of fish and the largest fish feed on the inshore side of the most windward of these reefs. Inshore reefs in more protected waters held smaller fish in fewer numbers.

Erdman concluded that fish diet probably accounted for the difference in bonefish size and abundance between these two habitats. Bonefish at windward reefs consumed clams and crabs in far greater numbers than their smaller counterparts on inshore reefs, where fish ate primarily snails. Erdman suggests that these differences in diet probably reflect differences in the natural availability of prey in these two habitats.

Why bonefish prefer to feed on the inshore side of the *outermost* windward reefs is still unclear. But after fishing the inside of these windy shoals successfully for almost two decades, I am convinced it occurs often. Apparently the combination of wind for cover, proximity to deep water, and prey availability, are especially appealing to the bonefish. Whatever the reason, along with turtle grass beds and mangroves, these reef areas have become one of my favorite places to look for fish. I especially like them on choppy days, when bonefish will come to them to mud or tail with abandon.

WHAT BONEFISH EAT

Bonefish feed both opportunistically and selectively. When tide and temperature are favorable and predators are absent, juvenile schooling fish will compete with each other for food and eat just about anything unlucky enough to be in their path. Other times, when they are full or have been chased by barracuda, the same fish will eat nothing you show them. Bigger, experienced, adult bonefish are often more selective. Both anglers and researchers describe many instances of watching large fish carefully pick out one form of prey while passing on others. Ideally, anglers want to know both the prey bonefish generally take, and the species of prey they choose when they feed selectively.

Fortunately, researchers have studied not only what bonefish eat in general, but which species they eat in two of the most popular bonefishing destinations in the world—the Florida Keys and the Bahamas. Two additional studies were performed in Puerto Rico and give us a window into feeding habits of the smaller fish more common in many Caribbean locations. Although some of these findings are far from conclusive, they are the result of examining stomach contents of nearly one thousand bonefish, and they go a long way toward answering the kinds of questions anglers have about this fish: what they eat the most; what they prefer the most; what the biggest fish eat; and what fish eat on different types of flats.

What Do Bonefish Eat the Most?

According to the research, bonefish of the Bahamas and eastern Caribbean eat many of the same prey. Both Dr. Douglas Colton in the Bahamas and Donald Erdman in Puerto Rico found that clams made up the bulk of the bonefish diet by volume, followed by crabs and shrimp. Worms, snails, fish, and other creatures are also eaten, though in significantly fewer numbers.

Dr. Colton counted both the number of prey consumed by each fish sampled and the volume of prey eaten. Prey counts tell much more than just gross volume measurements, because some bonefish eat many smaller prey, such as baby common shrimp and snapping shrimp. If only volume were considered, larger prey with bigger masses such as crabs and larger clams would overshadow smaller creatures. Table 2.8 shows the percent of prey numbers occurring on average in bonefish stomachs. It indicates that clams were clearly the leading prey consumed, followed by shrimp and crabs.

TABLE 2.6
SEASONAL VARIATION OF BONEFISH DENSITY

Bonefish Density	Jan	Feb	Mar	Apr	May	Jun	Jul	Aug	Sep	Oct	Nov	Dec
			High							High		
		Med							Med			
	Med			Med				Med			Med	
	Low					Low	Low	Low				

In contrast, a study on Florida bonefish showed that in the area from Biscayne Bay to Key West, bonefish consumed shrimp and crabs the most (found in 73 percent of bonefish studied), followed by clams and other small mollusks (28 percent), and small fish (15 percent). Gerard Bruger, who conducted the research for the Florida Marine Research Institute, attributes the differences in ranking to local availability of prey.

In spite of these minor differences in ranking, anglers should find it quite interesting that many of the prey in all locations came from the same *families*. Common shrimp (Penaeidae), snapping shrimp (Alpheidae), swimming crabs (Portunidae), and mud crabs (Xanthidae) are popular prey in all locations, even though the frequency with which they are consumed appears to differ.

TABLE 2.7
BONEFISH FEEDING ACTIVITY VERSUS WATER TEMPERATURE (°F)

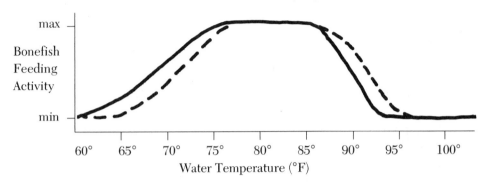

Bigger bonefish (solid line) are more likely to be found feeding on the flats at low temperatures (60° to 70°F) than smaller bonefish (dashed line), which can tolerate higher temperatures. Both big and small bonefish feed most actively in the 75° to 85°F range.

TABLE 2.8
WHAT BONEFISH EAT THE MOST

PREY FORMS	PREY EATEN (% OF PREY NUMBERS)
Clams (Bivalvia)	35.5%
Common shrimp (Penaeidae)	19.8
Snapping shrimp (Alpheidae)	13.0
Swimming crabs (Portunidae)	7.2
Mud & spider crabs (Xanthidae, Majidae)	6.9
Worms (Polychaeta)	6.1
Snails (Gastropoda)	5.0
Fish (Gobiidae, Batrachoididae)	4.4
Mantis shrimp (Squillidae)	2.1

SOURCE: *Colton and Alevizon, 1983*

Anglers want to find out not just what prey bonefish *eat* the most, but what prey they *want*. Over a nineteen-month period in the Bahamas, Dr. Colton examined 262 bonefish stomachs and compared their contents to 240 seine and core samples taken of the prey available on the flats on which those fish fed. Table 2.9 shows the results and it not only shows the percentage of prey eaten by the bonefish, but compares it to how available it was in each case.

In the Bahamas, bonefish not only consume clams in the greatest numbers, they prefer them the most. They consumed clams nearly six times as often as

TABLE 2.9
PREY MOST PREFERRED BY BONEFISH

PREY FORMS	PREY EATEN (%)	PREY AVAILABLE (%)	PREFERENCE RATIO
Clams (Bivalvia)	35.5%	6.1%	5.8
Common shrimp (Penaeidae)	19.8	8.7	2.2
Mantis shrimp (Squillidae)	2.1	1.2	1.7
Worms (Polychaeta)	6.1	6.5	0.9
Swimming crabs (Portunidae)	7.2	8.2	0.9
Snapping shrimp (Alpheidae)	13.0	22.0	0.6
Mud & spider crabs (Xanthidae, Majidae)	6.9	13.2	0.5
Fish (Gobiidae, Batrachoididae)	4.4	13.0	0.3
Snails (Gastropoda)	5.0	21.1	0.2

SOURCE: *Colton and Alevizon, 1983*

they were found on the flats. Since most of these clams are very small, bonefish probably eat so many of them because they are easy to catch. Common shrimp rank second in both number and preference. While harder to catch, they contain many more calories per bite. Snapping shrimp, which rank third in numbers, fall to sixth place in the preference rating because they were eaten only a little over half as often as they were available in nature. In contrast, the secretive and aggressive mantis shrimp, though taken in very small numbers, is a very meaty morsel and is high on the bonefish's target list.

Winter Versus Summer, Grass Flats Versus Sand
Should anglers expect a bonefish on a sand flat to have the same food preferences as bonefish on a sea grass flat? Or should a fish on any given flat in November have the same preferences as the fish that were there in May? Dr. Colton also examined bonefish feeding preferences by both types of flat (sand versus grass) and by season (winter versus summer) in the Bahamas. Table 2.10 shows the results for winter and Table 2.11 shows the results for summer.

As experienced flats anglers might expect, prey preferences differed substantially both by season and habitat. In winter, bonefish preferred common shrimp and clams on grass flats and clams, mantis shrimp, and snapping shrimp on sand flats. In summer, bonefish preferred clams, swimming crabs, and mantis shrimp on grass flats and clams and worms on sand flats.

Bonefish that were feeding on prey-rich sea grass beds discriminated far more selectively than fish feeding on bare sand flats. Researchers often

TABLE 2.10
BONEFISH WINTER FEEDING PREFERENCES

WINTER							
SAND FLAT				**SEA GRASS FLAT**			
	Prey Eaten (%)	Prey Available (%)	Preference Ratio		Prey Eaten (%)	Prey Available (%)	Preference Ratio
Clams (Bivalvia)	43%	1%	43.0	Common shrimp (Penaeidae)	28%	1%	28.0
Mantis shrimp (Squillidae)	7	1	7.0	Clams (Bivalvia)	22	6	3.7
Snapping shrimp (Alpheidae)	16	7	2.3	Worms (Polychaeta)	9	9	1.0
Mud/Spider crabs (Xanthidae/Majidae)	17	21	0.8	Mantis shrimp (Squillidae)	2	2	1.0
Snails (Gastropoda)	7	20	0.4	Swimming crabs (Portunidae)	5	6	0.8
Swimming crabs (Portunidae)	5	22	0.2	Snapping shrimp (Alpheidae)	19	33	0.6
Fish (Gobiidae, etc.)	4	18	0.2	Fish (Gobiidae, etc.)	6	12	0.5
Common shrimp (Penaeidae)	1	5	0.2	Snails (Gastropoda)	5	19	0.3
Worms (Polychaeta)	0	5	0.0	Mud/Spider crabs (Xanthidae-Majidae)	4	12	0.3

SOURCE: *Colton and Alevizon, 1983*

noticed bonefish picking out individual items, and even chasing and capturing fleeing prey in sea grass. Bonefish feeding in bare sandy areas foraged far less discriminately. They often processed large volumes of substrate, causing large muds as they excavated for limited amounts of buried prey.

What Big Bonefish Eat

All bonefish, large and small, consume huge quantities of small clams, shrimp, and swimming crabs. But only large fish are capable of eating the biggest, fastest, and most aggressive prey. In the Bahamas, Dr. Colton found that only large bonefish ate snapping shrimp, mantis shrimp, gobies, and toadfish. In Puerto Rico, Donald Erdman similarly found that small juvenile bonefish apparently did not eat other fish, but bonefish weighing 3 1/2 to ten pounds did, consuming two- to three-inch gobies, filefish, parrotfish, grunts, and eels. Erdman also found that bonefish size often relates directly to the size of the prey: larger bonefish eat larger prey; smaller bonefish eat smaller prey.

TABLE 2.11

BONEFISH SUMMER FEEDING PREFERENCES

| SUMMER | | | | | | | |
| SAND FLAT | | | | SEA GRASS FLAT | | | |
	Prey Eaten (%)	Prey Available (%)	Pref-erence Ratio		Prey Eaten (%)	Prey Available (%)	Pref-erence Ratio
Clams (Bivalvia)	44%	14%	3.1	Clams (Bivalvia)	49%	6%	8.2
Worms (Polychaeta)	6	3	2.0	Swimming crabs (Portunidae)	12	5	2.4
Mantis shrimp (Squillidae)	3	3	1.0	Mantis shrimp (Squillidae)	2	1	2.0
Mud/spider crabs (Xanthidae/Majidae)	11	12	0.9	Worms (Polychaeta)	4	5	0.8
Common shrimp (Penaeidae)	20	22	0.9	Common shrimp (Penaeidae)	11	16	0.7
Swimming crabs (Portunidae)	8	12	0.7	Mud/spider crabs (Xanthidae/Majidae)	6	12	0.5
Snails (Gastropoda)	6	17	0.4	Snapping shrimp (Alpheidae)	9	19	0.5
Fish (Gobiidae, etc.)	2	14	0.1	Snails (Gastropoda)	5	25	0.2
Snapping Shrimp (Alpheidae)	0	3	0.0	Fish (Gobiidae, etc.)	2	12	0.2

SOURCE: *Colton and Alevizon, 1983*

Larger bonefish also eat the same prey as smaller bonefish, in greater numbers. In his Bahamas research, Dr. Colton found that larger bonefish eat swimming crabs, spider crabs, and clams in substantially higher numbers than small bonefish do, at least at certain times of the year. Anglers report seeing large bonefish also take cusk eels, small urchins, and brittle stars.

What Bonefish Eat Where You Fish

Research studies give anglers rich insight into general bonefish feeding behavior. But how well do the findings apply to the particular places you might be fishing? Dr. Colton believes his 1983 Bahamas findings are valid for feeding behavior throughout the Bahamas, due both to his sample size and the relatively isolated geographic nature of the islands.

Gerard Bruger's work in Florida is probably valid for bonefish feeding behavior in the area from Biscayne Bay to Key West for similar reasons. A second Florida study is now underway, supervised by Dr. Roy Crabtree of the

Florida Marine Research Institute; it should add new insight into this important fishery.

For areas where no formal research has been done, I believe it makes most sense for anglers to use the research reported here as a *general* guideline. Bonefish prey are concentrated in a dozen or so families of clams, shrimp, crabs, worms, fish, and various other marine creatures. But bonefish prey preferences will vary among these families from location to location, depending on their availability. Also, while most of these families exist in nearly all of the bonefishing destinations around the world, different species often occur locally.

You can determine which species inhabit a specific bonefishing destination by close observation and some simple sampling techniques. You can use a sieve box or core sampler to investigate common feeding areas such as turtle-grass beds and sand flats (see the last section of Chapter 3, "What Bonefish Eat," for more on sampling).

PREDATORS AND BONEFISH DEFENSE BEHAVIOR

As a flats angler, you must understand not just what bonefish want, but also what they fear. Their defensive reactions can have a devastating impact on their feeding behavior — and therefore on your fishing.

Bonefish react to danger several different ways. Their most fundamental defense is their wariness. With their keen eyesight and acute hearing, little occurs on a flat without their knowing it. They startle violently, even with only slight provocation, making it very difficult for a predator to get close to them.

When bonefish "spook," they take off in an explosive run. Typically, a school of fish will flush all at once when the members sense danger. They communicate their alarm through a series of low-frequency toothy clicks and thumps produced by their swim bladders. These noises are a form of talking that warns bonefish of danger over a wide area, explaining why a flat can suddenly go completely dead when you spook a single fish.

Two different groups of predators stalk bonefish in the primary zones they inhabit. On the flats between the shoreline and the outer reefs, ospreys, barracuda, small sharks, and man prey on bonefish. In the deep shallows and channels beyond the edge of the flats, large sharks, porpoises, and big barracuda dominate.

Barracuda

Small and moderate size bonefish fear barracuda more than they do most other natural enemies, especially when they are feeding on the flats. Barra-

Large sharks like this six-footer often prowl the flats and will sometimes chase a hooked bonefish. An angler can usually drive these large predators away by slapping the water with a fly rod or a push-pole.

cuda are superb hunters, with protruding jaws and fang-like teeth. They swim even faster than bonefish, see better, and are well-disguised—they not only have a reflective camouflage similar to bonefish, but they can also change their color to match their surroundings to conceal themselves. Sometimes they cruise the shallows; other times they lie suspended near the bottom waiting in ambush. Either way they can lunge with lightning speed to pick off bonefish feeding with their heads grubbing in the bottom and tails standing tall.

Sharks

Small sharks cruise the flats and detect prey using a sophisticated combination of smell, vision, and electroreception. They will attack a bonefish if they can corner one. (I once saw a sand shark beach one on a shallow bar. The shark chased the bonefish onto the shoal until it was so far out of water it could no longer swim. Then the predator wiggled in behind the fish and devoured it.) But most of the time bonefish are too fast and too wary to be caught by sharks except when they are handicapped. If attracted by the thrashing sounds of a bonefish struggling on an angler's line, sharks will often chase the fish and cut it in half while it is still being played.

Porpoises or Dolphins

Porpoises swim as fast as twenty-nine miles per hour. They are more agile than any other bonefish predator and, in deep water, they are perhaps its most feared enemy. They detect prey with their excellent sight, hearing, and sophisticated sonar-like echolocation. They are voracious eaters that hunt in packs. They encircle entire schools of fish, trap them, and take turns lunging into the school to feed. Porpoises can run down even the largest bonefish just about anywhere, except on a tidal flat where the water is too shallow for their bulk.

Porpoises and dolphins can work to the angler's advantage. Because they attack bonefish in deeper water, they usually drive large numbers of fish onto the flats for safety. Even large fish that normally feel safer in the deep water will head for shallow flats when porpoises or dolphins are near. This is a rare opportunity to pursue these big bull bones in the thinnest water.

Ospreys

Ospreys often hunt on the flats, where the water depth makes fish vulnerable. Alert anglers are sometimes led to schools of bonefish by these solitary hunters as they watch prey from an island sea grape tree or cruise overhead. I know one cut in the Bahamas that connects an enclosed lagoon to the open flats where ospreys often hunt. Whenever I see ospreys in this area, I always find bonefish coming through the cut. Birds of prey are important to bonefish anglers in one other way, too. They have conditioned bonefish to be very sensitive to overhead movement, which is why the motion of a fly line whipping back and forth will often cause fish to spook.

Defensive Behavior

When in danger, bonefish home in on the shortest route to the safety of deeper water. The escape path is a straight line — allowing for channels and the contours of the flat — that follows the shortest distance to safety. Bonefish somehow keep themselves constantly aware of which channels lead them off the flat.

A second way that some bonefish respond to danger is by schooling. Smaller bonefish, in particular, almost always school up for safety, gathering in groups of ten, twenty, or even fifty at a time. This schooling improves their sensitivity to danger because it combines many sets of eyes and other sensors to detect predators. It also increases the odds of surviving attack by simply increasing the number of targets available to a predator.

Even larger bonefish, which normally swim alone, will sometimes school and feed with smaller fish, using them as a warning system to alert them of danger. In general, however, with their imposing size and faster speed, larger fish are less threatened by sharks and barracuda and do not need the protection of numbers.

LIFE CYCLE

While we know less than we wish about the bonefish's spawning period and earliest life stages, we *do* know quite a lot about the rest of their life cycle. Studies have found that bonefish spawn year-round. Their eggs hatch into a strange, transparent, ribbon-like larva that scarcely resembles a fish (except for a well-developed tail fin). For several months, the larva lives in the upper one hundred-foot layer of deep tropical oceans, where it grows to just over two inches long. Then through an extraordinary process of metamorphosis, the bonefish larva shrinks to three-quarters of an inch, its color changes from opaque to silver, and fins form. Throughout this shrinking stage, the larva's fins move progressively forward along the body until they reach their final positions. Then the larva begins to grow again, looking now like a complete but miniature bonefish. At about one inch, these juvenile fish migrate into the safety of inshore mangrove swamps where they live for the first year or so of their lives.

But we still do not know where and when the bonefish's spawning takes place and where the earliest stages of its life begin. Researchers offer two theories. One holds that bonefish spawn *inshore* during high tides; then currents and tides take the eggs offshore. Many weeks later as the larva develops, it returns to the shallows where it metamorphoses into a juvenile fish.

A second theory says that bonefish spawn *offshore*, in relatively deep water. The larva is then carried inshore to the shallows where it metamorphoses into a juvenile.

A most compelling description in support of the first theory (though it does not negate the second) comes in some unpublished observations passed along by researcher Dr. Douglas Colton:

"On two occasions during the course of this research, aggregations of several thousand bonefish were sighted (once by the senior author, the other time by a number of reliable witnesses) in shallow (3-5m depth) inshore lagoonal areas. Fish in these aggregations were observed to be unusually tightly packed, often rolling over and breaking the surface. These aggregations were observed to remain in a specific area for several days, showing no movements in response to tidal changes, an atypical behavior for schooling bonefish. The general behavior of the bonefish in these aggregations was also most uncharacteristic for the species, which is famous for being unusually wary and easily "spooked." These could be heavily fished, and even have boats driven through the aggregations, with almost no effect on behavior other than an immediate reaction to avoid being struck by the boat. Four of the five fish angled from one of these groups could easily be stripped of roe and milt. The activity was also found to coincide with high tide, suggesting that spawning might be timed to facilitate movement of fertilized eggs offshore with the immediate falling tide."

Once the spawning period is understood, it should help us better understand the whereabouts of bonefish at maturity and whether spawning has an impact on anglers. It should also help us protect this magnificent game fish and ensure its survival for future generations of anglers.

3

What Bonefish Eat

Bonefish eat a great variety of prey, and they eat often. They also eat what gives them the most nourishment for the least effort. Which species they eat at any given moment varies from one part of the world to another, from one tide to another, and even from one habitat to another. Florida Keys habitats are richer in shrimp and crabs than are flats in the Bahamas. Mangrove habitats hold different prey from sand flats. Shoreline tidepools offer prey only on high tides.

But for all this variation in diet and prey availability, bonefish feed on the same types of prey throughout most of their range. For fishermen, the most significant finding of the Bahamas, Florida, and Puerto Rico research on bonefish eating habits is that bonefish eat the same prey *families* at different locations. This means that at any given bonefishing destination, you are likely to find fish feeding on local species of the same dozen or so common prey families: snapping shrimp, mantis shrimp, common shrimp, swimming crabs, mud crabs, gobies, burrowing worms, errant worms, and clams.

In some instances, you will even find exactly the same species eaten by bonefish on opposite sides of the world; the red-backed cleaning shrimp (*Lysmata grabhami*), the golden mantis shrimp (*Pseudosquilla ciliata*), and the rock mantis shrimp (*Gonocactylus oerstedii*) are all found both in the Bahamas and on the flats near Christmas Island, for example.

Most of the specific species described in this chapter and its prey tables come from the feeding research performed in the Bahamas, Florida, Puerto

Rico, and Belize. While some of these same species also inhabit other locations, many species vary locally as diet, camouflage needs, and other survival demands differ from one destination to another. But by using these prey descriptions as a guide, you can focus your search on specific species in any locality. You can look for the prey signs described in this chapter and use sampling techniques like those detailed at the end of the chapter to find and identify local species, wherever you are.

The prey tables are organized by family and species. They include shape, color, size, habitat, and behavior data that should help you identify prey on the flats when you are fishing. This may help you select flies or even tie them to approximate the local species.

But even more important, this prey information should help you evaluate which flats have the richest concentrations of food and are most likely to attract bonefish. You may not, for example, want to tie a fly to imitate the small burrowing Caribbean tellin clam, but you may want to fish habitats rich in tellins with a Clouser Deep Minnow, a Bunny Bone, or a Gotcha to see if an opportunistic fish would like a little more bang for the bite.

PREY SPECIES

Shrimp Families

Shrimp contain one of the richest concentrations of calories per bite of all bonefish prey and are one of the fish's favorite foods. Distinctively shaped, most species look like insects of the sea. Their hard cape-like carapace covers a head and thorax that are fused into a single segment. Three pairs of antennae, a set of jaws, and five pairs of feeding and walking legs extend out of this upper body. The lower body or abdomen section contains several segments, including a fan-shaped tail or telson, and several pairs of swimming legs or swimmerets. Shrimp crawl across the bottom, on plants, and in grass. They also swim. They propel themselves forward with their paddle-like legs and backward by rapid jerky tail movements. Most shrimp are nocturnal, burying themselves in sand, mud, or crevices during the day. Sometimes you can spot shrimp by the small breathing holes they make, and occasionally you can see their pronounced eyes and eye stalks sticking up in the sand.

Common Shrimp (Penaeidae)

Common shrimp, including the commercial shrimp we eat, grow as big as eight inches long. These adults are too large for most bonefish to catch or eat, but young shrimp are a prime target. Once adult shrimp spawn offshore, juveniles are carried inshore by flood tides to shallow-water nursery grounds.

PINK SHRIMP
(*Penaeus duorarum*)

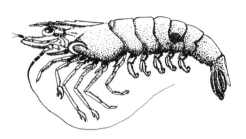

The pink shrimp (Penaeus duorarum), often colorless as a juvenile, burrows in hard sandy bottoms.

They live in mud-bottomed sea-grass beds and mangrove stands and eat algae, plant fragments, organic debris, and a variety of small animals and fish larvae. Common shrimp thrive in areas rich in vegetation and plant detritus. They burrow by day in the upper two to three inches of substrate and become active at night. If water temperatures fall below about fifty-nine degrees Fahrenheit, they either burrow and become inactive, or they migrate to warmer waters. Most penaeids taken by bonefish are two to 2 1/2 inches long. Within the family, bonefish eat primarily three species: the pink shrimp, the brown shrimp, and the pink spotted shrimp. Most are consumed during the day.

Mantis Shrimp (Squillidae)

Mantis shrimp resemble the preying mantis from which they get their name. They differ significantly in appearance from other shrimp. Two large overdeveloped forelimbs project forward. An unusual jointed head contains prominent eyes atop long stalks. The lower part of the body resembles other shrimp, except that the tail is larger. Behavior also differs from other species;

GOLDEN MANTIS SHRIMP
(*Pseudosquilla ciliata*)

The aggressive golden mantis shrimp (Pseudosquilla ciliata), usually yellowish-brown in color, is one of the most highly preferred prey of larger bonefish.

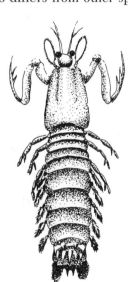

extremely aggressive, mantis shrimp are commonly categorized as either "spearers" or "smashers."

"Spearers," like the golden mantis, lance fish and other shrimp with razor-sharp forelimbs. Their attack is one of the fastest, most pugnacious movements made by any underwater animal—about thirty-two feet per second, or twenty-two miles per hour. This species burrows in mud or sand. With its eyestalks exposed, it sits in ambush, searching for prey on the bottom.

The "smashers" in the mantis family have blunter weapons. They club open clams, snails, and crabs with an enlarged blunt forelimb. Smashers typically live in rock or coral cavities and discard prey shell fragments in piles outside their residence, revealing their presence.

Two species of mantis shrimp are common bonefish food: the golden mantis shrimp and the rock mantis shrimp.

Snapping Shrimp (Alpheidae)

Shaped somewhat like small lobsters, snapping shrimp display one claw that is much longer than the other. This dominant claw, which is sometimes as large as the shrimp's body, contains a moveable finger that can be cocked open.

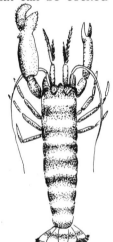

BANDED SNAPPING SHRIMP
(*Alpheus armillatus*)

*The banded snapping shrimp (*Alpheus armillatus*), with green and white stripes and one enlarged claw, makes a snapping sound to warn off predators.*

When released, it snaps loudly and stuns small fish and other prey. Large colonies produce crackling and popping sounds like a blazing fire, which you can hear when you drift or wade a flat. Bonefish consume primarily five species of snapping shrimp: the common snapping shrimp, the red snapping shrimp, the banded snapping shrimp, the long-clawed sponge shrimp, and the short-clawed sponge shrimp.

Small Shrimp (Hippolytidae, Palaemonidae, Gnatophyllidae)

Shrimp in this diverse group resemble the common shrimp in overall appear-

TABLE 3.1
SHRIMP

SPECIES	COLOR	MAX SIZE	BEHAVIOR	HABITAT	COMMENTS
Common Shrimp (Penaeidae)					
Pink Shrimp (*Penaeus duorarum*)	Juveniles gray, white, green, pink or colorless; adults variable: pink, brown, gray	8" long	Crawls along bottom; swims intermittently	Prefers hard sandy bottoms; scarce in soft mud; common in areas rich with detritus; shallow subtidal	Omnivorous; burrows during daytime, leaving breathing hole; nocturnal activity; very common in Florida and Mexico
Brown Shrimp (*Penaeus aztecus*)	Juveniles light grayish brown or speckled brown; adults variable: brown, orange, lemon	8" long	Crawls along bottom; swims intermittently	Prefers loose peat and muddy sand bottoms; common in areas rich with detritus; shallow subtidal	Omnivorous; burrows during daytime, leaving breathing hole; nocturnal activity; common in Florida; closely related species in Caribbean
Pink Spotted Shrimp (*Penaeus brasilensis*)	Juveniles brownish; adults pink or brownish-red; red spot on abdomen	8" long	Crawls along bottom; swims intermittently	Prefers soft mud covered with vegetation; common in areas rich with detritus; shallow subtidal	Omnivorous; burrows during daytime, leaving breathing hole; nocturnal activity; occurs in Florida; common in Bahamas and Caribbean
Mantis Shrimp (Squillidae)					
Golden Mantis Shrimp (*Pseudosquilla ciliata*)	Yellow brown, bright green or almost white	3–4" long	Burrows and spears prey; active free swimmer	Found on shallow banks with mud or sand bottom; sometimes intertidal, usually subtidal	Burrows in mud to wait for prey to ambush; also swims freely; feeds on shrimp and fish; less active than common shrimp; Florida, Bahamas, Caribbean and Indo-West Pacific

TABLE 3.1 (continued)

SHRIMP

SPECIES	COLOR	MAX SIZE	BEHAVIOR	HABITAT	COMMENTS
Rock Mantis Shrimp (*Gonodactylus oerstedii*)	Dark mottled green to black; also cream with green mottling	3–4" long	Crawls and batters prey	Found in coral and rock crevices; subtidal	Secretive; stalks prey, usually snails, hermit crabs and clams; less active than common shrimp; South Florida, Caribbean and eastern Pacific
Snapping Shrimp (Alpheidae)					
Common Snapping Shrimp (*Alpheus heterochaelis*)	Dark, translucent green with purple sides	1 1/4" long	Burrows; swims in short, rapid bursts	Soft mud in canals and mangroves; also among stones, shells and oyster reefs; shallow subtidal	Omnivorous; burrows during day, primarily active at night; Florida and Caribbean
Red Snapping Shrimp (*Alpheus armatus*)	Red or red-brown sometimes with golden highlights	2" long	Swims in short, rapid bursts	Lives beneath tentacles of ringed anemone; among rocks, coral and reefs; shallow subtidal	South Florida, Bahamas and West Indies
Banded Snapping Shrimp (*Alpheus armillatus*)	Abdomen has white and green bands	2" long	Swims in short, rapid bursts	Lives in rocky and reef areas; sometimes lives in sponges; subtidal	South Florida, Bahamas and West Indies
Long-Clawed Sponge Shrimp (*Synalpheus longicarpus*)	Translucent white with brown fingers	7/8" long	Swims in short, rapid bursts	Lives in interior of brown sponges; also in and under coral, rubble and shells; subtidal	South Florida, Bahamas, Caribbean and West Indies
Short-Clawed Sponge Shrimp (*Synalpheus brevicarpus*)	Light green with large red-tipped claw	3/4" long	Swims in short, rapid bursts	Lives in interior of sponges; subtidal	South Florida, Bahamas, Caribbean and West Indies

TABLE 3.1 (continued)

SHRIMP

SPECIES	COLOR	MAX SIZE	BEHAVIOR	HABITAT	COMMENTS
Small Shrimp (Hippolytidae, Palaemonidae, Gnatophyllidae)					
Arrow Shrimp (*Tozeuma carolinense*)	Variable: green or brown in grass; purple on corals; sometimes translucent	2" long	Swims vertically, then rests on grass blades	Usually lives in sea-grass beds; also found on corals; intertidal and subtidal	Very well camouflaged; feeds on organic material in corals and on grass; Florida, Caribbean and West Indies
Red-Backed Cleaning Shrimp (*Lysmata grabhami*)	Bright yellow with broad red stripe on back	2" long	Mobile and very fast	Found in crevices of reefs and among sponges and tunicates; shallow subtidal	Leaves shelter to clean parasites off fish that seek them out; south Florida, Bahamas, West Indies and Indo-West Pacific
Grass Shrimp (*Palaemonetes pugio*)	Transparent	2" long, slender	Swims intermittently from one grass blade to another	Lives on eel grass and turtle-grass blades, sometimes in sandy shallows; shallow subtidal	Sea grass is main diet; tolerates range of conditions from nearly fresh water to estuarine lagoons; Florida
Bumblebee Shrimp (*Gnathophyllum americanum*)	Yellow body with dark bands	4/5" long, thick	Commonly crawls	Sea-grass beds, corals and sponges; shallow subtidal	Feeds on urchin's tube feet; Florida, Bahamas, West Indies and Caribbean

ARROW SHRIMP
(*Tozeuma carolinense*)

*The sometimes-translucent arrow shrimp (*Tozeuma carolinense*), slender and about two inches long, clings to eel and turtle grass blades.*

ance. They are considerably smaller, however, and many reach only one-half inch in length. Bonefish prey most on those that live in sea-grass beds and reefs, such as the arrow shrimp, red-backed cleaning shrimp, grass shrimp, and bumblebee shrimp.

Crab Families

Crabs have a hard carapace or upper shell that shields their body from attack. The carapace can be oblong, triangular, or oval. All crabs have ten legs, usually two armed with claws and eight that are used for walking, swimming, or both. Many crabs display aggressive behavior and most, except some spider crabs, move very rapidly. Bonefish find crabs more difficult to catch than most other prey, but they also contain substantial food value.

At high tide bonefish prey on fiddler crabs that seek safety in small burrows such as these, which have a diameter about half the size of a #4 Crazy Charlie. At low tide, this pugnacious crustacean will come out of hiding to pick detritus and other nutrients out of the sand.

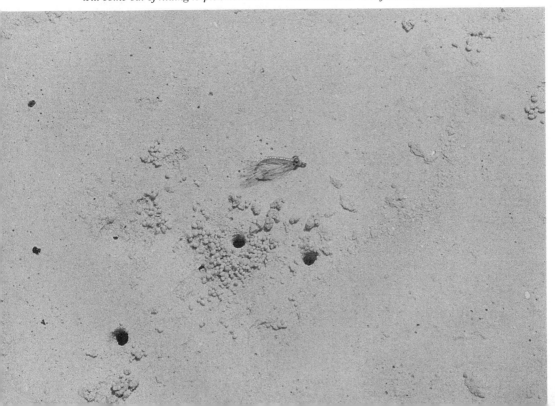

COMMON BLUE CRAB
(*Callinectes sapidus*)

The aggressive common blue crab (Callinectes sapidus), *usually pale gray-green or tan in juveniles, has distinctive paddle-shaped rear legs, swims in all directions and prefers muddy bottoms.*

Swimming Crabs (Portunidae)

The primary characteristics of the portunids are their wide carapaces and their distinct rear legs with flat paddle-like ends. To swim, they extend these back legs behind and above their body and push themselves forward, backward, and sideways with propeller-like movements. Portunids live on sandy or muddy bottoms between the shoreline and outer reefs. Fiercely predatory and extremely aggressive, many rear up with claws raised and attack any creature that approaches — including a human! They prey upon smaller fiddler crabs, juvenile fish, and tiny snails. Bonefish typically eat the common blue crab and the swimming crab.

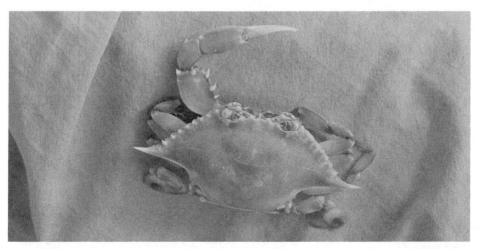

The common blue crab (Callinectes sapidus) *is often seen swimming in shallow water near shore. This two-inch juvenile lost a claw to a bonefish that was hunting in only six inches of water.*

FLORIDA MUD CRAB
(Cataleptodius floridanus)

The tiny Florida mud crab (Cataleptodius floridanus), only 7/8 of an inch long, has distinctive dark fingers and burrows in enriched muddy areas.

Mud Crabs (Xanthidae)

Mud crabs, or xanthids, usually have flat, oval carapaces, four pairs of walking legs, and two front legs with distinct claws. They usually move sideways, holding their black- or brown-fingered claws away from their bodies. Mud crabs typically inhabit muddy enriched bottoms or mangrove swamps. Bonefish prey on two species: the Florida mud crab and the common mud crab

Spider Crabs (Majidae)

Spider crabs, or majids, have a long, narrow triangular carapace, long spindly legs, and small claws. Majids live below the low tide line on a wide variety of

Finger-sized crab and shrimp burrows look small compared to an old, fist-sized bonefish feeding hole (upper right).

GREEN REEF CRAB
(*Mithrax sculptus*)

*The green reef crab (*Mithrax sculptus*) dark green, hairy, and barely one inch long, crawls slowly across reefs, rubble, or shell bottoms.*

bottoms, from sea grass to sand or coral, where they consume algae and detritus in large quantities. Three species of spider crabs are found in bonefish: the gray pitho, the southern spider crab, and the green reef crab.

Fish Families (Osteichthyes) and Spiny-Skinned Creatures (Ophiuroidea, Echinoidea)

Bonefish feed on a variety of small fish, ranging from adults of diminutive species such as gobies, to juveniles of larger fish such as snappers. Eight families of fish, all in the Osteichthyes class, are common bonefish food: snake eels, snappers, toadfish, gobies, cusk eels, grunts, mojarras, and false morays. Each of these groups comprises hundreds of individual species that vary in both appearance and behavior. Within the last six families, several individual species are identified as bonefish prey.

Bonefish also eat two other classes of invertebrates: brittle stars and sea urchins. Both are echinoderms, or "spiny-skinned" creatures that have internal skeletons covered with skin and spines. Their shapes vary with different species.

Brittle stars have small, flat, disc-shaped bodies with five flexible, plate-covered arms. Mobile, they crawl rapidly over the bottom using their arms like a serpent. Most feed at night on bottom dwellers such as bacteria, microalgae, larval fish, small mollusks, and tiny worms. Brittle stars collect food in their tube-like feet and pass it to a large mouth located underneath their body.

FRILLFIN GOBY
(*Bathygobius soporator*)

*The aggressive frillfin goby (*Bathygobius soporator*), drably striped olive-gray and blunt-shaped, rests on the bottom of tidepools and shallow-water shorelines.*

TABLE 3.2

CRABS

SPECIES	COLOR	MAX SIZE	BEHAVIOR	HABITAT	COMMENTS
Swimming Crabs (Portunidae)					
Common Blue Crab (*Callinectes sapidus*)	Blue-gray, white underside; red-tipped fingers	3 1/2" long; wider than long	Swims in all directions and walks on bottom	Common on sandy or muddy bottoms in bays and other low-saline water; subtidal	Extremely aggressive and carnivorous, eating fish, snails and small crabs; sometimes lies partly submerged; Florida, Bahamas, and West Indies
Swimming Crab (*Portunus depressifrons*)	Mottled light/dark gray; front legs bright purple or deep blue	1 1/4" long; wider than long	Swims in all directions and walks on bottom	Prefers shallow water with sandy bottoms; avoids hard-packed bottoms; subtidal	Closely matches colors of sand; sometimes lies barely submerged; Florida, Bahamas, West Indies and Caribbean
Mud Crabs (Xanthidae)					
Florida Mud Crab (*Cataleptodius floridanus*)	White or yellowish; red or brown spots; dark fingers	7/8" long; broad-fronted and oval-shaped	Moves sideways, holding claws up	Muddy bays and similar enriched areas; avoids hard-packed bottoms; intertidal and subtidal	Forages for algae during the day; South Florida and West Indies
Common Mud Crab (*Panopeus herbstii*)	Brownish green carapace; dark fingers	1 3/4" long; oval-shaped	Slow moving; moves sideways, holding claws up	Prefers soft mud, often oyster reefs and mangrove systems; intertidal and subtidal	Feeds primarily on small oysters and barnacles; active on high tides, burrows on low tides; Florida and Caribbean
Spider Crabs (Majidae)					
Gray Pitho (*Pitho aculeata*)	Gray	1" long; broad front wider than rear	Sluggish crawler	Common in seaweed shallows, rock and coral; subtidal	Defends itself by camouflage, draping seaweed over body; also called decorator crab; Florida and Caribbean
Southern Spider Crab (*Libinia dubia*)	Dull brown	3 1/4" long; longer than wide	Extremely sluggish	Common in seaweed shallows, all bottom types, especially muddy; subtidal	Scavenger; juveniles inhabit subumbrellar space of jellyfish; prefers quiet water; Florida and Caribbean
Green Reef Crab (*Mithrax sculptus*)	Dark green	1" long; slightly oval, with hairy legs	Slow crawler	Common on reefs, also among shell/coral pieces on shallows and flats and turtle-grass beds; subtidal	Very common crab; found in Florida, Bahamas, and Caribbean; identified in Puerto Rico research

Most brittle stars live in rocks, crevices, or shallow sand burrows that provide cover during the day. Their color varies both from adult to juvenile and from one locale to another. Size also differs considerably. Those most attractive to bonefish have arms up to two inches long and a body disc up to one-half inch wide.

Sea urchins grow in a great variety of forms, sizes, and colors. Many live on or just under the surface of the bottom. In spite of their often formidable appearance, juvenile urchins are quite vulnerable when flipped over to expose their soft underbodies. The best known of this family, the long-spined black urchin, has long, dark, threatening spines. It hides in crevices or lives in colonies on the bottom during the daytime. At night, it feeds on algae and turtle grass. The sand dollar urchin has a thin body with extremely short, fine bristles. It too lives on the bottom and can slide under the sand in seconds. Also common is the pencil urchin, a sluggish family member with large, blunt, cylindrical spines. Other urchins, such as the common heart or mud urchin, have rounded bodies covered with thin, fur-like bristles. They burrow easily into the substrate, and feed on small particles of food they inhale through a channel to the surface. The sizes of urchins vary considerably from specimens one to nine inches long. Bonefish mostly eat juveniles in the one-inch to three-inch range.

A shallow scoop sample taken in turtle grass reveals several lucine clams, snails, and an oyster shell.

TABLE 3.3
FISH & SPINY-SKINNED CREATURES

SPECIES	COLOR	SIZE	BEHAVIOR	HABITAT	COMMENTS
Snake Eels (Ophichthidae)	Often cream, tan or olive	Juveniles 2–3" long	Burrows, swims	Often prefers sea-grass habitats; shallow subtidal	Usually have a slightly pointed tail and no external caudal fin; sometimes have a stripe the length of the body; found in all bonefish destinations
Snappers (Lutjanidae)	Variable: red, tan or yellow; dark blotch sometimes below dorsal	Juveniles 2–3" long	Active swimmers	Common in sea-grass beds, mangroves and shallow reefs; subtidal	Color varies with environment; mainly nocturnal feeders; found in all bonefish destinations
Toadfish (Batrachoididae) Gulf Toadfish (Opsanus beta)	Mottled brown, tan and white	Juveniles 2–3" long	Bottom dwellers, often stationary	Common in sea-grass beds and rocky areas; also coastal waters; shallow subtidal	Large flat head, round caudal fin, large pectoral; belligerent, feeding on other fish and crustaceans; Florida, Bahamas and Caribbean
Gobies (Gobiidae) Frillfin Goby (Bathygobius soporator)	Drab gray body often with five dark stripes	3" long	Rests on bottom, then swims in spurts and darts	Abundant in rocky tidepools; also water's edge; shallow subtidal	Blunt-shaped, carnivorous, and aggressive hunter; secretive; often rests on bottom; Florida, Bahamas, and Caribbean
Cusk eels (Ophidiidae) Dusty Cusk eel (Parophidion schmidti)	Dusky brown	4" long	Burrows in soft bottom; swims snake-like	Common in turtle-grass beds; shallow subtidal	Top of head covered with large scales; continuous dorsal, caudal and anal fin; Florida, Bahamas and Caribbean
Grunts (Haemulidae) White Grunt (Haemulon plumieri)	Bluish white, with blue and yellow lines on head	Juveniles 2–3" long	Swims in perch-like fashion	Primarily in turtle-grass beds; shallow subtidal	Dark stripe along midside in young; gaily colored; Florida, Bahamas, and Caribbean

Where no individual species are identified, descriptions are only general.

TABLE 3.3 (continued)
FISH & SPINY-SKINNED CREATURES

SPECIES	COLOR	SIZE	BEHAVIOR	HABITAT	COMMENTS
Mojarras (Gerreidae) Yellowfin Mojarra (*Gerres cinereus*)	Body pale tan with silver; yellow pelvic fin	Juveniles 2–3" long	Swims primarily in schools	Common on non-reef areas including sand, mangroves, and grass; shallow subtidal	Protruding mouth for eating bottom-dwelling prey; Florida, Bahamas and Caribbean
False Morays (Xenocongridae) Atlantic Moray (*Kaupichthys atlanticus*)	Overall tan to brown	To 6 1/2" long	Snake-like swimming motion	Shallow water around coral reefs	Continuous dorsal, caudal, and anal fins; Bahamas, Florida and Caribbean
Brittle Star (Ophiuroidae)	All	Juveniles 3" overall	Often crawls rapidly; serpentine-moving arms	Habitat varies with species across all bottom types; intertidal and subtidal	Mostly nocturnal; feeds on variety of bottom food ranging from bacteria and microalgae to larval fish and small worms; found in all bonefish destinations
Sea Urchin (Echinoidae)	White, black or brown	1–3" overall; globular or flat	Burrows; sits or crawls on surface, or hides in crevices	Habitat varies with species across all bottom types; intertidal and subtidal	Teeth on underside scrape algae or eat detritus off bottom; often have prominent spines; found in all bonefish destinations

Where no individual species are identified, descriptions are only general.

Worms Families (Polychaeta)

Worms or polychaetes are a major source of food for bottom-feeders. They have segmented bodies with fleshy, bristly "legs" called parapodia. Polychaetes use these leg-like appendages to breathe, feed, and move. Some polychaetes stay and feed in one location. Others move about the bottom in search of food.

Some sedentary worms build tube-like dwellings on the bottom. Others construct their homes on coral, shells, and mangrove roots. Still others burrow into the bottom in tunnel-like holes. Both tube dwellers and burrowers obtain nourishment by filtering food from passing water currents or by eating pieces of detritus from the bottom. These sedentary worms usually have distinctive heads with long tentacles they use for both feeding and respiration. Their parapodia are seldom used for movement and appear as little more than bumps along their sides.

Wading anglers will often see the tube-like dwellings of polychaetes standing on the bottom. Some appear hard and calcareous, while others look leathery. Still others use shell fragments, sand, or debris for disguise. Bright-colored feeding tentacles, which inhabitants use to search for foods, often protrude from these tubes. Tube-dwelling polychaetes include various fanworms (Sabellidae), Christmas tree worms (Serpulidae), long-tentacled worms (Terebellidae), and mudworms (Spionidae).

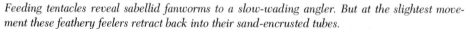

Feeding tentacles reveal sabellid fanworms to a slow-wading angler. But at the slightest movement these feathery feelers retract back into their sand-encrusted tubes.

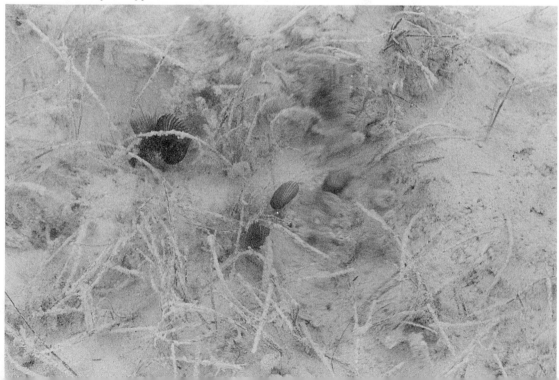

BANDED FEATHER DUSTER
(*Sabella melanostigma*)

*The banded feather duster (*Sabella melanostigma*) feeds at high tide with red-banded tentacles protruding from its tube.*

Burrowing sedentary polychaetes are much more difficult to spot than tube dwellers. Most, however, leave a breathing and feeding hole to the surface. Others leave two holes, one for feeding and one for waste. Burrowers range in shape from thin and earthworm-like to thicker species with elaborate crowns of feeding tentacles. Burrowing sedentary polychaetes include various threadworms (Orbiniidae and Capitellidae).

Unlike sedentary worms, the predatory errant polychaetes crawl or swim about freely in search of food. They feed on other worms and small invertebrates using well-developed jaws. Most have strong, prominent parapodia that they use to swim or burrow. As a group, these species vary little in appearance and are often difficult to distinguish from each other.

Errant polychaetes choose a wide variety of places to live. Several of the sandworms (Nephtyidae), bloodworms (Glyceridae), and threadworms (Arabellidae) burrow temporarily in muddy or sandy substrate when not foraging. But other errant worms, such as members of the Nereidae and Onuphidae families, live in tubes and leave them when they search for food. Still others, like the syllid threadworm, live freely in sand, coral, or sponges on the bottom.

While bonefish consume many polychaetes, researchers can seldom identify individual species as bonefish food. The polychaetes' unprotected bodies leave little to be identified after they pass through the crushing mouth of the bonefish. One polychaete species definitely identified as bonefish prey, however, is the errant, slender threadworm called the Atlantic palolo worm (*Eunice schemacephala*). During reproduction the end of this worm, called its epitoke, breaks off and swims to the surface, where eggs and sperm are discharged. Bonefish sometimes have feeding orgies among the swarming epitokes, usually during the last quarter moon in June/July off Florida, and in November/December on related species in the South Pacific.

TABLE 3.4
WORMS

SPECIES	COLOR	SIZE	BEHAVIOR	HABITAT	COMMENTS
Fanworms (Sabellidae)	Crown often yellow, red, brown or white; body often yellow, yellow brown or flesh	2–3" long; somewhat rounded or slightly flattened	Sedentary; tube builder	Attached to mangrove roots, coral, rocks, shells, pilings, buoys; intertidal and subtidal	Tubes leathery and cylindrical, covered with sand or mud; filter feeders; found in all bonefish destinations
Christmas Tree Worms (Serpulidae)	Crown often red, yellow or purple; body often purple, pink or reddish orange	2–3" long; worm-like	Sedentary; tube builder	Attached to rocks, coral, shells or other hard bodies; intertidal and subtidal	Tubes calcareous (Limestone) coiled or straight; filter feeders; found in all bonefish destinations
Long-Tentacled Worms (Terebellidae)	Crown often shades of red, bright to brownish; body often red, brown or flesh	2–3" long; worm-like, tapering posterior	Sedentary; tube builder	Attached to underside of rocks or buried in substrate; intertidal and subtidal	Tube membranous, covered with mud, shell or debris; direct deposit feeders, using tentacles to collect surface detritus; found in all bonefish destinations
Mudworms (Spionidae)	Body often flesh, mud or sandy	2–3" long; no crown	Sedentary; tube builder	Attached to oyster shells or rocks, or buried in soft substrate; intertidal and subtidal, especially in brackish water	Tubes soft and mud or sand covered; sweep bottom or water for food; found in all bonefish destinations

Where no individual descriptions are identified, descriptions are only general

TABLE 3.4 (continued)
WORMS

SPECIES	COLOR	SIZE	BEHAVIOR	HABITAT	COMMENTS
Threadworms (Capitellidae)	Body often reddish purple or red; sometimes lighter at posterior	2–3" long; earthworm-like; no crown	Sedentary; burrower	Burrows in soft mud; intertidal and subtidal	Most earthworm-like of all polychaetes; often ingests substrate; found in all bonefish destinations
Sandworms (Nereidae)	Body often iridescent; sometimes without color	2–3" long; elongate, rounded or flattened; no crown	Errant; tube builder; active swimmer	Buried in wide variety of muddy or sandy bottoms; intertidal and subtidal	Tubes often sticky, flexible and sand-covered; aggressive predators, leave tube to hunt for prey; found in all bonefish destinations
Syllid Threadworms (Syllidae)	Body often brown, purple, yellow or colorless	2–3" long; threadlike	Errant; often creeps along bottom	Found in sponges, under stones or on sandy bottoms; intertidal and subtidal	Usually not a tube builder, but free-living; presumed to be predacious; found in all bonefish destinations
Predaceous Tubeworms (Onuphidae)	Body often iridescent red	2–3" long; slender	Errant; tube builder; cautious outside	Buried in sand flat often with sea grass; intertidal and subtidal	Tubes often membranous, covered with shell and debris; carnivorous, often feeding on small worms; found in all bonefish destinations
Threadworm (Arabellidae) Atlantic Palolo Worm (*Eunice schemacephala*)	Body often iridescent reddish brown	Epitoke 2–4" long	Errant; active free swimmer	Lives in old coral reefs, just below low tide mark	Hind end breaks off and swims to surface where eggs and sperm are discharged; found in southern Florida Keys

Where no individual descriptions are identified, descriptions are only general

Clam Families

Bonefish consume clams heavily in some areas. In the Bahamas, for instance, bonefish eat clams more than any other type of prey.

Clams protect their soft bodies inside shells that consist of two halves normally hinged at the top or dorsal side. These typically sedentary creatures burrow vertically. They dig into sandy and muddy bottoms by extending a muscular foot down until it anchors, then pulling themselves downward.

To feed, clams filter plankton out of salt water by collecting the water through siphons, then pumping it through their bodies. Some siphons periscope up to the surface to take in and expel water. Other siphons crawl on the surface and suck up food like a vacuum cleaner. These siphons make holes in the bottom that anglers can sometimes use to locate clams. Some species also cause bowl-shaped depressions above their burrowing.

Tellins (Tellinidae)
Tellins have oval-shaped, shiny, delicate shells. They burrow fast and prefer fine, soft sediment. They feed by a flexible siphon that collects food directly off the bottom. Bonefish frequently prey on two species of tellins: the Caribbean tellin and the candy-stick tellin.

Lucines (Lucinidae)
Lucines, characterized by beaded ribs and thicker shells than tellins, use their siphons to pump water through their bodies and then extract plankton from it. One larger member of this family, the tiger lucine, feeds on rotting sea grass. Bonefish also eat the costate lucine, the Pennsylvania lucine, and the three-ridged lucine.

Solemyas (Solemyidae)
Fragile and tiny, solemyas differ from many other small clams. They can move by flapping their umbrella-shaped foot, causing an erratic swimming motion. One solemya species, the West Indian awning clam, has been identified as a common bonefish food.

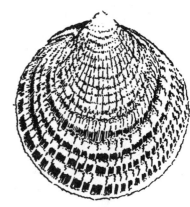

COSTATE LUCINE
(*Codakia costata*)

The costate lucine (Codakia costata), white and barely 3/8 of an inch long with circular flat ribs, prefers sandy bottoms and is consumed in great quantities by bonefish.

TABLE 3.5

CLAMS

SPECIES	COLOR	MAX SIZE	BEHAVIOR	HABITAT	COMMENTS
Tellins (Tellinidae)					
Caribbean Tellin (*Tellina caribaea*)	Glossy white, pink or orange	1" long; thin oval	Sedentary	Prefers fine muddy sand in grass or sandy habitat; intertidal and subtidal	Fast burrower; mobile siphon sucks material directly off bottom; Florida and West Indies
Candy-Stick Tellin (*Tellina similas*)	White or yellow, often with pink rays	1 1/8" long; thin	Sedentary	Prefers fine muddy sand, in grass or sandy habitat; intertidal and subtidal	Fast burrower; mobile siphon sucks material directly off bottom; south Florida and West Indies
Lucines (Lucinidae)					
Tiger Lucine (*Codakia orbicularis*)	White with rose or yellow at margins	3 1/2" long; many ribs; heavy	Sedentary	Prefers silty or muddy sand on protected beaches and subtidal bottoms	Filter feeder; often largest and most common clam in turtle-grass beds; feeds on bacteria; south Florida, Bahamas and West Indies
Costate Lucine (*Codakia costata*)	White	3/8" long; circular; flat ribs	Sedentary	Common on sandy bottoms and other habitats with deficiency of food	Filter feeder; most frequently consumed bonefish prey in Puerto Rico; Florida and West Indies
Pennsylvania Lucine (*Lucina pensylvania*)	Pure white	2" long, concentric ridges; deep fold	Sedentary	Common on sandy bottoms and other habitats with deficiency of food	Filter feeder; long channel to substrate kept open with foot; Florida and West Indies
Three-Ridged Lucine (*Lucina blanda*)	White, sometimes yellow or salmon	1/4–1/2" long; tri-angular; 3 folds	Sedentary	Common on sandy bottoms and other habitats with deficiency of food	Filter feeder; long channel to substrate kept open with foot; West Indies
Solemyas (Solemyidae)					
West Indian Awning Clam (*Solemya occidentalis*)	Shiny brown with yellow lines	1/4" long; thin	Swims in bursts	Prefers soft mud; intertidal or high subtidal	A rapid burrower and occasional swimmer; west coast Florida and West Indies

SPOTTING PREY, READING PREY SIGNS, AND PREY SAMPLING

Knowing what areas of flats hold the most prey and which prey species live there can make the difference between a productive and a fishless day of bonefishing. Before I fish a new area, I like to spend a few hours studying the bottom — wading when possible — to check out the most promising areas.

I start by looking at the places bonefish frequent. I look for flats peppered with feeding holes or muds, indicating recent or current feeding activity. Then I move over the entire area very slowly, looking for prey signs, even observing prey first-hand when possible. An 8X magnifying monocular fitted with a polarizing filter is a big help in spotting prey. A glass-bottomed "water box," a core sampler, and a seine box can also be very useful.

Reading Prey Signs

Prey signs tell where and what kind of prey is around. The most common signs are burrows, discarded prey remains, and fecal casts or piles. Worms leave good signs. They have six common types of burrows. The sedentary parchment tube worm (*Chaetopterus variopedatus*), a threadworm, constructs a U-shaped burrow with two sand-encrusted "chimneys" that stick up from the sand-flat floor at either end of the burrow. The one-inch diameter chimneys project two inches above the bottom and stand a little more than a foot apart.

A related threadworm, the trumpet worm (*Cistena gouldii*), also lives in a U-shaped burrow that creates two holes in the bottom. One becomes depressed as the worm sucks in sand and filters out nutrients. The other becomes mounded with fecal casts.

Several worms construct only single tubes that extend above the substrate. The errant onuphis worm (*Onuphis eremita*) makes a fine sand-grained tube about one-half inch wide and one to two inches tall. The errant plumed worm (*Diopatra cuprea*) builds a slightly larger tube covered with shell and debris fragments. It measures three-eighths inch wide and two to 2 1/2 inches tall, and can be either straight or periscope-shaped.

The errant bloodworm, *Glycera americana*, leaves still another surface clue. It lives in a branched interconnecting tunnel network that makes numerous thin, irregularly spaced holes on the surface. Some worms can be seen directly as they extend their fine feathery tentacles in active feeding. Buried in the substrate, species such as the sedentary terebellid *Amphitrite ornata* reach their tentacles directly onto the surrounding surface and gather detritus.

A number of other bonefish prey bury themselves and leave signs. Most clams dig very deep for cover, but large species leave visible siphon holes in the substrate surface. Lucines have only one siphon hole visible, up to three-eighths inch in diameter in the largest species such as the tiger lucine, *Codakia orbicularis*. Other clams extend two siphons to the surface, one to inhale and one to exhale. Tellins extend a mobile siphon out of the burrow to vacuum pieces of detritus off the substrate floor. But usually these siphons are too tiny — pencil-lead thick to one-eighth inch — to be detected by wading anglers.

Several burrowing crustaceans leave clues that reveal their presence. Some species of swimming crabs, such as the speckled crab (*Arenaeus cribrarius*), bury themselves in shallow water while hunting but leave their tiny eyes and antennae showing. Penaeid shrimp burrow during the day but leave an inhaling hole near the tip of their head.

Mantis shrimp, one of the bonefish's favorite prey, are extremely secretive and seldom seen. But even they leave signs. The golden mantis (*Pseudosquilla ciliata*) burrows in sand or mud and waits to ambush prey, but usually leaves its eyestalks visible. The rock mantis, *Gonodactylus oerstedii*, likes to hide in rock crevices and leaves discarded remains of crabs and clam shells near its retreats.

Many burrowing urchins make mounds on the bottom the size and shape of their outer covering. For example, the five-holed keyhole urchin, *Mellita quinquiesperforata*, lives just beneath the surface, creating a thin mound over its body.

Spotting Prey

Small creatures, such as those bonefish eat, do not survive long if they are not well protected. For many bonefish prey, their primary defense is camouflage. Small fish like grunts and silversides are disguised by reflective scales like those of the bonefish itself. Bottom-dwelling fish like gobies have dusty-colored bodies that blend in with the bottom. Spider crabs have earth-tone mottled colors and are further camouflaged by a rich growth of algae on their hard shells. Mantis shrimp are colored to match their environment — tan and gold over sand and green-black in coral. Many snapping shrimp are translucent and effectively blend into any environment. Most clams display pale cream colors to disappear into the bottom that forms their burrows. But in spite of all these effective disguises, if you know what you are looking for, and if you are patient and look closely, you can see many of the prey bonefish eat.

While gobies and cusk eels tend to lie partially buried on the bottom, their eyes and dorsal fin often protrude enough to be spotted. Many clams, snails, oysters, and other mollusks cling to roots of mangroves or coral outcroppings. Many of the shrimp that thrive in turtle-grass communities feed or rest on top of turtle-grass blades. Most, like the arrow shrimp and the grass shrimp, are well camouflaged. But if you hold still and watch closely you will sometimes see them. Crabs are also sometimes visible to the careful observer, especially since most varieties of swimming, mud, and spider crabs are active. While well camouflaged, if you remain still their movements will give them away. Some of the more pugnacious crabs like the blue, which is found worldwide, are less disguised as adults. Their bright appendages make them easier to see, but they are very fast and difficult to approach.

Another easily spotted prey is the urchin. While large adults are protected by their forbidding spiny exterior, bonefish occasionally prey on small, slow juveniles. Brittle stars are also relatively easy to see with their five long, snake-like legs.

Most of the worm species are difficult to detect directly. Some tube dwellers can be identified when they attach themselves above the bottom to objects like mangrove roots or reefs. Occasionally you can even see their colorful crown of tentacles if they are feeding and if you move slowly. And some of the free-moving errant worms are visible when they crawl and feed in turtle grass. But for the most part, many of these creatures hide in burrows, crevices, and holes and you must detect their presence indirectly, through other signs.

Prey Sampling

In addition to reading signs, you may want to sample the prey present. Two methods are most effective. A sieve box lets you examine a shallow upper-substrate area. A core sampler allows you to go deep into the substrate.

A good sieve box can be made with a one- to two-foot-square wooden frame and a galvanized mesh bottom. You can scoop sand or mud into the box and shake as if you were panning for gold, exposing trapped prey against the mesh.

For core samples, press a coffee can or a section of drain pipe about five inches deep into the substrate, then dig down and put a trowel across the bottom to extract the sample.

Whatever method you use, be aware that many burrowing prey, whether worms, shrimp, crabs, or clams, move very fast and many will escape before you can get them into a seine. Some, like swimming crabs and mantis shrimp, are quite aggressive. Others — like fireworms and urchins — sting and bite. They are better observed than handled.

4

Reading Bonefish Water

At first, bonefish flats appear inscrutable. These opaque fields of sand, grass, and reefs look unfathomable to eyes accustomed to reading water for trout, salmon, and bass. But you interpret saltwater flats the same way you assess fresh water sites — you find fish by looking for protective cover, concentrations of food, and holding areas.

You must also read bonefish water for its fishability. You have to determine which areas let you see the fish, get flies down to them, and play them without breaking off on coral or mangrove hazards. Of all these evaluations, by far the most important is understanding where fish go to find food.

WHERE BONEFISH FEED

Bonefish feed in three zones: along shorelines, on shallow-water flats, and in deep water. The shoreline zone contains three distinct types of bonefish feeding areas: mangroves, rocky shores, and sandy beaches. The shallow-water zone, which lies between the shoreline and deep water, holds food primarily in turtle-grass flats and sand flats. The deep-water zone also has sand and grass, as well as reef feeding areas. But with less light to sustain plant life and food chains, deep water offers bonefish far less calories per cubic foot than flats and shoreline areas.

Reading water in bonefishing is a matter of assessing which areas have the necessary prey, cover, and comfort to attract fish under different tide, temperature, and wind conditions.

Shoreline Mangrove Feeding Areas

Bonefish are attracted to stands of red mangroves, or *Rhizophora mangle*, more than any other area along the shoreline. Mangroves produce more food than any marine habitat except turtle-grass beds. They also have the advantage of offering protection from predators inside their large interlaced root systems. Mangroves give bonefish a rich array of prey that live off the decay of the plant's own leaf droppings.

The food chain that attracts bonefish begins with bacteria, mold, and other microscopic organisms that feed on dead mangrove leaves. These minute creatures become food for tiny copepods and other small crustaceans. They in turn form a rich nutritious soup that feeds shrimp, crabs, juvenile fish, and other small invertebrates. This creates a prey-predator hierarchy that extends upward to include bonefish, snappers, rays, and sharks. Bonefish typically eat mud crabs, snapping shrimp, fiddler crabs, mussels, and sea worms that inhabit this zone.

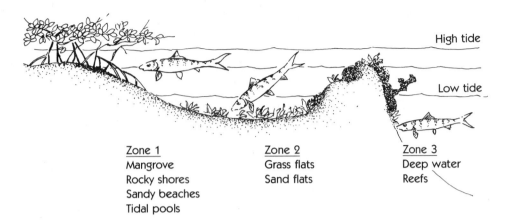

High tide

Low tide

Zone 1
Mangrove
Rocky shores
Sandy beaches
Tidal pools

Zone 2
Grass flats
Sand flats

Zone 3
Deep water
Reefs

BONEFISH FEEDING ZONES

Bonefish feed in three zones, moving inland as the tide rises. At the lowest tides, they rest or feed in the outer zone (Zone 3) in deep-water reefs and holding areas. As tides rise, they move into shallow sand and grass flats rich in food (Zone 2). At highest tides they feed along shorelines (Zone 1) on sandy beaches, tidepools, and in mangrove stands.

The red mangrove or Rhizophora mangle *habitat found along shorelines provides bonefish with ample food and shelter from predators.*

Rocky Shore Feeding Areas

Bonefish also hunt for prey along rocky shores, which are the remains of ancient coral reefs. Colored ocher and gray by the moss-like algae that grow on them, these craggy shoreline reefs range from a few feet to several miles long. Bonefish plunder them at the highest tides and favor two productive areas that contain prey: tidepools and reef walls.

Tidepools consist of deep, wide basins etched into the coral shoreline that receive fresh seawater twice a day. Their sturdy coral boundaries provide a stable, protective environment for marine algae, isopods, and amphipods. These in turn feed a variety of small fish that bonefish eat, including several members of the goby and blenny families. Among them bonefish especially favor the common frillfin goby, the tiny greenband goby, the pearl blenny, and the small blackfin blenny.

Bonefish also hunt along shallow reef walls. Submerged for all but two hours or so at slack low tide, this almost entirely marine environment harbors several prime bonefish prey. Reef crabs and rock mantis shrimp, two favorite bonefish food items, live here. Also, the red rock urchin hides in the reef's crevices for protection while it eats algae. Other prey include small shrimp, fish, worms, numerous bivalves, brittle stars, and whelks.

Sandy Beach Feeding Areas

Bonefish also feed along a third shoreline feeding area, the sandy beach. But these barren intertidal stretches of sand attract bonefish far less than the mangroves, tidepools, and reef walls. Sandy beaches contain neither the plant life necessary to sustain a food chain nor any protective cover. These spartan shoreline habitats look starkly empty compared to richer food-holding areas.

But there is an interesting twist for anglers here. The life forms that live on these intertidal beaches are blatantly vulnerable when feeding at high tide, and bonefish will cruise along the shore to feed on them. Sandy shores hold large colonies of polychaete worms, for example, that burrow and eat along beach areas. The fish come inshore and pick them off when the worms come out of their burrows to feed at high tide. Common species here include trumpet worms in sand-covered cases, parchment worms in U-shaped tubes, and ribbon worms.

Crabs are also abundant on sandy shores. Several species of surf and mole crabs are easy prey for bonefish here, as they sift out particles of food in their shallow burrows at high tide. Other sandy shore prey include coquina, razor, and tellin clams, along with small fish and swimming crabs that come inshore to hunt and become targets themselves.

Shoreline feeding areas can attract bonefish only during high tides. But

Rocky shores, actually the remains of ancient coral reefs, contain two bonefish feeding areas, tidepools and coral banks.

At high tide, sandy beaches provide large numbers of clams and worms for bonefish who venture into shallow shoreline waters.

other habitats like the deeper saltwater flats stay submerged. Bonefish can feed on them all through the tide cycle. These are some of the most important bonefish feeding areas of all.

Grass Flats Feeding Areas

Bonefish feed on sea-grass meadows more than any other marine habitat. Grass beds produce more food than most other habitats in the world and rival even corn fields in the amount of life they sustain. Especially attractive to bonefish, they not only harbor many of its favorite prey in great quantities, they also provide a variegated backdrop that makes the bonefish's camouflage most effective.

These underwater meadows that bonefish find so attractive consist of turtle grass, or *Thalassia testudinum*, and in the shallowest waters, shoal grass, or *Halodule wrightii*. Grass beds can range from carpet-sized patches that pepper the white expanses of sand flats to parking-lot-sized meadows that are acres in size. They grow wherever loose bottoms and protection from wind-driven currents and surf permit them. But regardless of their size or where you find them, they always attract bonefish. Their grass blades provide food and cover for enormous colonies of algae and tiny invertebrates. This forms the first link in a long marine food chain that feeds thousands of species of shrimp, crabs, clams, worms, and small fish that live there. These, in turn, become food for larger fish, especially rays and bonefish. Blue crabs, snapping shrimp, common shrimp, and golden mantis shrimp are but a few of the favorite prey bonefish find here.

Bonefish feeding holes pepper a prey-rich flat full of algae-encrusted turtle grass.

Sandy flats may look barren compared to grass flats, but they sustain a large variety of burrowing prey that attract bonefish.

Sandy Flats Feeding Areas

Sandy flats may look barren compared to grass flats, but many of them attract bonefish just as certainly as grass beds. These flats have a variety of bottoms suitable for prey, ranging from medium-soft mud and marl to coarse-grained sand. They permit small prey to burrow and feed by sucking nutrients and microscopic food forms out of the tidal flow. These lower-level members of the food chain then become food for larger prey that bonefish eat, including burrowing worms, clams, mantis shrimp, swimming crabs, urchins, and brittle stars. Like sandy shores, these plain-background areas give bonefish less cover.

Deep-Water Feeding Areas

Deep-water zones contain the feeding and resting areas bonefish must use when tides are low. They are similar to shallow-water flats areas except that they tend to offer less prey. Partially deprived of sunlight, they contain less plant life to sustain large food chains and to provide shelter. But when tides are lowest, look for bonefish in these deep-water areas. Of the three deep-water habitats, grass beds and reefs support more prey than bare sand for all the same reasons that they do in shallow-water areas. Typical prey here include grass shrimp, spider crabs, and juvenile fish. Because bonefish can be very difficult to see in these deep-water habitats, you may have to use indirect signs of their presence — such as finding muds — to detect them.

Looking for Active Feeding Areas

Once you know the different types of habitats that bonefish frequent, you should look for signs of recent prey activity and bonefish feeding to narrow your search for fish. Most bonefish prey leave signs, both where they burrow and where they eat. These signs will tell you if an area contains active prey. Small pencil- and bullet-sized holes signify worms, clams, and some shrimp. Tiny fecal piles and debris mounds indicate the burrows of members of the mantis shrimp and crab families. Larger two- to eight-inch-diameter mounds are signs of burrowing urchins.

Other signs can also indicate active feeding. The most promising of all are actual bonefish feeding holes — the lemon-sized to grapefruit-sized feeding cavities that bonefish leave in the bottom when they dig out prey. These crater-like holes are a sure sign that a flat has seen feeding activity. Marks that are distinctly formed and slightly darker than their surroundings indicate that

Bonefish feeding habitats often blend into one another. This cay's shoreline contains coral banks, mangrove stands, and sandy beaches.

they are fresh, that bonefish are near, and that you have found an active site (for more detail on bonefish feeding signs, see Chapter 5 "Finding and Seeing Bonefish").

Seeing other predators feeding can also indicate that a flat is active, especially if you see rays, sand sharks, nurse sharks, boxfish, and mullet that eat the same prey as the bonefish. If these fish are feeding, bonefish are probably feeding on the flat as well.

Two other indicators of likely feeding potential are water flow and bottom quality. Flats guides often say, "Dead water means a dead flat." Stagnant water does not supply the nutrients needed to sustain a food chain, and any flat with poor flow should be avoided. Look at the bottom closely to see if there is enough current to pull the turtle grass blades in one direction. Or kick some bottom up with a push-pole or your foot to see how fast the flow carries it. Areas with deep, soft sediment smother life, shutting out both the life-nurturing qualities of sunlight and the microscopic food sources suspended in the water column.

One of the reasons I like to wade is that it lets me quickly make these evaluations. Even when skiff-fishing, getting out to wade will let you check a flat for prey signs and bottom quality.

WHERE TO FIND BONEFISH ON DIFFERENT TIDES

Once you understand which areas hold food for bonefish, you can figure out where to find them on different tides. As tides cycle, fish will travel to graze on the richest areas unless predators or temperatures put them off. By focusing on when the tides give the fish access to their favorite areas, you can pick likely areas for them to feed. Then you can go look at these locations for the presence or absence of feeding signs to determine whether the fish are there.

Rising Tides

At the beginning of a rising tide, look for fish concentrated in either deep-water holes *on* the flats or in deep-water holding and feeding areas *off* the flats. As the tide begins to rise, fish will leave these crowded holding areas for more productive shallow-flats habitats.

Fishing a rising tide, you encounter many hungry fish that have been waiting for the tide to start rising so they can move onto the flats to feed. The earlier you fish this tide, the more you should concentrate your search along deep-water edges, because the flats will still be too shallow to offer fish enough prey and cover to attract them.

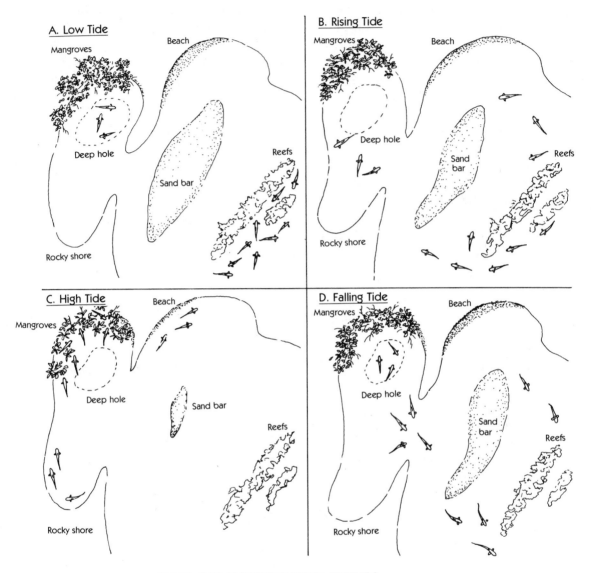

A. Low Tide
Mangroves
Beach
Deep hole
Sand bar
Reefs
Rocky shore

B. Rising Tide
Mangroves
Beach
Deep hole
Sand bar
Reefs
Rocky shore

C. High Tide
Mangroves
Beach
Deep hole
Sand bar
Reefs
Rocky shore

D. Falling Tide
Mangroves
Beach
Deep hole
Sand bar
Reefs
Rocky shore

FINDING FISH ON DIFFERENT TIDES

You can find bonefish on any phase of the tide — if you know where to look. At the lowest tides (A), look in the deep-water edges of flats or in on-flat holes. On rising tides (B), fish come onto food-rich shallow flats and scatter to feed on grass beds and around sand bars. At high tide (C), fish move into the shoreline areas that hold the most food, especially mangrove stands, tidepools, and sandy beaches. Falling tides (D) cause fish to return to deeper water, and if you wait for them where routes constrict, you can ambush them as they leave.

But as the tide rises and begins to flow over flats, tidal currents will bring fresh plankton and microscopic organisms into the tidal shallows. Turtle-grass meadows and sand flats will come alive as thousands of species of shrimp, crabs, clams, worms, fish, and other organisms begin to feed actively. When the prey start feeding, they become vulnerable and bigger predators start feeding. Schools of bonefish begin cruising into them to graze. As the tide continues to rise, hunt for bonefish schools even farther inshore along the sandy beaches, tidepools, and mangrove stands.

If you fish mostly in skiffs and have never done it before, you must sometime wade a food-rich sand and grass flat as the tide rises. Observe the changing activity of marine life as it begins to feed. This is one of my favorite times in bonefishing and it is one you can learn much from, by just watching the natural cycles of the saltwater flat.

Flood Tide

As the tide reaches its fullest point, some fish will travel deep into mangrove backwaters. Anglers are often surprised that such spooky fish travel so far away from the safety of deep water. But once there, the mangroves offer bonefish both food and protection. On one trip to Andros, I listened to big bonefish brazenly popping crabs off mangrove prop roots in stark midday sunlight. They were hundreds of yards from the safety of the nearest deep-water channel, but no angler, barracuda, or osprey could possibly get to them in their red-rooted stockade-like shelters.

At flood tide, grass flats and sand flats deepen. You will continue to find some fish here, but they require different fishing strategies. Some anglers switch to sinking lines in these conditions and fish deep-cruising schools or muds on these deep, flooded flats. Those who prefer to stay with shallow-water techniques will use these high-water periods to search the highest flats often found in shoreline areas and in higher-elevation sounds.

Ebbing Tides

As the tide turns and tidal currents begin flowing off the flats, you will find fish turning back out from shorelines to feed on the flats again. Fish that have been feeding throughout the tide cycle may be partially sated, but most will continue searching for food along the way. Since they have been eating, they may not display the eagerness of fresh, hungry fish on an incoming tide. But this can still be a productive time. Fish will be crossing the flats in great numbers on their way back to their deeper holding areas.

On these falling tides, outbound tidal currents concentrate dislodged prey, and you should always hunt for bonefish along cuts and channels and on the inland sides of reefs where large fish often wait to feed.

Slack Tides

During the lowest part of the tide cycle, especially during spring tide periods, you can find fish congregated in large holding schools as they wait along the edges of flats or on the perimeter of reefs in atoll-flat areas. Anglers usually turn to deep-water techniques to reach these deep-holding fish. But some fish may have opted to wait out the tide cycle in deeper holes on the flats. Look for them by scanning the pale-colored flats for dark blue and dark green pockets. Then search these areas for muds.

WHERE TO FIND BONEFISH AT DIFFERENT TEMPERATURES

Water temperatures, like tides, also let you predict where fish will be. In general, you will usually find bonefish actively feeding in any prey-rich area on the flats as long as water temperatures stay between seventy-five and eighty-five degrees Fahrenheit. But above eighty-eight, you will begin having

When water temperatures rise above eighty-eight degrees Fahrenheit or fall below sixty-eight degrees Fahrenheit, bonefish usually disappear from the flats.

difficulty finding many fish of any size — and you probably won't see any big bonefish at all. Similarly, below sixty-eight degrees, you will find few fish, although big bonefish sometimes stay on the flats a little longer than smaller ones as temperatures fall.

Warm Weather Holding Areas

When prolonged summer temperatures heat the bonefish's shallow-water feeding areas above about eighty-eight degrees, look for fish in cooler, deeper water, usually off the edges of the flats. You can fish for them with sinking flies and lines to search for deep-water mudding fish. You can also adjust your schedule to fish very early in the day when waters are coolest. Concentrate on places where channels, holes, and other deeper-water configurations tend to hold water at slightly lower temperatures. Also look along the edges of flats where colder, deeper water from offshore may attract bonefish.

Cold Weather Holding Areas

When cold winter winds drop the water temperatures on the flats below about sixty-eight, fish swim to warmer waters. Offshore, hunt for them just under the surface layer offshore. The large mass of deep water in the ocean keeps this layer from chilling as rapidly as the changeable thin layer of tidal flat water. This offers bonefish a temporary shelter during short-lived cold spells. On the flats, look in deep lagoons and sheltered areas along the shoreline where thinner, less turbulent water retains higher temperatures. And concentrate your looking in the warmest part of the day when the sun is high.

Cold spells usually cause fish to stop feeding, if water temperatures get down to about sixty-eight degrees or lower. But as temperatures rise after a cold spell, look for fish starting to feed again in waters as low as sixty-two. The fish will be hungry and will tolerate more cold.

Smaller bonefish are more susceptible to cold than are larger fish. This represents an interesting opportunity for anglers, because cold tends to drive small fish off the flats first. This creates a window during the first stages of a cold spell when you can fish to primarily large fish.

Prolonged high or low temperatures like those that occur with seasonal changes cause fish to migrate to waters in their preferred temperature range. Fish in the northern end of Florida, for example, migrate south from Key Biscayne in the fall to warmer waters in the lower Keys. Seasonal factors like these do not affect the way you read water on a trip, but they may well affect where you take a trip at certain times of the year.

Squalls can quickly drop shallow-water temperature eight to ten degrees and drive bonefish off the flats. But since large fish tolerate cold better than small fish, anglers may find the beginning of a cold front offers a special opportunity to search for the biggest targets.

WHERE TO FIND BONEFISH IN WINDY CONDITIONS

Wind, like tides and temperatures, also affects where bonefish feed. Transitory winds from storms have one effect, while constant or prevailing winds have another.

When cold fronts and other weather systems cause *temporary* winds to lash a saltwater flat, this initially drives most bonefish to seek shelter in leeward holding areas behind reefs and islands. Here they can avoid turbulent waters and falling temperatures that come with roiling seas. But once a storm passes, bonefish will usually move into the places that were heavily pounded. These areas will hold an abundance of prey that became dislodged by rough seas, and they provide a rich feeding opportunity.

Trade winds and other long-lasting or prevailing air currents that churn waters day after day, provide a special case for bonefish. Little prey is able to live in windward shore areas that receive constant wind and wave action. In these location, bonefish will hunt on the leeward side of reefs and cays where habitats are protected and prey can thrive. Often choppy and turbid, these areas provide enough cover that fish will feed in very shallow water and tail with abandon.

Two other fish-holding areas that are often affected by wind are channels and cuts. After the strong winds of a storm have pounded a food-rich sand and turtle-grass flat, look for bonefish lined up along the cuts and channels that lead off the flat. The outgoing tides carry an especially rich mix of dislodged prey through these natural constrictions. They concentrate the food and often become especially productive feeding stations for waiting schools of fish after storms.

The arcing reefs that rim the flats of atoll-type areas like the Turneffe Islands of Belize and Los Roques, off Venezuela, also trap and funnel prey unearthed by wind-driven currents. Outgoing tides carry the prey against these bulwark-like barriers and then drain lengthwise along their inshore sides, as they empty off the flat.

WHERE TO FIND BONEFISH IN WIND
One of the favorite haunts of bonefish during prevailing windy conditions is on the inshore side of reefs. The largest concentrations are found behind the outermost windward reefs.

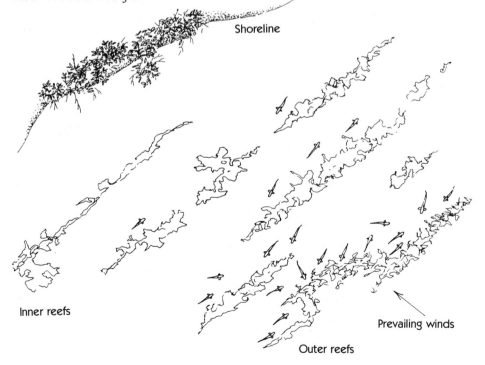

Shoreline

Inner reefs

Prevailing winds

Outer reefs

Bright sunlight on a light-colored sand flat provides one of the best situations for seeing bonefish — but the fish tend to be very wary under this vulnerable condition.

WHERE TO FIND BONEFISH ON SUNNY AND CLOUDY DAYS

In the brightest sunlight, look for bonefish feeding in areas that will provide cover and make their camouflage most effective. Under such conditions, you will often find fish in grass beds, in mangroves, and in deep or cloudy water. Also on bright days, you may find fish in clear shallow water or on light sandy bottoms, as long as these highly vulnerable areas hold food and have comfortable water temperatures. But because they offer little cover, fish found on them in bright sun will usually be wary and difficult to entice.

Cloudy days usually offer more places to search for bonefish — as long as the clouds don't accompany winds that drop water temperatures below the fish's comfort range. In low light, prey feed more actively, and you will find bonefish feeding more actively as well. Most flats will contain more fish and hold them longer. Also, cloudy days offer you a special opportunity to fish areas where fish usually spook on sunny days. Bright-bottom sand flats, sand bars, and shallow-water flats may fish well in cloudy weather. Also look for more tailing on cloudy days.

USING COVER AND ESCAPE ROUTES TO FIND BONEFISH

You can also use bonefish hiding places and escape routes to locate fish. Whenever fish feel threatened by predators, bright light, or shallow water, look for them in the most protective areas. Sea-grass beds, coral reefs, and other variegated backgrounds allow bonefish to conceal themselves. Wind-driven choppy or muddy water also provides cover in otherwise vulnerable waters. Mangroves are the best of all, but can only be reached at the highest tides.

Escape routes can also help you predict where fish will be. Fish use these underwater highways when spooked because they offer the fastest, safest, and

USING ACCESS AND ESCAPE ROUTES TO LOCATE BONEFISH
Bonefish are constantly aware of the entrance and escape paths that lead on and off flats. They follow these paths on rising tides to reach feeding grounds. They also retreat along them on falling tides or when spooked, in order to escape to the safety of deeper water.

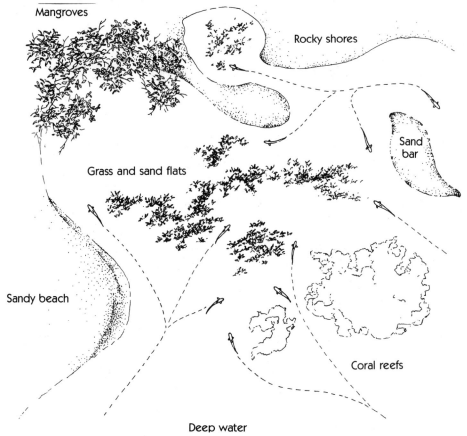

Mangroves

Rocky shores

Sand bar

Grass and sand flats

Sandy beach

Coral reefs

Deep water

shortest paths to on-flat and off-flat sanctuaries. You can find these potential escape trails by walking flats when the tide is dead low, especially during spring tides. Emptied of water, you can easily distinguish the channels, cuts, and holes bonefish will use to take refuge or to leave the flats for deeper water. You can also see some of these channels and deep-water sanctuaries during high tides by looking for the dark blue waters that indicate depth, but this is much cruder than reading flats at low tide.

One way that escape routes help you predict fish locations is by telling you which flats they will favor or avoid when they sense danger. Bonefish will generally prefer flats where deep water or mangroves border their perimeter. They also like large, wide flats laced with deep-water channels that offer many paths of escape and deep-water sanctuaries. On the other hand wide, shallow flats that lack deep holes or channels are less likely to hold fish long. Small, confined, lagoon-type flats and others bounded on most sides by shoreline are also nervous places for bonefish. Any fish found in these areas is likely to be very skittish.

But just because a flat is dangerous for bonefish does not mean you should ignore it. There is one small cul-de-sac flat in the Bahamian out islands where I fish that is so full of food it holds great schools of bonefish. If spooked, the fish will ride over each other's backs in their rush to escape through the narrow entrance. Yet the food concentration here is so high, they will come right back to it on the next tide.

USING PREDATOR PRESENCE TO FIND BONEFISH

If you see bottom-feeding sharks, rays, mullet, and other predators that prey on crustaceans and mollusks working a flat, consider it a good indication. These predators seldom bother bonefish and since they feed on the same prey, they confirm the presence of food that will attract bonefish. But ospreys, frigate birds, fish-eating sharks, and large barracuda that run down bonefish are bad signs on a flat. Any bonefish you find nearby will be nervous and will spook at the least noise or movement. Once I see these predators around, I usually move to another flat or to another area on large flats.

One of the bonefish's most dangerous enemies can be a good sign for anglers, however. Schools of fast-swimming porpoises encircle and attack bonefish. But their large bodies prevent them from coming into the shallowest parts of flats. When under attack, even large bonefish will take refuge and hold for hours in unusually shallow waters. So if you see packs of these big gray submarines patrolling offshore, look for large bonefish on the back edges of flats and in mangrove areas if the water is high enough to reach them.

FISHABLE WATERS

In addition to choosing waters for their fish-holding potential, you should also select waters for their fishability. Water depth, fish visibility, wading dangers, and fish-playing hazards all affect your ability to stalk, hook, and play fish.

Depths Suitable for Fly Fishing

Most anglers prefer hunting bonefish in waters between about one and four feet deep. These depths permit you to both see the fish well and to get flies down to them quickly. In areas with two equal daily tides, you can normally follow the daily flow of rising and falling tides and find optimum fishing depths throughout the fishing day. You simply fish prime depths as they move back and forth between the shoreline areas and the flats.

But some anglers prefer to fish deeper areas, such as on-flat holes and channels and off-flat reefs and shoulders. You can reach fish in these holding areas with long leaders and heavy flies or, better yet, with sinking lines or sinking tips and short leaders. While less exciting — because you cannot see fish as well — this technique can offer good fishing when the flats are too warm, cold, or dangerous for fish. Deeper waters offshore from flats or outside the reefs that rim atolls are probably better left to other methods of angling.

Fish Visibility

Most anglers fish best if they fish to the limits of their vision. On cloudy days or when it is windy and choppy, you increase the odds that you will see bonefish by picking areas with good bright bottoms and shallow depths. Fish will frequent these areas more and be calmer under the cover of clouds and rough or turbid water. You are far more likely to spot them there than if you hunt in hard-to-see places like grass beds and reefs in low-light conditions.

But on bright days, you should favor the places where fish can best conceal themselves or feel most protected. Mangrove areas, grass beds, and deep-water areas, especially grassy ones, can all hold fish when bright light and shallow water make them most vulnerable.

Wadable Bottoms

If you fish mostly on foot, you will have to avoid some promising waters because of bad bottoms and currents. Cul-de-sac flats often have soft sediment and can wear you out with laborious wading. Sinkholes can be as treacherous as quicksand on some flats. Also watch out for rips and cuts that can sweep you off your feet (see Chapter 9, "Wading for Bonefish," for more on reading flats for wading).

Fish-Playing Hazards

Hazards should seldom prevent you from fishing a promising flat, but they may determine how you position yourself to fish it. You should keep coral reefs, bars, and sharp-edged sea-razor beds inland of you so they can't sever your fly line when a hooked fish runs for deep water.

In mangrove areas, fish will often run into the protective spider-like legs of the root systems. You should position yourself between the fish and the mangroves to encourage the fish to run seaward.

In areas with abundant reefs, like many of the atoll flats areas, hooked fish will drag your line across the sharp coral and break off. Since you are sur-

A barnacle-encrusted mangrove shoot can cut you off if a bonefish drags your line across it.

rounded by reefs in some of these areas, you cannot always put yourself between the fish and the hazard. You may have to take your chances, giving the fish slack line and wading toward it to free the line when necessary.

Some areas present so many hazards that they are just not worth the risks. Inshore mangrove flats peppered with fresh barnacle-encrusted mangrove shoots hold treacherous fish-playing hazards. They will almost certainly separate you from a hooked fish. Some reef areas have so much sharp coral they will cost you a new fly linnne every time a fish escapes across them. Better to look for fish elsewhere.

TIDES: A PRIMER

Tides are critically important to bonefishing anglers. They affect the behavior of fish and they determine how and where you fish. They also vary, not only from day to day and week to week, but also from one location to another.

How Tides Work

Most bonefishing destinations have twice-daily tides with highs and lows spaced about six hours apart. Some places have two equal high tides every day, while others have two unequal high tides every day: one strong and one weak. Still others have only one high tide a day, period.

What makes tide cycles vary from place to place and from week to week is complex, but tides have such a great effect on bonefish behavior that all bonefish anglers should understand how they work.

Tides result from the gravitational pull of both the moon and the sun. But the moon affects tides the most; even though it is much smaller than the sun, it is located so much closer to the earth that it exerts a far stronger pull on the earth's surface and its oceans. The massive gravitational forces of the moon combine with the earth's own centrifugal spinning forces to form an enormous ring-shaped bulge in the waters on the earth's surface. This bulge encircles the earth, creating two high tides — one on the side of the earth closest to the moon and one on the side farthest from it.

Every day, the earth passes through these two high-tide bulges as the planet revolves. This causes two complete tide cycles daily: two high tides and two low tides.

If the moon stayed fixed in one spot while the earth turned below it, these highs and lows would each occur at the same times every day and take place six hours apart. But the moon orbits the earth very slowly. It travels in the same direction that the earth rotates and it moves forward in its orbit by only fifty minutes each day.

Thus, every day it takes the earth twenty-four hours and fifty minutes to rotate far enough to catch up to the same position it held yesterday. This orbital lag is what causes the same tidal condition that occurs in Bimini today at 9:10 A.M. to occur in Bimini tomorrow at 10:00 A.M. and on the next day at 10:50 A.M.

This typical tide cycle, commonly found in most Bahamas and Florida bonefishing waters, contains two high tides and two low tides spaced approximately six hours and twelve minutes apart (twenty-four hours and fifty minutes divided into four equal parts). Such cycles vary water depths all day long and almost always provide anglers with fishable depths for some portion of the fishing day.

Once-a-Day vs. Twice-a-Day Tides

Many popular bonefishing destinations that border large expanses of uninterrupted ocean — such as Florida and the Bahamas — experience the "typical" twice-a-day tide cycle. But some flats areas have only once-a-day tides. Usually these limited daily tide cycles occur in areas where large bodies of land, islands, and reefs shield flats from the full tidal effects of the open ocean. Some Gulf of Mexico and South American locales, for example, have single daily tide cycles. You must plan your fishing carefully in such areas. If you arrive at a once-a-day tide location when the lowest tides occur during the peak sun periods you need for visibility, you may not have enough water to hold fish. Book these areas through an agent who has fished there and can tell you how to plan for tides.

Spring and Neap Tides

One other tidal condition, which is caused by the sun, can affect the time of month you should fish. While the moon accounts for most tidal activity, the sun has one important effect on tides. During full and new moons, the moon is in line with the sun and the earth. The combined gravitational forces of the sun and moon create the most exaggerated tides, called "spring" tides; they have the highest high tides and the lowest lows. In between, in the weeks of the first- and third-quarter moons, the sun and moon are at right angles relative to the earth. This causes the weakest, or "neap," tides to occur.

Depending on location, spring tides can help or hurt fishing. In places like the Bahamas and Florida, high water from spring tides makes bonefish feel more secure by deepening the shallowest backwaters and creating stronger current flows on falling tides that sweep more food off the flats. Also, some favorite bonefish prey in the shrimp and worm families time their spawning

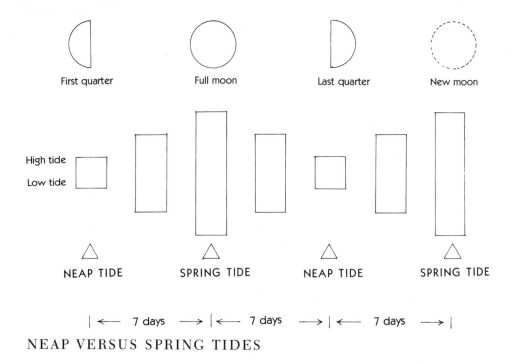

First quarter   Full moon   Last quarter   New moon

High tide

Low tide

NEAP TIDE   SPRING TIDE   NEAP TIDE   SPRING TIDE

|←— 7 days —→|←— 7 days —→|←— 7 days —→|

NEAP VERSUS SPRING TIDES

Following the phases of the moon, tides change from the lightest (neap tides) to the heaviest (spring tides) every seven days, greatly altering the amount of tidal acreage available to bonefish.

with the highest tides, causing fish feeding frenzies during new and full moon periods. But in other places, such as Christmas Island, the spring low tides fall so low that water disappears off the flats, making them virtually unfishable for anglers unfortunate enough to be there.

Neap tides, with their more subdued tidal swings, usually offer more periods of favorable water depths. In the Bahamas, you can usually fish the entire tide cycle during neap periods. But these weaker tides do not churn as much prey and create the feeding sprees that spring tides do.

Planning Your Trip Around Tides

The more you understand the tides at a location, the better you can plan a trip to fish there. Tide knowledge is especially critical for places with once-a-day tides or unequal twice-a-day tides, where a whole week of fishing with the best sunlight conditions can take place during the worst water conditions. Even in good twice-a-day tidal areas, knowledge of tide times and depths will help you better plan the tackle you need and the times to fish. This is one area where a booking agent can offer anglers a really useful service by staying on top of tidal information and providing up-to-date charts along with your airline ticket.

5

Finding and Seeing Bonefish

Finding and spotting moving fish is what sets bonefishing apart from other angling. Trout and salmon fishermen may cast to sighted targets, but their quarry hold fixed locations. Bonefish do not. They roam wide expanses of tropical flats in search of food. You must track them down and see them before you cast your fly.

Bonefish zigzag across flats, digging out crabs and shrimp. To make a fly attract them, you must anticipate their path, cast your fly in front of them, and let it sink to the bottom. As they approach it, you retrieve your line to get their attention and to make the fly move like a shrimp or crab going for cover. But you cannot do all of this fast enough unless you first see the fish.

At first, finding bonefish and seeing them may frustrate you. These are unusual skills. No other fishing — at least none familiar to most of us — prepares you with the unique hunting, tracking, and spotting experience you need to stalk this well-camouflaged creature.

But you can learn these abilities like those required by any other complex sport: you break them into components and master each one in turn. Once you do, it may change you. You will find that these very skills and challenges that were so difficult in the beginning, are what draw you back to the flats and this ephemeral fish year after year. If you are not careful, they will also ruin your other fishing.

FEEDING SIGNS AND HOW TO READ THEM

Many predators feed on the bottom of the saltwater flats. But the bonefish eats in a unique way, leaving distinct feeding signs that can be quickly identified. As bonefish burrow into the mud to root out crustaceans and mollusks, they expel a jet of water from their mouths that blows mud and sand away from their prey. This debris forms a rim around the edge of each feeding hole that looks like a little volcano. These crater-shaped cavities, about the size of lemons, oranges, and grapefruits, mark the path of a feeding school. Each hole indicates a place where a fish stopped to eat.

A small group of two or three fish or a single fish traveling alone will leave only a few feeding cavities. A large school will pepper acres of tidal flat with hundreds of crater-shaped holes. In either case the definition, color, size, and shape of these signs tell an experienced angler how many bonefish have been there, how big they were, how recently they were there.

Feeding Cavity Depth and Color

The distinctiveness and definition of a bonefish feeding cavity tells how recently it was made. Fresh feeding marks are typically deeper than older ones.

The mud inside and around the edges of fresh bonefish feeding holes often appears slightly darker than the surface that surrounds the cavities.

Tides and currents have not yet washed sediment back into them, and they still retain their distinct outlines. Often the mud inside and around new cavities appears slightly darker because the underlying substrate contains dark-colored decaying organic matter. In contrast, older holes often look lighter in color as pale sediment settles into them.

Feeding Cavity Size

Big bonefish make big feeding holes — sometimes eight inches across. Small bonefish make smaller cavities, three or four inches in diameter. Uniform-sized feeding holes indicate feeding by a group of fish that are all about the same size; different-sized holes usually mean a school of fish of many sizes is feeding. Hole size is important because it tells you what to look for next. If the feeding signs indicate a great many small fish, you should start to look for the broad muddy clouds given off by many fish feeding in a large school (see page 89 for a description of muds). But if the feeding cavities suggest the presence of a few large fish, you must look for individual puffs of mud. These are indicative of big fish, which tend to feed alone or in small pods of twos and threes.

Feeding Cavity Shape

The bonefish pushes its conical head into the mud as it excavates prey with a hydraulic jet-stream technique. Its feeding holes are basically round. But most holes are slightly oblong and have more debris at one end than the other. This build-up of sediment at one edge of the hole comes from the fish pushing and thrusting to grasp prey and blowing sediment away from it. These uneven rims are unique to bonefish and a definite sign of their presence.

False Signs

Many forms of life burrow in the substrate of the flats for protection. A few of them, such as larger shrimp, crabs, and other fish, make cavities that resemble those made by bonefish. The diameter of these holes ranges from two to four inches — similar in size to the feeding cavities of smaller bonefish. But their depth is shallower, their bottoms have a distinct burrow hole, and their walls appear bowl-shaped. Bonefish feeding cavities have solid bottoms, no burrow hole, and distinct near-vertical walls.

Anglers sometimes misread the cavities made by long the push-poles fishing guides use to propel their boats. But push-pole holes are too angular, deep, and uniform in shape to look like bonefish signs. They are also usually too linear in direction and too regular in spacing.

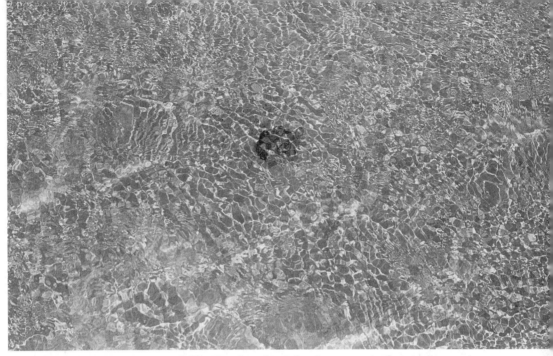

Unlike bonefish feeding signs, a guide's push-pole makes holes that appear uniform in shape and regular in spacing.

READING MUDS

Feeding cavities show you where fish *were* feeding. Muds tell you where fish *are* feeding, now or within the last few minutes.

Muds are clouds of silt, sand, and coral dust particles. They hang suspended in the water column where bonefish have been churning the bottom and feeding. Normally these clouds disappear quickly. Their particles settle back to the bottom or dissipate in the current until they can no longer be detected.

Muds tell you three things: where, when, and how many fish are feeding.

Fresh Muds

A fresh mud looks more intense in color than an older mud. The sediment may color it dark gray, milky ocher, or dusky pink, depending on the make-up of the bottom and the brightness of the day. The more recent the mud, the richer and darker the hues of the colors it contains. A fresh mud also looks distinct. It will hang intact in the water.

Older Muds

Older muds dissipate as tides and currents disperse them. They look like chalky water. The more time passed since the fish were feeding, the paler or

When a large number of bonefish school together to feed, they leave a sprawling, chalky mud-cloud in the water. This one stretches half the length of a football field behind a group of about thirty medium-size fish.

less intense the mud will appear. When you see old muds, look for the darkest or densest part. Then scan beyond it for a fresh, new mud that indicates the next place the fish are feeding.

Small Muds

Single fish, doubles, and triples leave a trail of small individual puffs as they feed. These puffs march across the flat like little explosions, following the trail of the grazing fish. As you get closer to them you should be able to pick out the forms of the fish themselves.

Large Muds

When a lot of fish feed, their puffs merge into a large, chalky cloud that follows them. Sometimes large schools make muds that cover two or three acres. But no matter how large or small the mud, look for fish where the cloud appears most intense. That is where they are feeding. Sometimes this darker area occurs at one edge of the mud as the school migrates from one feeding site to another. Other times it shows up in the center when fish congregate in a food-rich area and stay in one place. When you cannot see the fish in one of these deep muds, cast "upstream" of it and let the tide carry your fly into it — bonefish usually will be feeding into the tide.

False Muds

Some muds are false alarms. Rays disturb the bottom by flapping their large wing-like bodies as they feed. From a distance, this churning may look like bonefish mudding. But you can easily identify the large, distinct, black shape of a ray as you get closer. Don't break off your search immediately, however. Bonefish often trail rays, feeding on overlooked food kicked up in their foraging. You can sometimes see very nice fish following in a ray's wake.

Smaller fish like mullet and little sharks also sometimes make muds. But most of these other fish are easier to see than bonefish. If you watch the area around these muds for a few seconds you will see what made them. Some larger shrimp, brittle stars, and crabs kick up bottom sediment, but the size of these mini-muds tells you bonefish did not make them. Whenever you are not sure what made a mud, however, make a trial cast and retrieve your fly through the cloudy area. Sometimes you will be rewarded with the solid tug of a bonefish.

Color of Feeding Holes and Muds

Fishing locations vary in their geologic make-up, and this affects the color of feeding holes and muds. Shell and coral fragments color feeding holes and muds in the Bahamas various shades of ocher and dusky rose. A mixture of yellowish-colored coral and quartz make feeding signs in the upper Florida Keys pale ocher. Those of the lower Keys often appear snow-white, since most of the bottoms there contain limestone.

Even different habitats at the same location can affect the appearance of signs. Feeding holes and muds in mangrove flats look tea-colored or charcoal, stained by root tannin and leaf detritus in the sediment. Signs on turtle grass or mud flats take on a gray cast from organic detritus sediment, while signs on coarse sand flats display the natural color of the base sediment.

SEEING THE FISH

After you track feeding cavities and muds to the area where a school is feeding, you have to see the fish to aim your cast. But if you are new to bonefishing, you probably won't be able to see the fish at all. You will stare at the water. You will see every detail of the surface. You will see chop. You will see glare. You will see the contour of the pale gray-green bottom. You will even see moving shapes and shadows. You will see everything except the fish. The problem is that you won't even know what you are looking for. Are the fish silver like their scales? Or dark like their backs? Are they dull or shiny?

Blue-gray or silver-white? Chalky or ocher? Or bottle-green? Are you looking for one fish or five or fifty?

Seeing bonefish is one of the hardest skills for beginners to learn. They don't know what to look for because they don't understand that the bonefish's appearance changes constantly.

The bonefish's camouflage is so effective that it prevents you from catching more than a glimpse of its body, a wisp of its shadow, or the quickest glimmer of its side as its body turns against the sun. If you are going to spot this fish, you have to carry a large inventory of visual patterns with you, and you must constantly scan the flat for every one of them.

Most of the time, seeing a bonefish requires making a positive match with a known bonefish pattern. You learn the different disguises or "looks" a bonefish adopts. Then you scan the water until you lock onto one of these disguises long enough to identify it as a fish. But other times you will see a negative cue—a pattern breaker—that is not part of the background. You catch a glimpse of bonefish color, shape, pattern, and movement that says, "There is something here that does not fit."

Bonefish Markings

Close-up, three aspects of the bonefish's distinctive appearance can give it away. When sighting conditions are extremely difficult, spotting one of these hard-to-conceal markings may be the only way to detect their presence. The fish's great black eye will sometimes stand out starkly against the pale translucent background. The bonefish's oversized tail, which always seems twice as large as it should be, will also break its cover. The tail has a large black outline that appears as a distinct hard-edged shape against the watery surroundings. The pattern of black bars on the bonefish's back blend perfectly with turtle grass and mottled bottoms. But these too can break a fish's cover when you see it against plain surroundings like sand, or when you see it up close.

Seeing The Fish Whole

Seeing an entire bonefish in quiet, clear water is rare. Usually this occurs when fish feel safe, as when they tail in low light or in calm backwaters around protective mangroves. When the fish feed in such clear, still water, you see them in incredible detail. They stand almost vertically, with their mouths to the bottom. Puffs of mud rise and slowly drift away on the tide. The fishes' white bellies and black-barred backs do not blend with either mangrove roots or uniform sand-covered bottoms when they tail. You can see them so plainly, you wonder how it was that you ever had trouble seeing them before. Then they will lower their tails, resume their normal horizontal

Large exposed tails glistening in the sun are the easiest sign of bonefish for an angler to spot. But tailing fish are also especially wary and difficult.

swimming position, and glide off toward their next grazing site, disappearing before your eyes.

Tailing Fish

When bonefish feed in shallow water with their heads down, they stick their tails out of the water. If the sun is strong, the tails give off little reflective flashes. Sometimes the tails even make noises as they splash in the water in the excitement of feeding. You hear the kind of slapping sounds that a light chop makes when it smacks into a dock piling. Bonefish tails, exposed and glistening out of the water, provide you with one of the easiest cues in bonefishing—and one of the most promising. When fish tail, they show you exactly where they are, and they tell you they are hungry. But tailing fish are also very wary and selective. This is the most nervous of all feeding conditions. It is a time for long leaders and quiet flies.

Nervous Water

Nervous water is caused by a school of fish cruising or mudding just below the surface of shallow water. This cue usually signifies schools of small- to medium-sized fish that are erratically cruising and darting back and forth, competing for food. Larger fish tend to feed alone and move more deliberately. They make more subtle wakes or finning bulges in thin water.

Both tailing and nervous-water cues are good signs when you see them. But beginning bonefish anglers should be warned that these easily seen fish signs usually represent a small percentage of the fish present on the flats. Learning to see through the water to pick up the cues of subsurfacccsh will reveal many more targets.

Side Flash

Many fisherman will recognize this easy-to-spot underwater cue. It occurs when sunlight bounces off a fish's mirror-like gill-plate cover or its side as it turns. You see this sign only on bright days, and it may signify something other than a bonefish. A barracuda may have made it, or even a boxfish or school of shad. But side flash always reveals the presence of fish and tells you to look for a match with other bonefish cues.

Zigzag Grazing Behavior

When a school of fish cruises a flat in search of food, it zigzags. You see the erratic motion of the fishes' shapes and their shadows moving across the bottom. Sometimes they search and feed slowly. Other times their movement is fast— almost frenzied—if competition for prey is intense. You should consider this swirling movement an especially favorable cue. When a pod of six or eight fish feed below the surface, they eat aggressively and attack flies hard. (See p. 96)

A compound cue, zigzag grazing behavior consists of two different motions at the same time. Within the school, fish move like boiling water. Each fish constantly changes its position relative to the others as they each vie to beat others to the next morsel. Second, the whole school will drift back and forth as it moves from one food site to the next. This pattern of a school of cruising fish jaggedly darting across the flat, with individual fish boiling around inside, is a sure sign of bonefish *feeding*. Because they are deeper and feel more protected, they eat flies more aggressively than do tailing fish.

Straight-Line Run

The flushed path of spooked fish contrasts starkly with the busy patterns of grazing behavior. At the first sign of danger, a school of bonefish breaks into a

A mirror-like plate covers the bonefish's gills, and hundreds of silver scales sheathe its body. Together this reflective armor gives off side flashes in bright sunlight, creating one of the easiest bonefish looks for anglers to spot.

Even on bright days, the side flash made by a bonefish as it turns into the sun is brief. If you see one, look for the shape of the fish behind the flash and lock onto it.

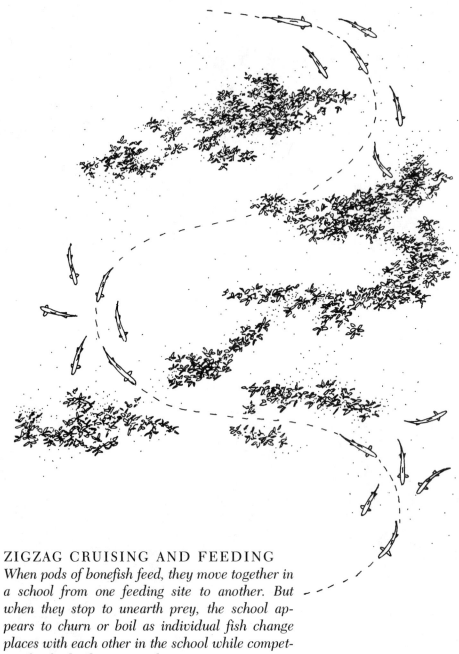

ZIGZAG CRUISING AND FEEDING

When pods of bonefish feed, they move together in a school from one feeding site to another. But when they stop to unearth prey, the school appears to churn or boil as individual fish change places with each other in the school while competing for food. This stop-and-go, zigzag pattern is a sure sign of feeding fish and is easy to spot even in water that is four to five feet deep.

sudden, straight-line run to open sea. They make no boiling or darting motions — they just take off in a single streaking run. Like subway cars blasting through a tunnel, the fish will scream past you toward deep water. You won't have any trouble spotting them. But most of the time you won't get them to stop to look at your fly, either. Once in a while, however, a fly that lands noisily alongside a flushed school will cause fish to dart over and grab it. I have gotten into the habit of casting to spooked fish and found it works perhaps twenty percent of the time. Not great odds, but what have you got to lose when the fish have already spooked?

EFFECT OF DIFFERENT COLOR AND LIGHT CONDITIONS

To see bonefish, you have to hunt for all of the basic patterns of bonefish shape, motion, and behavior. You must look for them in a constantly changing framework of backgrounds that varies with brightness of sun, water depth, color of bottom, color of water, angle of sun, amount of glare, and amount of chop on the water.

The reflectivity of the bonefish's body magnifies the effect of all these conditions. Not only are you limited to partial glimpses of this shy fish, but these partial glimpses are constantly changing in color, shape, texture, and brightness as the background changes.

The Chameleon Effect

The bonefish's coat of several hundred tiny mirrors echoes everything around it. This scattering of scales not only reflects its surroundings, it aims each reflection at a slightly different angle. This breaks up the image of whatever pattern it mimics, sending the angler a fragmented vision of the tidal flat. Worse, through chemical changes in their outer skin layer, bonefish can alter their hue to blend with both light and dark backgrounds. In combination, this reflectivity and ability to vary hue make the bonefish one of the most difficult creatures in the world to see.

In the world of solid shapes, colors, and flat planes we live in, the mirrored bonefish would stand out like a billboard. But in the irregular, variegated world of the shallow flat, the mottled patterns it imitates blend perfectly. The fish is no color and all colors. It is no pattern and all patterns. It is five hundred little reflections of the color and pattern of everything around it.

When sighting conditions are extremely difficult, the distinct black outline of the bonefish's caudal fin and the faint shadow of its body may be the only cues you can see.

Bright Days

On really bright days, with good sun overhead, bonefish reflect their surroundings so well that they are almost invisible. You see the *shadow* of a fish before you see the fish that made it. So a fish's first appearance will be dark, almost black. If you lock onto the zigzagging path of this approaching shadow, you will see the fish itself. It will vary in color and brightness as it passes over different bottoms and through different intensities of sunlight:

- In bright sun on a white sandy flat covered with small patches of turtle grass, fish will appear white with flecks of gray-green, just like the grass.
- In bright sun on a muddy flat with a bottom of ocher coral mud, a fish looks chalky dirty-yellow.
- When you find a fish in deeper turquoise water, it will appear pale blue-green.
- In bright sun on dense, dark turtle grass, a fish takes on the dark blue-green of an old Coke bottle.
- In bright sun and chalky or muddy water, a bonefish looks like a vague, milk-colored shape the same hue as the mud—the classic bonefish phantom.
- Sometimes you encounter a dark-hued fish in a light area, or vice versa. This is a fish that altered its color while feeding in one area for

a long time and that just moved to a new area. While sometimes easier to spot, its reflectivity usually offsets its contrasting hue so it appears as a slightly darker or lighter reflection of its surroundings.

Dark Days

On dark days you will not see fish from as far away as on bright days, when you can spot their high-contrast shadows eighty or one hundred feet away. Otherwise, appearance varies with color and level of brightness just as on sunny days:

- On cloudy days when little sun reflects off a fish's scales, it appears as a slightly darker reflection of its surroundings: brown shape on a tan bottom, tan shape on an ocher bottom, gray shape on a white bottom, etc.
- On very dark days, a bonefish appears as a dark gray shape. This is different from seeing its black shadow on the bottom on a bright day. Here the *shape* of the fish appears dark.

On a cloudy day in thin water, a bonefish against a pale sand bottom (center of photo) looks white and is nearly invisible with no shadow to give it away.

TABLE 5.1

**HOW BONEFISH COLOR CHANGES WITH DIFFERENT
LIGHT, WIND, AND FEEDING AREAS**

WIND	FEEDING AREAS	BRIGHT LIGHT	LOW LIGHT
Calm	White sand flat	White	Cream
Calm	Sand/turtle grass flat	White with gray-green flecks	Cream with gray-green flecks
Calm	Turtle grass flat	Blue-green	Dark blue-gray
Calm	Mud flat	Chalky dirty yellow	Dark ocher
Calm	Reef shoreline	Gray	Dark gray
Calm	Deep water	Pale blue-green	Dark blue-green
Windy	All areas	Color of sediment	Darker color of sediment

Bright Light: sunny days and mid-day sun. Low-light: cloudy days; early morning and late afternoon on sunny days

FALSE VISUAL CUES

Several flats dwellers give off cues similar to bonefish and can be mistaken for them.

Barracuda

Barracuda appear similar to the bonefish but do not display their erratic grazing behavior. Instead they alternate between cruising in a straight line and lying in ambush. Blending with the color around them, they look like ice-green torpedoes suspended a few inches beneath the surface, always ready to attack anything that looks vulnerable.

Like the bonefish, barracuda also use reflection to blend with the background. But their larger silver scales give off pronounced reflections, uncommon with bonefish. Bonefish flash like broken glass, while barracuda emit flashes like a hand-sized signal mirror. Also, barracuda tend to be larger than bonefish. They have a broader profile and big square tails. Bonefish have thinner, forked tails.

Sharks

Almost all members of this well-known family are larger and darker than bonefish. Their dull skins do not reflect light. Even light-colored species such as the lemon shark usually look like dark shadows.

Sometimes on a bright day, however, the lightest-colored sharks can be deceiving. Only their characteristic undulating swimming motion gives them away under these conditions. Sharks swim with their whole bodies and display a snake-like rhythm in their swimming, a kind of wiggling motion that looks distinctly different from the tail-propelled cruising of bonefish and barracuda.

Rays

Rays sometimes make muds that look like those of bonefish. But usually their mudding is continuous and takes on a long, straight-line pattern, in contrast to the sporadic muds of a school of bonefish. The large black shape of this common flats feeder also makes it stand out, even at a distance, easily distinguishing it from bonefish as the source of a mud.

Boxfish, Shad, Grunt, Needlefish, and Others

Most other flats fish have characteristic shapes and colors that distinguish them from bonefish. Needlefish appear as long, slender, electric-green shapes on the surface. Boxfish display a chunky, bluish-green, milk-carton profile

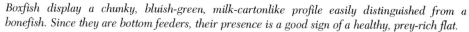

Boxfish display a chunky, bluish-green, milk-cartonlike profile easily distinguished from a bonefish. Since they are bottom feeders, their presence is a good sign of a healthy, prey-rich flat.

easily discriminated from bonefish. Most members of the grunt family are gaily colored in yellows and greens, and it would be hard to confuse them with the silver phantom. But mullet share both the silver color and torpedo shape of bonefish. They also feed on the bottom, make muds, and at times can look like a school of small bonefish. But no other fish of the tidal flat display the erratic, darting swimming behavior of a school of feeding bonefish. This pattern more than any other visual cue identifies them.

Bottom

When you fish with the sun in front of you or to the side, shadows of objects on the bottom often look like the long shapes of fish. Because you are moving, the shapes appear to move. If you are wading, you can stop. A few seconds of watching for movement will tell you if the shapes are fish. But if you are drifting in a skiff, you must learn to look away *for three or four seconds* and then look right back. If the shadows or shapes have not moved more than the small distance accounted for by the boat drifting, then you are looking at bottom. This technique is not difficult, but it takes practice to get the feel for the effect of the boat drifting.

SIGHTING BONEFISH IN DEEP WATER

Three special spotting situations merit some brief discussion. They all occur in deep water — uncommon territory for fly fisherman. But when flats predators are present or temperatures are too hot or cold, you may sometimes find fish only in deep-water schools. Also, large swarms of bonefish occasionally teem near the surface of very deep water, providing an opportunity that is too good to miss.

Large Schools Swarming on Top of Deep Water

Sometimes dozens, scores, even hundreds of fish will swarm in the *upper* layer of water nine to fifteen feet deep. You seldom see mudding during swarming, but occasionally you can see and smell milky clouds of milt, indicating spawning activity. You can pick out individual fish in these swarms. They will change back and forth from black to silver to green as their angle to you and the sun changes. You can also see frequent side flashes when they swarm, sometimes almost like a battery of flash bulbs going off. You can cast to individual fish swimming in the surface swarm.

Deep-Water Muds

Spotting deep-water muds is easy. Sighting the fish is not. Muds can be dark blue-gray, chalky-white, or yellow-ocher, depending on the color of the bottom that the bonefish are digging up and the amount of sunlight. You may see occasional side flashes from a mud, which is good confirmation that it's caused by bonefish. Depending on the intensity of sun and the cloudiness of water, you may be able to see fish. If not, you will have to fish the mud, aiming at the darkest, freshest areas.

Deep Clear Water

The last and most difficult deep-water sighting situation is one of the most perplexing and frustrating. It is like trying to pick out a clear glass bottle sitting in the bottom of a glass tub filled with three feet of gin. The problem is that this is one of the very rare times that a bonefish is not reflecting something else. You can make out all of the detail of the fish: the eyes, the barred back, the tail, dorsal and pectoral fins are all plainly there, but it looks as if it is all made of glass. There is no flash, no texture, no reflected color, no shadow to break the pattern of the background.

The effect is total invisibility. Some guides can see such a fish. I cannot — even when I am standing right on top of one with the guide pointing at it with his push pole. I may see it for a second, but if I blink I lose it.

IS ALL THIS REALLY NECESSARY?

These then are the many feeding signs, visual patterns, and deep water cues you should search for. You should focus especially on those most likely for the light and color conditions on the flat you are fishing. Also try to avoid being fooled by all the other objects and creatures that can look like a bonefish in this shadowy world. The key to sighting a bonefish is to look for *all* of their patterns and *all* of their disguises *all* of the time.

If you are looking only for black shapes, you won't see the silver ones, or the white ones, or the ocher ones, or the green ones, or the transparent-as-glass ones. Or you will be blind to the big fish sitting there stark still, reflecting the mottled turtle grass or mangrove roots, as it rests eight feet in front of you before it moves on to dig out another big flat-browed mud crab.

One of the cardinal rules bonefish guides first teach you is never to take your eyes off a fish once you have seen it. If you do, it will disappear into the background and you won't be able to pick it out again. I still marvel every time I return a fish to the water at how quickly and totally it disappears, sometimes when it is no more than *two feet* away!

You may wonder why you should learn all of these stalking and sighting skills if you are going to fish with a guide. After all, isn't it his job to find the fish?

It is true that many guides will usually get you into the vicinity of fish. But unless you know what you are looking for, you may not see fish even when a guide points them out to you. If you cast, you will often cast blindly, aiming where the guide tells you.

You may well hook and land a fish, but chances are greater you will over-cast and spook them. Or you will under-cast and the fish won't bother to go after the fly. Even more likely, the fish will change direction as you are casting. By the time your fly has landed, the school will be off on another path. They will never even see your fly, and it will be too late to make another cast. Had you seen the fish when they changed direction, you could have re-aimed in time to put your fly where it would have intercepted their new path.

In the beginning, you will not read signs and see fish as well as your guide can. But if you watch the area you are drifting or wading for both muds and fish, eventually you will learn to see them. Once you do, you will never be the same again.

Even today, I still remember the first time I spotted a fish on my own before the guide did. I was fishing off Eleuthera with Joe Cleare at midday. We were fishing the upper end of Inner Sound below Devil Hole, and the sun was high and the fish scarce. The bottom was soft and very white. Sometimes after fish mud, the water has a chalky cast that makes it hard to see even shadows. I spotted a tail flash first and then picked up a black eye. As cocky as a ninteen-year-old on the way to the senior prom, I made a cast. Then I heard Joe say, "You see something?" just as the whole school scattered. I was so excited that I had seen a fish on my own, that I lined the closest fish and spooked the whole school.

But I still remember that fish today. It was the first time I knew for sure that I could see bonefish on my own. After that, I started working harder at spotting them and now I get as much thrill out of seeing a fish as hooking it. Hunting fish is, after all, half of what bonefishing is all about. If you don't learn to stalk them, you're missing much of what makes this sport what it is.

6

Selecting
Bonefish Flies

Bonefish flies must suggest some form of food to fish. They have to cast well, land quietly, and sink quickly. They should not snag bottom or spook fish and they must also work in many different habitats and water depths. Few other game fish require flies to do so many things at one time. But once you understand the basic characteristics that cause bonefish flies to mimic prey and to function properly, you will be able to choose patterns that will work in most situations.

HOW BONEFISH FLIES LOOK LIKE PREY

Flies portray food by emulating the shape, color, size, and movement of prey. Some flies mimic prey in all these characteristics. Others key on just one or two traits that their designers believe will trigger a fish to eat them.

You can fish with flies that range from almost exact copies of prey to those that only vaguely suggest a meal. Some patterns, like Carl Richards' latex crabs, mimic prey so precisely they look like they could crawl off the hook. Others capture the look of only a few key body parts, like the McVay Gotcha with its bulbous eyes, reflective carapace, and pink head. Still other patterns are even more general. They display a vaguely shrimpy-crabby-fishy look that can portray many different types of prey depending on the size and color you select and the action you give the fly. Different colors of the Clouser Deep

Selecting bonefish patterns requires you to understand how a fly should look in order to portray prey and how it should function in order to get down in front of fish without spooking them.

Minnow, for example, will mimic mantis shrimp, common shrimp, and baitfish. The Bunny Bone patterns look equally suggestive as either crab or shrimp species. The original Nasty Charlie has probably been mistaken by bonefish for every shrimp species on the face of the earth.

Some fish require flies to do a better job of simulating prey than others. Older, experienced fish in heavily pounded areas have seen many patterns. They discriminate better and are less likely to take a swipe at a poor imitation than are young bonefish. In some places that see little fishing traffic, like Ascension Bay or South Andros, juveniles will jump on almost any fly you throw.

But no matter where you go, you will usually have more successful fishing when you assume you are stalking at least somewhat sophisticated bonefish. If you always use flies that suggest the prey that the local bonefish normally see and eat, you will greatly increase the likelihood of deceiving and hooking the largest and most experienced among them. Your choice of fly shape, color, size, and action are critical to that deception.

How Fly Shape Suggests Prey

For the first fifty years of bonefishing, nine out of every ten bonefish flies imitated some member of the shrimp family—mostly the common and snapping shrimp. Shrimp represent a highly nutritional package for bonefish and are avidly sought by them. But bonefish also eat great numbers of crabs, worms, juvenile fish, and other unusual shrimp species like the members of the mantis family. They also gorge themselves on many smaller shrimp such as the grass, arrow, and sponge species. Fly designers now create patterns for all these prey categories. Taking along a few of each of them will improve your chances of having something to interest the fish in each habitat, water depth, and location you find them.

Listed below are the major prey families commonly eaten by bonefish at most fishing destinations, along with some fly patterns whose shapes suggest them. (Most of these flies appear in the color plate section of this book, and general descriptions for each are listed at the end of this chapter; Chapter 12, "Tying Bonefish Flies," contains pattern recipes and a material list for each.)

Common Shrimp, Snapping Shrimp, and Small Shrimp Patterns: Nasty Charlie, Crazy Charlie, Ben's Epoxy, Slider, Bonefish Short, Bunny Bone Natural, Pops' Bonefish Bitters, Mini-Puff, Horror, Barber Pole Shrimp, Cockbone, Piggy Back Shrimp, Gotcha, Peacock Angel, Bonefish G.P., Hare Trigger, Wiggle Shrimp, Common Shore Shrimp, Clouser Deep Minnow, Jim's Golden Eye Shrimp, A.K. Bonefish Fly, Shallow-H_2O Fly.

Mantis Shrimp Patterns: Slider, Jim's Golden Eye Shrimp, Apricot Charlie, Clouser Deep Minnow, A.K. Bonefish Fly, Mantis Shrimp, Bonefish Special, Ben's Epoxy, Saltwater Sparrow, Bunny Bone Grizzly.

Crab Patterns: Turneffe Crab, Blue Crab, Black-Tipped Mud Crab, Green Reef Crab, Chernobyl Crab, Borski Wool Crab, Beady Crab, Diamond Bitters, Charlie Bunny Bone, Bunny Bone Grizzly.

Worm Patterns: Rubber Band Worm, Orange Annelid, Pink Polly, Dick's Fanworm, Woolly Bugger.

Eel, Forage Fish, and Juvenile Fish Patterns: Elver, Soft Hackle Streamer, Glimmer, Magic Minnow, Clouser Deep Minnow, Wiggle Shrimp, Saltwater Sparrow, Goby Bugger, Rubber Band Worm.

Other Prey Patterns: Black Sea Urchin, J.G. Chiton, Winston's Urchin, Punta Squid, Sea Lice.

How Fly Color Suggests Prey

Unless they burrow, few prey survive long in bonefish territory without camouflage. The majority of the shrimp, crabs, fish, eels, and worms that

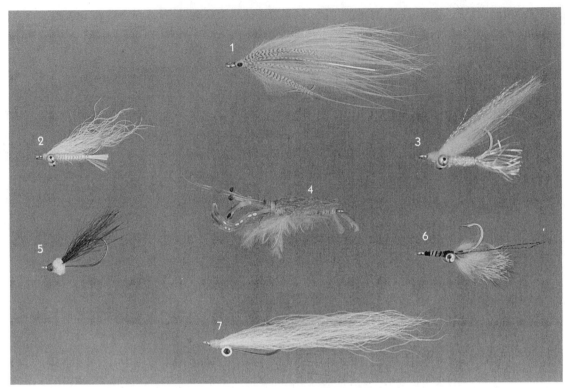

Some flies such as Carl Richards' Mantis Shrimp (4) imitate prey species precisely, while some such as the Soft Hackle Streamer (1) and Clouser Deep Minnow (7) mimic prey more loosely. Others, such as the Crazy Charlie (2), the Gotcha (3), the Horror (5), and the Bunny Bone Grizzly (6) are simply suggestive of a general shrimpy-crabby look.

bonefish eat blend almost completely with the turtle grass, sand flats, reefs, mangroves, and other habitats where bonefish hunt. You will increase the natural look of most flies if you choose them in earth-tone colors, variegated patterns, or reflective exteriors that best conceal themselves in whatever habitat you are fishing.

When fishing over turtle-grass beds, choose fly patterns in medium grays, greens, and tans to blend with the natural colors of the grass bottom. Tan or green versions of weed-proof flies like Ben's Epoxy or slow-sinking flies like the Bunny Bone Natural, the Borski No Name Shrimp, or the Hare Trigger will blend well over grass without getting hung up on the blades. Crabs like the green Turneffe Crab, the Chernobyl Crab, and the green Beady Crab will also look natural in grass. Worm patterns, however, will often appear more natural in brighter colors such as pink, orange, or red, since many of these species burrow and they are much more gaily colored. Bright-colored patterns that mimic snapping shrimp and some other small species may also look natural in grass beds since many of them conceal themselves on garish-colored anemones and sponges.

Somewhat surprisingly, reflective patterns can also work well over grass. The mirror-like surfaces of flies like the Gotcha, Crazy Charlie, and the Peacock Angel adopt the natural gray-green of their surroundings and look natural. Have them tied blind — without the bead-chain eyes — or cut the eyes off if you use them over grass, or they will sink too fast and snag.

On sand flats, you should choose camouflaged patterns that portray the many creatures living on or in the surface layer, such as swimming crabs, mantis shrimp, and common shrimp. But choose brighter-colored patterns to mimic the worms that burrow in sand and mud flats. For crabs, flies like Del's Merkin, the Richards' Juvenile Blue Crab, the Borski Wool Crab, or the Beady Crab will suggest natural-looking swimming crabs — one of the bonefish's favorite sand flats prey. You can mimic another sand flat favorite, the mantis shrimp, with tan patterns such as Jim's Golden Eye Shrimp or a tan Clouser Deep Minnow.

As was true with grass flats, reflective patterns such as the Apricot Charlie, McVay Gotcha, and the Charlie Bunny Bone will also mimic natural colors on sand bottoms. Their mirrored bodies reflect local color and blend with it perfectly. Wing materials must also be chosen to blend. Jim McVay tells me he ties his blond-winged Gotcha pattern with a duller orange wing for one flat in Andros (Moxey) that has an especially dark bottom.

When selecting fly color for reef areas, let the local hues of the reef and sand behind it dictate your choice. If you are fishing a shallow reef wall, darker colors often will best approximate the prey that hides there. The gray Saltwater Sparrow or the gray-green Goby Bugger can mimic species of the goby family, such as the dark-banded frillfin, which lives in tidepools. Dusky patterns such as the Bunny Bone Grizzly can suggest the darkly camouflaged reef-dwelling rock mantis shrimp. Dark-colored urchin flies like the Black Sea Urchin are also appropriate here.

Reef areas are not uniformly dark and drab, however. Many contain light-colored patches of coral and colonies of bright-colored inhabitants such as anemones. They harbor gaily hued shrimp, fish, and other creatures that blend with the color of their hosts. Flies fished along the bottom that match the gay colors of these local species and look natural to the bonefish may trigger aggressive strikes. Bonefish often feed on these more visible and mobile species when strong winds and currents pound reef areas, churning prey and separating them from their cover. Reflective fish patterns like the Glimmer and dark-winged reflective shrimp flies like the Peacock Angel may also appear natural in reef areas.

Mangroves, like grass beds and reefs, sustain many different families of prey, including shrimp, crabs, and fish. Colors such as dark brown, tan, and burnt red dominate the background here and most crabs and shrimp adopt these colors to survive. But while most mangrove prey use camouflage, several of the crabs that live along mangrove shorelines burrow for protection. They display bright red, purple, and yellow splashes of color on their carapaces, and crab patterns in these hues will sometimes work here. Crab flies such as Richards' Black-Tipped Mud Crab, the Beady Crab, and Borski Wool Crab patterns in these colors may also be effective here. Mangroves also serve as nurseries that harbor many juvenile fish. Drab-colored Soft Hackle Streamers and reflective patterns like the Glimmer can look natural here.

How Fly Size Suggests Prey

The size of the fish and the size of the prey in the area you plan to fish should, more than any other factor, determine the size of your flies. Smaller flies in #6, #8, and #10 will approximate prey eaten by the small schooling fish seen regularly at Ascension Bay, Boca Paila/Pez Maya, and Belize. Larger sizes of #2 and #1 are commonly used to match the large shrimp and crabs eaten by Florida's and Bimini's trophy bonefish. Locations such as Andros and the Bahamas out islands, as well as Christmas Island and Los Roques require mid-range sizes of #6, #4, and #2 to best match the wide range of prey and the broad range of fish sizes found at these locations.

An unusual destination in terms of hook size is the Turneffe Islands, which require small #8 to #16 flies for stalking large fish in the thin water of the atoll's flats. When fishing Turneffe's deeper reefs or its mangrove areas, however, anglers have successfully used #4, #2, and even #1 patterns.

How Fly Action Suggests Prey

An angler's stripping action is the primary determinant of how a fly moves. But a fly's design and materials also influence its action. Some flies are built to dive like a burrowing shrimp, or to wiggle and swim like a small goby, or to skitter and crawl sideways like some crabs. With so many different types of prey moving in different ways, anglers must select patterns with natural action as well as natural shape, color, and size. Several of the mantis patterns illustrate the different ways flies interpret prey action. The Bonefish Special, Apricot Charlie, the tan Clouser Deep Minnow, Jim's Golden Eye Shrimp, and the Carl Richards Mantis Shrimp patterns all suggest the same species — the

Recently anglers have been using both larger and smaller bonefish flies. On the left, all tied on small #6 to #10 hooks, are the Sea Lice (1), Pops' Bonefish Bitters (2), the Rubber Band Worm (3), Ben's Epoxy (4), and Carl Richards' Grass Shrimp (5). On the right, all tied on size #2 to #1 hooks, are the Clouser Deep Minnow (6), the Beady Crab (7), the Slider (8), Ben's Epoxy (9), and the Mantis Shrimp (10).

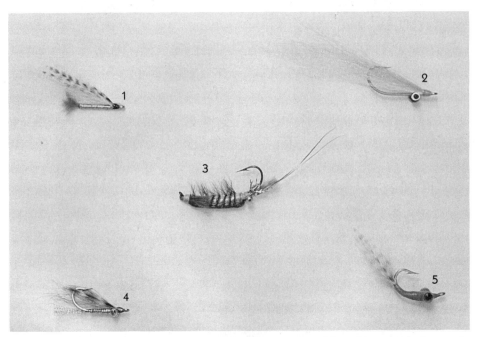

These five patterns all suggest some aspect of the shape or color of the golden mantis shrimp: the classic Bonefish Special (1), the Apricot Charlie (4), the tan Clouser Deep Minnow (2), A.K. Bonefish Fly (5), and Jim's Golden Eye Shrimp (3).

golden mantis, *Pseudosquilla ciliata*, one of the bonefish's favorite prey. All of these flies, however, have different actions.

The venerable Bonefish Special, with its early, simple, inverted-wing design, sinks down and then swims with a very slight jump when stripped. The Apricot Charlie, with its metal bead-chain eyes, sinks faster and moves with a more pronounced up-and-down, jig-like action. The tan Clouser Deep Minnow, with even heavier lead eyes, sinks faster still and bumps the bottom hard between each jump when stripped. In contrast, when you strip the Jim's Golden Eye Shrimp, it jerks backward and wiggles—its profile is tied backward on the hook and it has an off-center tail that jiggles it side to side. Carl Richards' latex version of the mantis shrimp has yet another action designed into it: it sinks and then appears to wiggle and crawl across the bottom when retrieved.

Each of these flies suggests some of the natural movements of the mantis, and each of them may be effective at different times. But patterns that display the prey movements fish expect to see when they attack should work best. The action of Jim Orthwein's Golden Eye Shrimp, for example, is fairly close

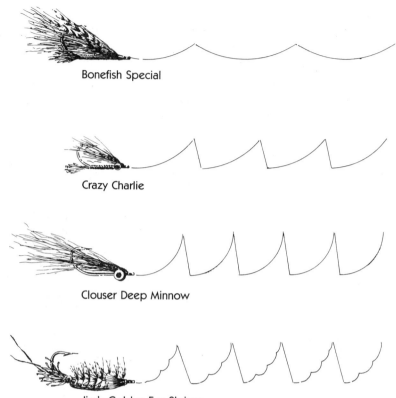

Bonefish Special

Crazy Charlie

Clouser Deep Minnow

Jim's Golden Eye Shrimp

FLY ACTION

Different flies can have very different action. The unweighted Bonefish Special moves in a slight up-and-down, wave-like path when stripped. The heavier bead-chain and lead eyes of the Crazy Charlie and the Clouser Deep Minnow yield even more pronounced wave-type actions. Jim's Golden Eye Shrimp, which is tied backward and has an off-center tail, wobbles backward in addition to jumping and diving.

to the aggressive escape posture of the mantis — it tends to counterattack any attacker. Perhaps this is why this fly has taken three world-record fish and hooked two others that were judged to be even bigger.

For other shrimp species, the jig-type action of metal-eye patterns has proven its long-term effectiveness. Also, the wiggling action of material like rabbit in the Bunny Bone flies is effective.

When selecting fly action for other prey, different actions may fool fish. Mud crabs skitter sideways; select flies to imitate them that have bodies tied sideways to the pull of the hook, like the Beady Crab. Swimming crabs, however, move every way — they crawl and swim up, down, forward, and back as well as sideways. When attacked, they often face and counterattack like mantis shrimp. Look for swimming crab patterns tied to face the fish, like the Borski Wool Crab and Richards' Blue Crab.

Many of the smaller fish that bonefish eat have natural swimming action that streamer patterns such as the Soft Hackle Streamer, Magic Minnow, or Glimmer imitate well. Others, like gobies, which skip across the bottoms of tidepools, are better portrayed by Woolly Bugger-type patterns with metal eyes that make them rise and fall, such as the Sparrow and Goby Bugger.

Liveliness is one additional aspect of fly action you should consider when you buy flies. Flies that try to emulate prey in a rock-hard static form are seldom productive patterns. No matter how precise they appear in the vise, they are usually too stiff in the water to look like they are alive, especially compared to the pulsating appearance of patterns that use the interplay of light, pattern, and moving parts.

HOW BONEFISH FLIES GET TO THE FISH

Bonefish flies must not only look like food to the fish. They should also get in front of the fish without spooking it. This means you must choose flies that cast well in the wind, land quietly, and sink at whatever rate is necessary for the water depth you are fishing.

Ease of Casting

You should have no difficulty finding flies in most prey categories that cast well. Most bonefish shrimp, worm, and baitfish patterns are streamlined and sparse. They cast well even in strong head winds. Most crab patterns, however, do not throw well. Their large body bulk and heavy weighting tend to make them unwieldy. Newer patterns like Carl Richards' latex-body crabs have thinner profiles that are less bulky (thus requiring less weight to sink them), and cast more easily. Wool bodies that suck up water and require less weight, as in the Del's Merkin and Borski Wool Crab patterns, also cast well.

Flies that use the largest lead "barbell" type weights for eyes have proven difficult for some casters. Many popular patterns use these fast-sinking eyes, but you will have to adjust your casting to deliver their weight long distances.

Sink Rates

In a single day's bonefishing you may fish in water depths from eight inches to over four feet. For fish cruising in moderate depths, the ideal presentation

Fly tiers control sink rates by varying eye material and hook size. Here Ben's Epoxy pattern is shown with six different eye-and-hook combinations: Styrofoam eyes on a #4 hook (1), plastic eyes on a #4 hook (2), bead-chain eyes on a #4 hook (3), 1/50th-ounce lead eyes on a #4 hook (4), 1/50th-ounce lead eyes on a #2 hook (5), and 1/36th-ounce lead eyes on a #2 hook (6). Lead eyes flip the heavier patterns over, decreasing their tendency to snag.

gets the fly down in front of the fish fast — you don't want to give them long to think about it. For tailing fish in shallow water, the best presentation drops the fly quietly and places it close to the fish. Then the fly must sink slowly so it doesn't snag. Fish in the deepest water (say four feet or more) require sink rates that balance all these variables of spooking, snagging, and getting noticed, as well as where the fish are in the water column. You must vary sink rate to accommodate how much you lead the fish and how deep they are feeding.

Fortunately, bonefish flies come with many different sink rates today. Most of them adjust the sinking speed by adding metal eyes of different sizes or by putting different amounts of lead underneath the fly's body. Metal eyes are more common than lead-wrapped bodies because they also give natural action to flies.

In most bonefishing destinations, you need flies with at least four or five different sink rates: unweighted, lightly weighted, medium-weighted, heavily weighted, and neutral density. You use unweighted flies for fish feeding or cruising in very shallow water. Some have heavier dressings and almost float, like Lefty Kreh's Shallow-H$_2$O Fly. Others, like Craig Mathews' Turneffe Crab or Ben's Epoxy with Styrofoam eyes, just land quietly and slowly sink to the fish's feeding level.

For fish in water of medium depth, flies should have enough weight to sink them fast before the fish come to them. Heavier dressings with medium bead chain, or very light dressings with larger-sized hooks, will usually sink flies rapidly enough for one- to two-foot depths, yet still land them quietly and not spook fish.

Deeper water of two to four feet requires heavy bead chain, small lead eyes, or lead-wrapped bodies. For bottom feeders in the deepest waters, 1/24-ounce or heavier lead eyes, or double-wrapped lead bodies and sparse dressings, will sink fastest.

Fish cruising above the bottom in deep water require a different weighting strategy. Flies that balance heavier weights with very bulky bodies, like the Borski No Name Shrimp and some of Ben Estes' Epoxy patterns drop very slowly in the water column and let anglers "hang" them in front of fish at intermediate depths.

TABLE 6.1
FLY WEIGHTS FOR DIFFERENT WATER DEPTHS

WATER DEPTH/FISH FEEDING BEHAVIOR	FLY WEIGHT	FLY DESIGN
Less than 12 inches (tailing fish)	None	Heavy dressing, no additional weight added
12 to 24 inches (mudding fish)	Light	Heavy dressing, weighted with bead-chain eyes, or light dressing with larger hooks for weight
2 to 4 feet (mudding fish)	Medium	Moderate to sparse dressing with large bead-chain eyes, small lead barbell eyes, or lead strips in body
More than 4 feet (mudding fish)	Heavy	Sparse dressing with very heavy 1/24-oz. or larger lead barbell eyes, or lead in body
Variable depths (cruising fish)	Neutral density	Heavy dressing to balance weight of hook and eyes so fly hangs in the water column or sinks very slowly

Splashdown impact versus sink rate is always a trade-off. Light patterns with fluffy materials like the Bonefish G.P. (1) and the Shallow-H$_2$0 Fly (2) land delicately and sink slowly. Medium-weighted flies like the Mini-Puff (3), the Dr. Taylor Special (4), and the Crazy Charlie (5) sink fast enough for calf-deep to thigh-deep water and make a small "plip" when they land. Heavy patterns like the Clouser Deep Minnow (6) and Bonefish Bomb (7) sink very fast and get down in deep water, but they splash and make too much noise for calm, thin conditions.

Use Table 6.1 as a rough guide for selecting flies with the correct amount of weight for the various depths normally fished. If you like to fish a single pattern, you can use different eyes in it to achieve each of these different sink rates.

Splashdown Impact and Noise

Most heavy flies splash so hard and make so much noise that they spook fish in calm shallow water. Metal-eye patterns like the Clouser Deep Minnow and the Charlies work best in moderately deep water and on breezy or cloudy days. But on calm days and in thin water, they make a harsh little plip that spooks fish. Many flies reduce this splashdown noise by using soft materials such as chenille, wool, hair, and hackle to muffle the effect of weight when they land. Use them when you are fishing in very shallow water on calm, bright days. Some of the most effective of them include: the Rusty Bunny Bone, the Bunny Bone Natural, the Borski Wool Crab, the Shallow-H$_2$O Fly, the Bonefish Soft Hackle, the Turneffe Crab, the Dr. Taylor Special, and the Hare Trigger.

Other Negative Characteristics: Shine and Snagging

Shine attracts bonefish because it is often a sign of prey. But too much shine turns fish off and sometimes spooks them. Flies with an abundance of shine, like Charlies and Gotcha patterns, attract fish well in low-light or cloudy water. But on bright days and in clear water these shiny patterns sometimes look artificial. For experienced fish, you may have to switch to duller patterns, such as a Slider, Clouser Deep Minnow, or Piggy Back Shrimp.

The unnatural action of a fly that snags will also alert experienced fish to danger. Most bonefish flies are snag-proof and should have no hang-up problems. They use metal eyes that flip them on their backs, or they have inverted wings or weed guards to keep their points from catching in grass or coral. But some flies, especially those used on sand or for tailing fish, have exposed hooks and ride with the hook point down like a streamer fly, such as the Orange Annelid, Pink Polly, and Hare Trigger. These patterns are effective in water of moderate depth or over sand, but should be avoided when fishing deep or in shallow water over grass and coral beds.

SELECTING FLIES FOR DIFFERENT KINDS OF FISH, PLACES, AND CONDITIONS

Once you understand what bonefish flies must look like and what they must do, you can develop guidelines to select flies that fish well for most different flats situations. Most anglers find that the major considerations in fly selection for any destination are the prey eaten by the fish, the size and sophistication of the fish, the types of habitat, and the light, water, and wind conditions.

Prey and Flies that Suggest Them

When you fish for bonefish that seem to favor certain prey or find an abun-

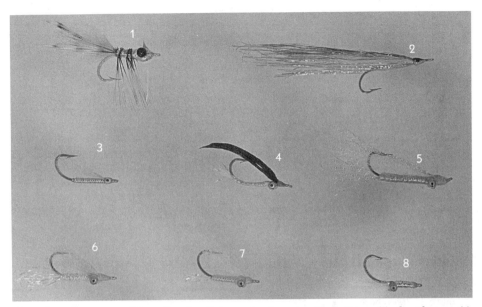

These shiny flies attract fish well in low-light or cloudy water: Ben's Epoxy (1), the Glimmer (2), the Blind Charlie (3), the Peacock Angel (4), Joe's Mantis (5), the Gotcha (6), the Crazy Charlie (7), and the Charlie Bunny Bone (8). But be careful on bright, calm-water days when reflective patterns may flash and look unnatural. (Note, however, that the clipped, palmered hackle in Ben's Epoxy and the small-faceted Diamond-braid material in the Gotcha greatly reduce this tendency.)

dance of some known bonefish favorite such as mantis shrimp, blue crabs, or reef crabs in an area, you will probably want to use patterns that suggest them. You may find it useful to familiarize yourself with some of the major bonefish prey commonly found at most destinations and some of the patterns that suggest them. Table 6.2 lists prey descriptions along with many of today's fly patterns. As more prey are discovered each year and many new patterns are tied, you will want to add to this listing.

Size and Sophistication of Fish

About fifteen percent of the time, bonefish take almost any reasonable fly you show them. Another fifteen percent of the time they will take no fly pattern — no matter how enticing it is. Selecting flies in these two conditions is irrelevant. During the other seventy percent of the time, fly selection is critical, and nowhere is it more important than with large, sophisticated fish. The more flies and fishermen the fish see, the more precisely you must select your fly. With sophisticated fish, flies must get to their feeding level without

TABLE 6.2
FLY PATTERNS AND PREY FORMS

PREY CATEGORIES	PATTERN NAME	PATTERN COLORS
Common Shrimp Long body with head and thorax covered with hard carapace and lower segmented abdomen. Somewhat large eyes. Wide tail, five pairs of legs, several pairs of swimmerets. Often blends with habitat, sometimes taking on color of bottoms; sometimes colorless.	Madonna Pink Nasty Charlie Charlie Bunny Bone Bunny Bone Natural Slider Gotcha Wiggle Shrimp Crazy Charlie Mini-Puff Ben's Epoxy Clouser Deep Minnow Jim's Golden Eye Shrimp Piggy Back Shrimp Pops' Bonefish Bitters Bonefish Short	Pink Reflective White Tan Tan Pearlescent and pink Pink, tan, white Pink, tan, white Pink, tan Pink, tan, translucent Tan Gold and tan Tan, gray, pink Amber Tan
Mantis Shrimp/Spearer Unusual jointed head with prominent eyes on long stalks. Large spearing forelimbs and very broad tail. Three pairs of walking legs. Usually golden yellow or white to blend with sand.	Slider Mantis Shrimp Jim's Golden Eye Shrimp Apricot Charlie Clouser Deep Minnow Bonefish Special A.K. Bonefish Fly Wiggle Shrimp	Tan Golden yellow Gold and tan Gold and orange Tan Gold Golden tan Tan
Mantis Shrimp/Smasher Like golden mantis except forelimbs are blunt, for smashing prey. Usually dark gray, green, or black to blend with coral rock habitats.	Slider Clouser Deep Minnow Ben's Epoxy Saltwater Sparrow Bunny Bone Grizzly Wiggle Shrimp	Tan Tan Green Dark gray Gray Black
Snapping Shrimp Similar in appearance to common shrimp, except smaller, to 2" long. Pronounced claws, one often as long as shrimp's body. Color varies; dark green, reddish, orange, translucent, banded.	Nasty Charlie Peacock Angel Big-Clawed Snapping Shrimp Borski No Name Shrimp Mini-Puff Crazy Charlie Horror Ben's Epoxy Cockbone Dr. Taylor Special Hare Trigger Bonefish G.P.	Reflective Silver and green Tan and orange Tan Orange, yellow, tan Tan Yellow Yellow-green Tan and orange Orange Green Orange

TABLE 6.2
FLY PATTERNS AND PREY FORMS

PREY CATEGORIES	PATTERN NAME	PATTERN COLORS
Small Shrimp Similar in appearance to common shrimp except extremely small, sometimes less than 1" long. Color varies; red brown, green, yellow, transparent, banded.	Nasty Charlie Shallow-H$_2$O Fly Wiggle Shrimp Yucatan Charlie Barber Pole Shrimp Ben's Epoxy Grass Shrimp Common Shore Shrimp	Reflective Chartreuse Chartreuse Chartreuse Red and white Green Green White
Swimming Crabs Carapace wider than long with three pairs of walking legs, two large forelegs with claws, and two paddle-shaped swimming legs. Mottled blues, greens and grays to blend with sand bottom.	Blue Crab, Juvenile Borski Wool Crab Beady Crab Turneffe Crab Diamond Bitters Charlie Bunny Bone Shallow-H$_2$O Fly Bonefish Soft Hackle	Pale green-gray White and tan White, tan, green White White White Chartreuse Tan and green
Mud Crabs Flat, oval carapace, first two legs have claws with dark fingers. Four pairs of walking legs. Many mottled dull colors; white, yellow, brown, green to blend with mud. Some with reddish spots.	Black-Tipped Mud Crab Chernobyl Crab Beady Crab Bunny Bone Grizzly Mini Puff Piggy Back Shrimp	Brown Tan Tan, green Gray Tan Tan
Spider Crabs Long, narrow, triangular carapace. First pair of legs has claws, sometimes small. Four pairs spindly walking legs. Mottled beiges, tans, and grays to blend with sea grass.	Green Reef Crab Turneffe Crab Pops' Bonefish Bitters Beady Crab Bunny Bone Grizzly	Green Green Amber, gray, green Tan, gray Gray
Baitfish and Minnows Dark back, pale or silver sides and prominent eyes. Back often blends with bottom. Sometimes transparent.	Glimmer Soft Hackle Streamer Magic Minnow Clouser Deep Minnow Nasty Charlie Wiggle Shrimp Gotcha Rubber Band Worm Shallow-H$_2$O Fly	Multi and reflective Tan and white Tan Tan, green White White Pearlescent Tan Chartreuse
Gobies and Toadfish Thick-headed "tadpole" profile. Often browns, grays, yellows, and greens to blend with bottom.	Clouser Deep Minnow Saltwater Sparrow Goby Bugger Wiggle Shrimp	Tan Black Dark green and gray Black

TABLE 6.2

FLY PATTERNS AND PREY FORMS

PREY CATEGORIES	PATTERN NAME	PATTERN COLORS
Eel-Like Fish Long slender eel-like fish, often with continuous dorsal, caudal, and anal fins. Colors often dark gray or brown, sometimes cream or olive, to blend with bottom.	Soft Hackle Streamer Clouser Deep Minnow Elver Rubber Band Worm	Tan Tan Tan Tan
Worms Bristly segmented bodies, some with well-developed appendages for swimming; others are sedentary without appendages. Bodies often iridescent, sometimes brown, red, or colorless. Sometimes in tubes, sometimes free-swimming.	Orange Annelid Rubber Band Worm Pink Polly Woolly Bugger Dick's Fanworm	Orange Tan Pink Tan, pink Tan and orange
Urchins Spiny-covered bodies, often round. Some burrow, others remain on bottom surface. Black, brown, or cream	Winston's Urchin Black Sea Urchin Bonefish Soft Hackle Pops' Bonefish Bitters	Tan, red Black Olive Amber, orange

spooking them. They must look like prey that live in the area where you are fishing. These smarter fish are doubly difficult when you can see them well—when the wind is calm, the water is shallow, and the bottom is bright and sandy. Under these conditions, fly selection becomes even more important.

Less experienced fish usually require far less concern with fly selection. Often traveling in schools for protection and having seen fewer anglers and flies, unsophisticated fish frequently compete to take any fly that even remotely suggests a meal. These fish also often tolerate negative fly characteristics such as too much shine or splashdown noise.

In heavily fished areas such as Islamorada and Biscayne Bay, most bonefish are sophisticated regardless of size. But in remote areas like the backcountry of Ascension Bay or the south end of Andros, where fish seldom see anglers, both small and large fish may jump on flies with abandon. In most situations, however, larger fish will be more discerning than small ones. Casting to schools of mixed sizes almost always results in hooking smaller fish, even when you cast to the larger ones.

One other aspect of fly selection that may be especially important with large bonefish is pattern size. Large fish must consume a lot of calories — either a small number of large prey or a large number of small prey. Research on the eating habits of large bonefish shows that they eat greater percentages of large baitfish and shrimp than their smaller counterparts. Anglers fishing for large fish may want to consider using patterns that suggest large prey species like snapping shrimp, mantis shrimps, and gobies, which provide the greatest amount of protein for the least amount of effort required to catch and crush them.

But in areas like the Turneffe Islands, which have an abundance of smaller prey and where fish appear especially wary, you may find small fly patterns more effective on large fish. Big fish in these areas may well eat both large and small prey. But smaller flies will spook them less.

In any case, whether you pursue large fish with large or small flies, you should avoid patterns that put these wary fish on notice by splashing too much, snagging too often, and shining too brightly to resemble natural creatures.

Flies for Different Feeding Areas

You should fish a bonefish feeding area with flies that suggest the prey natural to it, and avoid patterns that imitate species never found there.

When fishing a destination with many different types of feeding areas, be aware that some prey species live in only certain habitats. Gobies and blennies, for example, are found only in tidepools and shallow beaches. But for the most part, if you avoid blatant violations, most of the types of flies that suggest general prey forms in Table 6.2 will work in most feeding areas. If you are after large, experienced fish in areas that see a lot of pressure, however, be prepared to be more prey-specific in your representations. As time goes on this may become more important on all bonefish at all destinations. Table 6.3 should serve as a guide to show the major prey families living in different types of bonefish feeding areas.

Choosing Flies for Different Conditions

In addition to the effects of fish size and habitat on fly selection, conditions such as water clarity, sunlight, and wind can all influence the pattern you choose.

Flies avoid snagging in a variety of ways. The Gotcha (5) and the Clouser Deep Minnow (7) have metal eyes that flip them over on their backs. Ben's Epoxy (4) uses a mono weed guard, while the Turneffe Crab (6), the Bonefish G.P. (8), and the Black Sea Urchin (1) employ hackle weed guards. The Pink Polly (3) with no snagging protection was designed for sand flats, but Pete Perinchief's Horror (2), the first pattern to use the weed-proof, reverse-wing design can be cast anywhere.

Different Light Levels and Water Clarity

Reflective flies sometimes blend well and look camouflaged in almost any habitat. Also, since the outer covering and shells of many bonefish prey reflect at least some light, a little flash in a fly will often attract fish. But too much shine can turn fish away, especially on bright days and in clear conditions when artificial materials reflect far more light than the scales of any fish or the carapace of any shrimp. Flies with flash work best in low-light conditions early and late in the day, and in muddy water. As the daylight increases or as the water clears, you may have to switch to duller flies.

Selecting flies with the correct amount of shine is especially critical with large, sophisticated fish, which sense negative cues of unnatural appearance

TABLE 6.3
PREY MOST COMMONLY FOUND IN DIFFERENT BONEFISH FEEDING AREAS

FLATS AREAS		SHORELINE AREAS		
GRASS FLAT	SAND FLAT	MANGROVE STAND	SANDY SHORE	ROCKY SHORE
	Clams	Clams	Clams	
Common Shrimp	Common Shrimp	Common Shrimp		
Mantis Shrimp (spearer)	Mantis Shrimp (spearer)			Mantis Shrimp (spearer)
Snapping Shrimp		Snapping Shrimp		Snapping Shrimp
Small Shrimp				Small Shrimp
Swimming Crabs	Swimming Crabs		Swimming Crabs	
Spider Crabs		Spider Crabs		Spider Crabs
	Mud Crabs	Mud Crabs		
Fish	Fish	Fish	Fish	Fish
Worms	Worms	Worms	Worms	Worms
	Urchins			Urchins

far better than inexperienced fish do. The negative aspects of shine are also magnified in very thin water and over open sand, where fish feel especially threatened and vulnerable.

Wind

Wind is a mixed blessing for fly selection. On the one hand, wind demands flies with low resistance that are easy to cast. But wind also makes fish more tolerant. Big, splashy flies that you would never use on a calm day may be highly effective in the cloudy, choppy waters of a wind-pounded flat. Since wind also churns and muddies water, flies with more color or shine will often produce better on these days than they would in calm conditions.

A fish mudding in two to four feet of water can be reached with sparsely dressed, bead-chain-weighted flies or with heavier lead-eye patterns.

Bonefish feeding in skinny water on a bright day call for anglers to use light or unweighted flies with little splashdown noise and, in some locations, for patterns without any shiny elements.

SELECTING AND ORGANIZING FLIES FOR A TRIP

The size, diet, and experience of bonefish varies from one flats location to another. Some flies work better at some destinations than others, depending on the prey that are present, and the prey preferences and sophistication of the fish. Also, since all bonefish locations have changing tidal, weather, and habitat conditions, you must take along fly patterns of different sink rates, color, and brightness to let you adjust to changing conditions.

How you organize your flies for a trip can differ from one destination to the next depending on which variables are most important where you are going. Sometimes you may be more concerned with certain prey the fish prefer. Other times some color that predominates in most local prey may seem more important — white for Christmas Island, orange and gold for the Bahamas, chartreuse for Belize.

Also, some anglers like to fish almost exclusively with one pattern. They carry it in many different colors, sizes, and weights so they can fish it in all conditions. Others carry many different patterns: one box of patterns for grass, another for mangroves, and a third for sandy flats. Some arrange their flies by dark and light patterns to make it easy to match flies to flats as they move from grass to sand to mangroves. Some put shiny patterns into one box for low light or muddy water and dull patterns into another for bright conditions and clear water.

If you fish a place often and know the patterns likely to work there, you will probably carry a smaller number of patterns. In this case, you might want to organize them to adjust to changing water depth, clarity, bottom color, and fish size. But if you are going to a new location and have little information on what patterns work, you may carry many flies. You will be better off organizing them by types of prey, size, and color, until you can determine which categories work best.

STAINLESS HOOKS, BARBLESS HOOKS, SHARPNESS, AND OTHER CONSIDERATIONS

Almost all commercial bonefish flies are tied on stainless steel hooks, primarily because hooks of other materials corrode rapidly in salt water. Non-stainless hooks discolor fly patterns after only a few hours of exposure. Some anglers disagree with this practice and prefer flies tied on hooks that corrode. They believe a plated steel hook like the Mustad 3407 sharpens better than a stain-

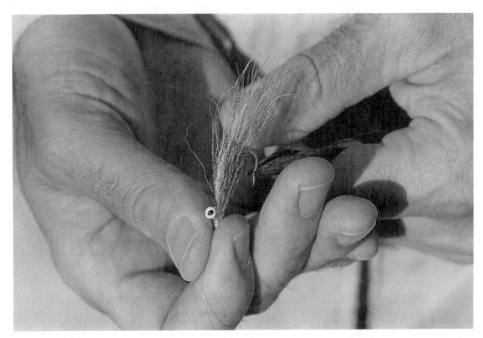

Hooks with crushed barbs penetrate deep, hold well, and increase the survival odds of any fish that breaks off—every angler should use them.

less steel hook like the 34007. Some also feel the 3407 gives fish that break off a better chance of surviving.

I have found no conclusive data on how long it takes salt water and fish excretion to corrode hooks to the point that they fall out of a fish's jaw. But if all anglers just mashed down the barbs on all their flies, fish would survive regardless of hook material by rubbing the hook out of their lips. Points with crushed barbs also penetrate deeper and hold better. Many anglers pursue other challenging game fish with debarbed flies without losing any more fish than normal.

The only time a barb might be effective in bonefishing is when fish run into hazards like coral formations, forcing you to slacken up on your line to clear it. But that's a small price to pay for the knowledge that any fish you break off can recover safely.

Sharpness: The toughness of the bonefish mouth demands sharp hooks. For sharpening, use a fine-toothed file to shape the point to a three-sided or four-sided edge. The point should be fine enough to catch on the surface of your thumbnail.

SEVENTY GOOD BONEFISH FLIES

Listed below are seventy flies that are described in this book and shown in its photographs. Some are old standbys, some are new. Some are highly imitative, others are suggestive. Some are light, some are dark, some bright, some dull. Most can be tied in unweighted, modestly weighted, and heavily weighted versions. Most are also available commercially. For those that are not, materials and pattern descriptions are listed at the end of Chapter 12, "Tying Bonefish Flies." At the end of this chapter is a list of some sources for flies.

A. K. Bonefish Fly *(A. K. Best pattern)*

Mustard-colored plastic body suggestive of shrimp and crabs. Dull finish good for bright days, clear water. Good tailing fly.

Apricot Charlie *(Bill Hunter pattern)*

One of the best ever Crazy Charlie patterns. Good low-light and cloudy-water fly. Effective in the Bahamas. Suggests golden mantis shrimp as well as common shrimp.

Barber Pole Shrimp *(Craig Mathews pattern)*

Quiet-landing shrimp pattern. Suggests the banded coral shrimp and some of the cleaning shrimp that inhabit reef areas. Craig says he fishes it with rapid six- to eight-inch strips.

Beady Crab *(Author's pattern)*

Good for medium-depth water. Effective in Bahamas. Can suggest swimming and mud crabs, depending on color. Also effective with longer legs as spider crab species. Two strands of bead chain (four beads each) perpendicular to hook sink fly fast while chenille body cushions landing.

Ben's Epoxy *(Ben Estes pattern)*

Ben Estes has stalked bonefish for over forty years in the Yucatan, Christmas Island, Andros, and the Florida Keys. He has used this fly almost everywhere and ties it in more sizes and sink-rate variations than you could ever imagine. It has taken fish up to twelve pounds.

Big-Clawed Snapping Shrimp *(Carl Richards pattern)*

Latex imitation of one of the most desirable and widely distributed bonefish prey. Can be tied in many color combinations to match local species, which vary to blend with colors of different habitats.

Black Sea Urchin *(Jack Gartside pattern)*

Simple but novel black urchin imitator uses black deer hair and stiff, black saddle hackle for spines.

Black-Tipped Mud Crab *(Carl Richards pattern)*

Highly realistic latex imitation of the crab species found on sand flats and in mangroves. Can be tied in many color combinations to match local species, which vary to blend with colors of different habitats.

Blue Crab, Juvenile *(Carl Richards pattern)*

Close imitation of one of the bonefish's favorite foods, made with Carl's innovative Rub-R-Mold technique. Usually designed to sink well with less weight than many conventional crab designs.

Bonefish G.P. *(Author's pattern)*

Light-tailing fly patterned after the classic Atlantic salmon prawn pattern. This unweighted fly lands quietly, sinks slowly, and suggests dusky shrimp and crab species found on darker bottoms.

Bonefish Short *(Tim Borski pattern)*

Epoxy-body fly used for tailing fish. Large-profile, slow-sinking fly effective in the Florida Keys.

Bonefish Soft Hackle *(Craig Mathews pattern)*

This unweighted pattern is used by Craig to imitate crabs and urchins. Soft partridge or pheasant hackle makes it look *very* alive.

Bonefish Special *(Chico Fernandez pattern)*

Long-time standard that is still effective. Body probably suggests golden mantis shrimp as well as snapping shrimp.

Borski No-Name Shrimp *(Tim Borski pattern)*

Designed for cruising fish in the two- to five-foot depths (adjust size of lead eyes). Large profile of this very buggy fly attracts fish from far away, when winds blow your cast or fish change direction. Nice silhouette. Good in Florida.

Borski Wool Crab *(Tim Borski pattern)*

Very light crab pattern for tailing fish uses wool body, palmered hackle, and burnt mono eyes to increase bulk and reduce weight while maintaining a crabby profile. Tim says it works well with the *slowest* of forward movements.

Bunny Bone Grizzly *(Jeffrey Cardenas pattern)*

Very light body and lead eyes make this fly an effective fast-sinking pattern for deep-cruising fish. Rabbit fur gives it lifelike motion even when stationary.

Bunny Bone Natural *(Jeffrey Cardenas pattern)*

A heavily dressed yarn body and buoyant rabbit-fur fan-tail wing are combined with light plastic eyes in this shallow-running tailing fly that lands quietly and sinks slowly.

Charlie Bunny Bone *(Jeffrey Cardenas pattern)*

Suggestive shrimp and crab pattern for hard sandy bottoms. Similar to Charlie styles except Jeffrey uses rabbit instead of calftail for livelier action. Reflective body adopts color of surroundings.

Chernobyl Crab *(Tim Borski pattern)*

Large fly for big Keys bonefish. Especially good for mudding situations. Also effective for permit.

Clouser Deep Minnow *(Bob Clouser pattern)*

One of Lefty Kreh's favorites and fast becoming a deep-water standard for bonefish in the Bahamas and Keys, especially in tan and chartreuse. Suggests both shrimp and small fish.

Cockbone *(Jack Gartside pattern)*

Grizzly saddle wing and coon or bucktail collar give this attractor a profile suggestive of many bonefish prey. Jack says he uses this fly as a searching pattern and fishes it many different ways. Can vary eyes to control sink rate.

Common Shore Shrimp *(Carl Richards pattern)*

Imitative, realistic but lively shrimp pattern that suggests one of the bonefish's favorite prey forms, found on sand flats and on mangrove-lined mud flats.

Crazy Charlie *(Bob Nauheim derivative)*

All-time classic pattern that made bead-chain eyes an essential component of bonefish fly design. Has taken fish at every bonefish destination. Originally tied as the Nasty Charlie to suggest the glass minnow, but used worldwide as a shrimp imitator.

Del Brown's Permit Fly or Del's Merkin *(Del Brown pattern):*

While developed for permit, few experienced bonefishing anglers go without a couple of these very effective crab patterns. Good mud and spider crab pattern.

Note: This pattern, received too late to appear in the color plates, is included in the pattern listing in Chapter 12 to provide readers with the ingredients necessary to tie it.

Diamond Bitters *(Craig Mathews pattern)*

Craig ties this pattern in green, amber, blue, tan, and orange to suggest crabs and urchins on Belize's Turneffe Flats atoll. The pattern has no weight and is for very shallow water on the reefs and flats.

Dick's Fanworm *(Author's pattern)*

Simple pattern suggestive of worms that live in tubes and feed through long feathery tentacles. Commonly fished on sand flats.

Elver *(Jack Gartside pattern)*

Good sand flat and sandy shore pattern suggestive of eels and baitfish.

False Mantis *(Carl Richards pattern)*

Realistic latex imitation of a favorite bonefish prey, has lifelike, pliable body parts for legs, tail, and claws. Can be tied in many color combinations to match local species, which vary to blend with colors of different habitats.

Flash Urchin *(Craig Mathews pattern)*

Sparkling lime, olive, copper, or peacock pattern lands very quietly. Craig uses it for the nervous fish and thin waters of Belize.

Flat-Browed Snapping Shrimp *(Carl Richards pattern)*

Lifelike latex imitator of this species that has similar-sized claws and lives on sand and mud flats. Can be tied in many color combinations to match local species, which vary to blend with background.

Flats Master *(Mike Wolverton pattern):*

Popular, effective pattern suggests common, snapping and mantis shrimp species. Also used in yellow, white, chartreuse, and pink.

Note: This pattern, received too late to appear in the color plates, is included in the pattern listing in Chapter 12 to provide readers with the ingredients necessary to tie it.

Glimmer *(Jack Gartside pattern)*

This translucent, sparkling forage fish pattern can be a good searching fly for mudding fish or spawners rolling in large swarms. Also effective at the deepwater edges of flats. Jack says this is the most effective streamer-type fly he has used for bonefish.

Goby Bugger *(Author's pattern)*

Gray-and-green-banded pattern suggestive of gobies, found in tidepools and along shorelines. Can be stripped once or twice across sand and mud bottoms and then stopped to mimic darting pattern of the fish.

Gotcha *(Jim McVay pattern)*

Very bright shrimp pattern that has been extremely effective at Andros. Especially good low-light fly. Suggestive of common and other transparent shrimp.

Grass Shrimp *(Carl Richards pattern)*

Imitates *Palaemonetes pugio,* which lives on turtle-grass blades. Translucent greenish body blends with natural environment.

Green Reef Crab *(Carl Richards pattern)*

Mithrax sculptus is a small hairy-legged crab that inhabits reef areas and coral heads. This fly is an effective imitator.

Hare Trigger *(Author's pattern)*

Rabbit fur gives this light shrimp pattern lively action. Unweighted and somewhat bulky, it lands quietly and sinks slowly for tailing fish.

Hover Bugger *(Jack Gartside pattern)*

Foam carapace floats this novel pattern, used for fish cruising just below the surface. Swarming fish will also come up and smack floating patterns like this.

Horror *(Pete Perinchief pattern)*

First popular bonefish pattern to use the reverse-wing style to make the fly snag-proof. Created by Perinchief in the 1950s, when he fished with Joe Brooks, the Horror is still a very effective fly for shallow- to medium-depth water (also see Lefty Kreh's chartreuse version, the Shallow-H_2O Fly). Probably suggests small crabs and some shrimp, depending on color.

J.G. Chiton *(Jack Gartside pattern)*

This clever little brown-colored mollusk pattern, like so many Gartside patterns, suggests other prey as well, including small mud crabs and worms. Good sand and mud flat pattern.

Jim's Golden Eye Shrimp *(Jim Orthwein pattern)*

Large shrimp pattern on a conventional long-shank freshwater hook, tied with an offset tail, which makes it wobble when stripped. Has taken three world-record bonefish. Suggests golden mantis or common shrimp.

Madonna Pink *(George Hommell pattern)*

Effective Florida Keys pattern sinks well for cruising fish. Mono weed guard allows use over grass as well as sand.

Magic Minnow *(Jack Gartside pattern)*

Lifelike small fish or eel pattern. Very quiet and slow sinking. Good along sandy shores and reefs.

Mantis Shrimp *(Carl Richards pattern)*

Imitating one of the most highly prized of all bonefish foods, Carl uses his Rub-R-Mold technique to tie this large, realistic mantis. Claws, legs, and tail all move in lifelike fashion.

Mini-Puff *(Nat Ragland derivative)*

This "mini" version of Ragland's original large Puff permit fly suggests many crab and shrimp species. It sinks well, while its chenille puff-ball head dampens landing splash and noise. Various versions in yellow, pink, and orange have probably taken more fish in the Bahamas over the years than any other fly.

Nasty Charlie *(Bob Nauheim pattern)*

The granddaddy of bead-chain eye patterns, this original "Crazy Charlie" was tied by its originator with a thin mono-wrapped body and white saddle hackle wing. It is still an effective shrimp pattern, and even imitates small baitfish. Especially good on sand. Bob ties it blind (no eyes) for grass.

Orange Annelid or Bristle Worm *(Jack Gartside pattern)*

Effective blend of color, sparkle, and long-shank shape make this a good pattern for suggesting many polychaetes.

Orange Buck Bone *(Bill and Kate Howe pattern)*

Bright orange-gold shrimp pattern good for cloudy days and muddy water. This sparse pattern lands quietly and sinks well with its small bead-chain eyes.

Peacock Angel *(Jack Gartside pattern)*

Flashy body, good for low light and cloudy water. Peacock sword wing is an effective attractor. Good for one- to three-foot depth with bead-chain eyes. Jack says this pattern is especially effective in the Yucatan and areas where blue-green crabs are found.

Piggy Back Shrimp *(Jack Gartside pattern).*

This buggy-looking pattern combines Jack's spine-like technique for attaching bead chain with soft marabou for a lively and quite different shrimp imitator. May also suggest species of mud crabs.

Pink Polly *(Author's pattern)*

Suggestive of many polychaetes, including clam worms and fire worms, this is a good shallow-water pattern to use along sandy shores. These species live and feed on invertebrates, including other worms.

Pink Shrimp *(George Phillips pattern)*

The deer-hair carapace on this very old fly buoys its bulk, so it sinks slowly through the water column. Good shallow-water tailing fly.

Pops' Bonefish Bitters *(Craig Mathews pattern)*

Imitates small crabs, urchins, and shrimp. Named after Belize guide Winston "Pops" Cabral, its creator has used this fly for large cruising fish at Turneffe Flats.

Punta Squid *(Craig Mathews pattern)*

White Spandex legs give this juvenile squid pattern lively action. Craig fishes it with rapid six- to eight-inch strips.

Rubber Band Worm *(Jim Orthwein pattern)*

Simple but innovative pattern that can suggest worms or baitfish. Elastic band gives it novel and realistic action. Dull body makes it a good bright-day fly.

Rusty Bunny Bone *(Jeffrey Cardenas pattern)*

Another of Jeffrey's effective "tarpon nose" designs, this one uses plastic eyes and a buoyant wool body to yield an almost neutral-density fly. It hangs in the water for bones tailing on skinny flats over grass, and it doesn't snag.

Saltwater Sparrow *(Jack Gartside pattern)*

Bonefish version of Gartside's highly effective trout pattern. It can suggest either tidepool gobies or darker-colored shrimp like the rock mantis, found in reefs.

Sand Flea or Amphipod *(Jack Gartside pattern)*

This pattern mimics amphipods found in beach areas and can be used along sandy shores. Beady eyes also suggest crabs found there.

Sea Lice *(Craig Mathews pattern)*

Small, unweighted cream and chartreuse pattern used in shallow Turneffe Flats waters. Craig fishes it in the water column.

Shallow-H₂O Fly (*Lefty Kreh pattern*)

Lefty designed this fly for spooky fish cruising shallow shorelines or edges on falling tides. He dresses the fly with a heavy (twice normal) wing and soaks it in dry-fly oil before fishing it so it drops like a milkweed pod. He says he can put it within inches of shallow cruisers, then just tug it to get it under the surface, where it hangs as the fish comes to it. Pattern probably suggests crabs, grass shrimp, and baitfish.

Slider (*Tim Borski pattern*)

This suggestive, vaguely Muddler-like fly uses deer hair to cushion the impact of lead weight. Its large profile also pushes water to get the fish's attention. Borski says he's had several fish eat this while it was sitting still on the bottom.

Soft Hackle Streamer (*Jack Gartside pattern*)

This saltwater version of Gartside's effective marabou streamer can suggest small cusk eels and other baitfish. Tan and pink version works well in Florida and Bahamas. Olive and other colors also effective.

Dr. Taylor Special (*Phil Taylor pattern*)

Mini-Puff style with bright orange head is a good attractor pattern that is very effective in the Bahamas, especially on windy, cloudy days. Can vary the sink rate with type of eye; chenille head quiets splashdown noise.

Turneffe Crab (*Craig Mathews pattern*)

This rubber leg and chenille crab casts better, lands quieter, and sinks faster than most deer-hair crab flies. In olive, tan, and chartreuse, it effectively suggests small reef crabs like *Mithrax sculptus*.

Ultra Shrimp (*Bob Popovics pattern*):

Good common and mantis shrimp pattern.

Note: This pattern, received too late to appear in the color plates, is included in the pattern listing in Chapter 12 to provide readers with the ingredients necessary to tie it.

Victor's Candy (*Bill Hunter pattern*):

Snapping shrimp pattern proven in Boca Paila, Florida, and the Bahamas.

Note: This pattern, received too late to appear in the color plates, is included in the pattern listing in Chapter 12 to provide readers with the ingredients necessary to tie it.

Wiggle Shrimp *(Author's pattern)*

This simple marabou "Cardinelle-style" fly can suggest shrimp, crabs, and baitfish, depending on size and color. Good bright-day fly in duller colors. Lime-green version suggests grass shrimp, tan version suggests common shrimp or mantis shrimp, black suggests gobies. Like the Bunny Bone family, it has lively action even when sitting still.

Winston's Urchin *(Craig Mathews pattern)*

This novel urchin pattern is made from rubber legs or Spandex material and a hot glue "bubble head" body.

Woolly Bugger *(Russell Blessing pattern)*

This ubiquitous freshwater pattern, in its original olive and black colors, is a good goby imitation for shoreline and tidepool areas. In tan or flesh colors, it is also effective as a polychaete worm pattern.

Yucatan Charlie *(Jan Isley pattern)*

When Jan and his wife Ina opened the Ascension Bay Bonefish Club on Mexico's Yucatan Peninsula in Mexico, he developed this chartreuse version of the Charlie; it's been effective in both Mexico and Belize.

SOURCES FOR FLIES

American Angling Supply
Capt. Dave Beshara, Al Bovyn
23 Main St.
Salem, NH 03070
(603) 893-3333

L.L. Bean
Freeport, ME 04033
(800) 221-4221

Bills Fly Shop
Bill Wilbur
85 Gardner Road
Hubbardston, MA 01452
(508) 928-5638

Blue Ribbon Flies
Craig Mathews
P.O. Box 1037
West Yellowstone, MT 59758
(406) 646-7642

Tim Borski
P.O. Box 122
Islamorada, FL 33036
(305) 664-9367

Clouser's Fly Shop
Bob Clouser
101 Ulrich Street
Middletown, PA 17057
(717) 944-6541

The Fly Shop
Mike Michalak
4140 Churn Creek Rd.
Redding, CA 96002
(800) 669-FISH

Jack Gartside
10 Sachem St.
Boston, MA 02120
(617) 277-5831

Bill and Kate Howe
c/o The Fly Shop
4140 Churn Creek Rd.
Redding, CA 96002
(916) 222-3555

Hunter's Angling Supplies
Nick Wilder
Central Square, Box 300
New Boston NH 03070
(800) 331-8558

International Angler
503 Freeport Rd.
Pittsburgh,PA 15215
(800) 782-4222

Kaufmann's Streamborn
Randall Kaufmann
P.O. Box 23032
Portland, OR 97223
(800) 442-4359

Orvis Boston
Chris Ryan
84 State Street
Boston, MA 02109
(617) 742-0288

Orvis Shop of Wayland
Bill Sullivan
213 W. Plain St.
Wayland, MA 01778
(508) 653-9144

The Orvis Company, Inc.
Historic Route 7A
Manchester, VT 05254-0798
(800) 548-9548

The Saltwater Angler
Jeffrey Cardenas
219 Simonton St.
Key West, FL 33040
(305) 294-3248

World Class Outfitters
Randy Towe
P.O. Box 1571
Islamorada, FL 33036
(305) 852-3177

World Wide Sportsman
George Hommell
P.O. Box 787
Islamorada, FL 33036
(800) 327-2880

7

Casting to Bonefish

Bonefishing requires you to cast a fly to a moving target thirty to eighty feet away. You must frequently cast into winds, and you often have to recast when a fish changes course. You must also make no noise or motion that can spook the fish. And usually, you have to do everything fast.

You don't *always* have to cast long distances in bonefishing. Sometimes twenty or twenty-five feet will do just fine. Other times only an eighty- or ninety-foot cast will reach your target. But if you can throw fifty to eighty feet consistently, with and without winds, you can catch fish. You will also have a good base from which to extend your range and build your other casting skills for bonefishing.

CASTING FROM A BOAT

In classic poled-boat bonefishing, the search window and the boat stance form the foundation for all casting. They allow you to stay balanced, comfortable, and relaxed. They keep you constantly ready to cast to any target in front of the boat that comes into range. Learning to use the search window to focus your pursuit is one of the most important early disciplines of bonefishing.

The Search Window

Search strategy in bonefishing is ruthlessly simple. The flats are enormous, and the fish can appear anywhere. When you meet fish, you may have only twenty or twenty-five seconds to sight, aim, and cast. You have to concentrate your search in an area you can reach. You also need to stay alert. Only then will you be ready to cast when you find a school of fish.

The fan-shaped search window extends forward of the boat to the edge of your fish-sighting ability. It reaches somewhere around one hundred to one hundred fifty feet for most of us, though I have fished with guides who can see fish even farther away. The window takes in a fairly wide view. Going from about seventy-five degrees on your right to seventy-five degrees on your left, it covers about eighty percent of the area in front of you. You focus both your searching and your casting readiness on this window. And your guide positions the boat so fish will pass through it.

Occasionally a fish will slip around the edge of the window. Sometimes they will even come up behind you. But most of your chances to cast to fish will first appear in the search window. Unless you develop the discipline to keep yourself focused on it, you will miss many opportunities for fish.

An angler's ability to spot bonefish varies widely with different sunlight, bottom color, and wind conditions (see Table 7.1). In low-light conditions, such as early- or late-day fishing or on cloudy days, light-colored sand flats may be easier to fish. But on bright days, even fish in the heavy cover of turtle grass may be visible. Wind can also reduce fish visibility, but anglers can often get closer to fish that feel protected by wind-driven choppy water.

The Boat Stance

You also need to concentrate on the way you stand in a skiff. Even calm days, when the water looks as flat as a farm pond, can wear you out. If you stand on the bow for too many hours, your legs will lock, your arms will ache from holding the rod too tight, and your eyes will lose their focus. Rough water demands even more. When the wind blows, the water kicks into a brisk chop and a little bonefish skiff bucks like a young goat. You must learn how to stay balanced, relaxed, and ready to cast in both situations.

The balls of your feet and your knees hold the secret to a stable boat stance. If you plant your weight down solidly onto your heels and stand erect with your knees locked, you tire quickly and your legs ache. You soon lose your balance and your concentration. But if you learn to flex your knees slightly, to spread your feet, and to shift your weight between the heels and balls of your feet, you will develop a stance that keeps you both relaxed and ready. The dynamics of this stance are not very different from those of a skier or surfer.

TABLE 7.1
LIMITS OF ANGLERS' SEARCH WINDOW (FEET) FOR DIFFERENT LIGHT, WIND, AND FLATS CONDITIONS

FLAT TYPE	BRIGHT LIGHT			LOW LIGHT		
	CALM	LIGHT BREEZE	WINDY	CALM	LIGHT BREEZE	WINDY
All Sand Flat	125	100	75	75	50	25
Sand & Grass Flat	100	75	50	50	25	15
All Grass Flat	75	50	25	25	15	10

Flats veterans adopt this position so naturally, it looks effortless. It is also as stable as a rock.

The upper part of the boat stance focuses on casting and line handling. Once your feet and knees are balanced and flexed, you learn how to keep your rod ready and your line clear. Start by holding your rod in your casting hand and stripping out enough line to make the *longest* cast you can throw. In the beginning, try only about forty-five feet of line on a calm day or twenty-five feet on a rough, windy day. Start by using much less line than you can really control. Once you have adjusted to flats casting, you can increase the range in ten-foot increments until you reach your limit.

Make a trial cast and then strip your line back in, letting the surplus fly line fall into loose coils on the deck in front of your feet. Hold the fly in your non-casting hand (hold it by the bend, behind the hook point, so you don't get

Guides and anglers fishing from skiffs should focus their search and casting readiness in the direction that the boat is drifting. In bright sun, wearing neutral clothing and standing on the lower deck will reduce your visibility to the fish.

Fishing in a skiff has the advantage of letting anglers spot bonefish at greater distances than wading.

pricked) and shake out enough line so you have about twenty-five feet (twelve feet of leader and thirteen feet of line) beyond the rod tip. (It should look like a semi-circle between the end of your rod and your non-casting hand, which is holding the fly.) With another twenty feet of fly line at your feet, you are now ready to shoot out forty-five feet of line in a few quick casting movements: (1) snap your rod forward into a brief roll cast that frees your line from the water and sends it forward as you release the fly; (2) make a quick false cast to the rear, and then make a false cast forward, aiming and building up power in the rod; (3) finish with a good solid backcast, then a forward cast that shoots out your surplus line.

Keeping Your Line Clear

In bonefishing, your fly line must always be clear and ready to shoot. Keeping a line free of twisting and tangling is a constant job. A boat always seems to have one deck cleat too many, or the stray end of a bow rope that grabs your fly line every time the wind moves it. Duct tape will cover many hazards. Or throw an old towel, jacket, or bait net over the whole area to create a safe zone.

Even with a clear area, you must watch your fly line. Wind always blows on the flats. It tumbles the coils of surplus line over themselves on the deck, twisting them into an impossible mess. Loops of line also manage to creep under your feet as you shift your weight from leg to leg. The segments of line that hang from your reel and from the stripping guide on your rod twist

Wind will blow a fly line until it wraps around your rod's butt and breaks off any fish you hook.

Only constant vigilance will keep you from stepping on fly line. This is one of the most common causes of lost fish.

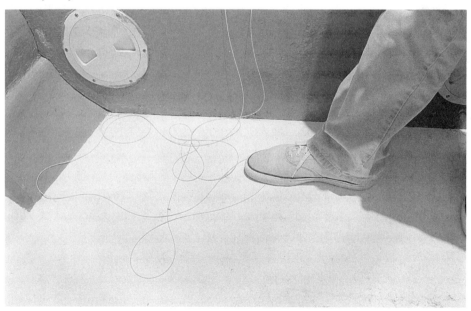

around each other. On especially windy days they will flap in the wind until one of them catches around the butt of your rod or the handle of your reel.

Worrying about all this line twisting business may seem compulsive. It probably is. But things happen fast in bonefishing. Few other mistakes in life make you feel dumber than missing a bonefish you have stalked for three hours because you are standing on your fly line. And you feel even worse when you hook a fish and break it off seconds later because the line is wrapped around the butt of your rod.

Only by paying constant attention to your line can you prevent such accidents. You probably won't do it at first. But after you've lost a couple of good fish to lack of attention and felt the heavy stare of a skiff guide on your neck, you'll watch it and keep it clear.

As you gain experience in bonefishing, you will learn to cast more line than in the beginning. You will begin to cast and shoot line without false-casting. You will try casting from both the platform on the upper bow and the lower deck inside the boat. You will also master casting to the side, to the rear, and into head winds and crosswinds. But if you just focus on perfecting the basic stance and the casting position, you will be able to get the fly to fish. In the beginning, that will seem like an accomplishment in itself.

Casting from a boat has the advantage of giving you a higher casting platform. It lets you see and cast farther, than if you were standing in the water next to the boat. But there are many places where all bonefishing is done by wading. There are many times, even in skiff-fishing, when shallow water will not permit a boat to drift. You must get out to pursue fish. You may also step out of the boat and cast from a wading position when fish are especially nervous. Sometimes the shape and "push" of the boat in the water will spook the biggest fish.

CASTING WHILE WADING

When you step over the side of a skiff and onto a flat, you can no longer see as far, and your search window shortens. But you can move in any direction, so your search window also widens. You will find you can scan and search more areas around you — even those behind you.

Casting strategy changes in wading. On foot, the difficulty of keeping your surplus fly line clear and ready to shoot increases. Without the benefit of a dry deck to store it on, surplus shooting line must be held in your hand, in a stripping basket, or even in your mouth.

Anglers new to wading often strip out too much line. If you keep out as much as you do when fishing from a boat, it will twist and tangle in your hands or jam in the stripping guides when a fish starts to run. But you seldom need this much line. Wading lets you to get closer to fish, allowing shorter casts. Usually thirty to forty feet of line is enough.

When you wade, you must protect yourself from hazards such as sinkholes and rip currents. You should also shield your feet from urchins, rays, and other perils. Since you wade wet, instead of in neoprene or rubber waders, watch out for over-exposing your legs if you are in shorts. Use lots of sunblock and make sure it's waterproof. Many veterans wear long pants for protection while wading (additional dangers are covered in Chapter 9, "Wading for Bonefish").

When you wade you must keep your legs stable and balanced. Take small steps, much the same as you would when you wade a shallow river or pond. Otherwise, fishing on foot is much the same as from a boat. You wade with the fly held in your non-casting hand. At the sign of a fish, snap it forward, false-cast, and then deliver the final cast to the fish.

Once you have learned where to focus your search and how to keep yourself ready to cast, you are ready to concentrate on the cast itself.

CASTING TECHNIQUES

The descriptions here are intended to help anglers adapt their casting to bonefishing. No book can substitute for casting instruction. If you do not already know how to fly-cast, you should take lessons or learn from a videotape. Once you know the basics of fly casting, then you can learn the special techniques you need to adapt them to bonefishing.

The Forward Cast

Probably sixty to seventy percent of fly casting for bonefish uses some form of the forward cast. But bonefishing puts a few unique requirements on this cast: you must do it quickly, accurately, and quietly. The erratic path of the fish may require rapid and repeated recasting to place the fly in the path of the fish.

To make a forward cast quickly, find a stance that is comfortable. Keep your line clear and stay focused on your target. Then roll-cast your line free of the surface and snap it into a backcast. Take aim, making allowances for the movement and direction of the fish (see "Aiming Your Fly," later in this chapter), and try to place your fly so it falls quietly onto the surface. Check frequently to make sure your fly line is clear. Keeping it free of tangles is the most common problem for newcomers to bonefishing.

You must place your fly close to fish, but not so close that it spooks the fish. Smaller and softer-landing flies and delicate presentations will allow you to

Bonefish feeding in clear, calm, and shallow water require long casts and delicate presentations.

get close. Quiet presentations also give you the option to cast a second and sometimes even a third time to a fish that did not see the original offering.

Strong and ever-present winds challenge most anglers in bonefishing, and you should adjust your forward cast to handle them. When you throw with the wind directly behind, you can use its power to help you lift line farther. While casting downwind is easier than casting upwind, it does require some adjustments. If you angle your backcast low and aim your forward cast high, the wind will lift and carry your line forward, giving you more distance. You must, however, drive your line forward with enough force to keep it under *your* control and not the wind's. If you don't, you will lose accuracy.

If you are in a skiff in a strong breeze, you have to allow the boat to drift more with the wind than against it. But you also need to keep the sun at an angle that lets you see fish. This usually results in putting the wind behind you at an angle or across you from one side. Guides encounter this situation so often that they intentionally position the boat to favor tail winds from right or left (depending on whether the angler is a right- or left-handed caster). Right-handers want the wind coming over their left shoulder so the fly is carried away from them rather than toward them. The guide will position the boat with its bow's port side facing downwind. This allows the angler to cast in a normal plane and drive the line down and across the wind to its target on the forward cast. With good line speed and tight loops, the angler can make long, accurate casts this way even in moderate wind. Really strong crosswinds, however, may require shortening casts twenty to forty percent.

Sometimes you will have to cast directly into a head wind to reach fish. Keep your backcast high and your forward cast low. You will be able to drive the line down onto the water in a tight loop on the forward cast. This locks the line onto the water's surface so fast it can't blow back at you. While you may have to shorten your line considerably to cast directly against a head wind, bonefish are often less spooky with the protective cover of choppy water. You may do better on windy days with a short line than on calm days with long casts.

The Single Haul

Once you learn to make the standard forward cast and adjust it for wind and other conditions, you can farther extend it with a *short* single haul to increase line speed. Single hauls can especially help you overcome strong head winds. They can also add distance when you need it.

Single-hauling on the forward cast does not require complex skills. Getting the timing right can take a bit of practice, though. The single haul is simply a small tug you make on the fly line just as you apply power to your forward cast. You apply this tug or haul to the section of your fly line that hangs just below the bottom line guide. As you reach the end of your backcast, you should be holding the line just below the bottom guide with your line hand. When your casting hand goes forward, give the line a sharp tug (make the tug toward you). This pull lasts only a second or two and usually pulls only about four to six inches of line from the rod.

You make this tug similar to making a short strip when you retrieve line, but you apply it *while* you are casting. Usually the hand that makes the tug (the line or stripping hand) comes back toward your casting shoulder rather than toward the center of your body or your left side, as it does when you strip line. When going for the highest line speeds, however, many casters apply the haul with their line hand pulling down dramatically to the side and going far back behind their waist.

As you experiment with the single haul, you will start to feel the fly line pick up speed noticeably as you get the timing right. This added speed cuts crosswinds and drives into head winds. By casting high behind you and by sharply applying a haul to a downward forward cast, you will drop the line onto the water fast so it stays there.

Double Haul

This cast commands a partially deserved reputation for being hard to learn. It requires precise timing to coordinate the two little tugs that speed up your

To make the first half of a double haul, tug line forward to load rod on your final back cast.

To make the final half of a double haul, tug the line a second time, this time pulling back toward your shoulder, as you forward cast.

line. (In the beginning, everyone seems to make the pulls too long.) But you will find it well worth the effort to master this cast. It can punch your line to a fish too far away to reach with any other method. It will also cut through winds and let you cast to upwind fish that you would normally have to ignore.

The average fly caster can learn the basic moves of the double haul fairly quickly. The first haul is similar to a movement you have made thousands of times when you retrieve your line to recast. At the end of the retrieve, your casting hand lifts the rod into a backcast. Your retrieving hand, which has been taking in line, normally stops stripping and holds the line firmly so the upper part of the line can load the rod. Right at this point, most anglers make a small little pull on the line with their retrieving hand to help load the rod better and speed up the line as it goes into the backcast. Follow this tug by letting your retrieving hand drift backward over your casting shoulder with your casting hand. This feeds line into your backcast and executes the first half of a double haul.

To make the other half of a double haul, you drive the line into a forward cast. Simultaneously, you must make a second tug or haul on the fly line below the stripping guide. This will speed the line a second time and shoot it forward. Your line hand should come back toward your body as it makes the second haul, just as was described earlier in the single haul.

Many anglers find the timing of the double haul difficult to master. But you can make it easier by breaking it down into two segments. Learn the backcast haul and the forward haul separately. Then combine them into the full double haul.

Several casting videotapes teach the double haul. Both Lefty Kreh's *All New Fly Casting Techniques* and Mel Krieger's *The Essence of Fly Casting* demonstrate the timing and the length of the pulls for effective hauls.

The Backward Cast

An accurate backward cast can let you reach fish behind you. In the typical boat stance, you normally face the direction the boat is drifting. You stay alert and ready to make a cast whenever a fish enters your search window. But sometimes a school of fish will sneak up on your rear or come at you from the side. When this happens, the backward cast can save you.

Say you are facing north and want to cast south. You proceed just as you would to make a normal forward cast: false-cast behind you to the south and then forward to the north. Then make your normal backcast to the south, but follow it with a forward cast to the north that is much higher than normal. Don't let it land in front of you. Instead, turn your upper body halfway around to the south and make a final cast in this now-forward direction.

A good way to practice this cast is to stand alongside a tall wall. It forces you to turn completely around to make the final reversed cast.

The Spring Cast

The spring cast can be useful when your line is sitting in the water on one side of the boat and fish suddenly appear on the other side. This occurs frequently when you are retrieving line after casting to a fish in front of you and another fish sneaks up behind you. Lifting your line into a backcast above the approaching fish will spook it. Instead, strip the slack out of your fly line just to the point where you feel the pull of the water's surface tension and stop. Now, look over your shoulder to the side of the boat the fish is on and aim. Begin a sharp abrupt forward cast *toward the fish*, loading the rod as it pulls the line up off the water. Then *simultaneously* apply a small, quick, single haul. This shoots your line into a spring cast and drives it to the fish's side of the boat. With a bit of practice it is both quiet and accurate for short distances.

The Lob Cast

If you have always been a fly caster, you may find the lob cast harder to execute than it should be. But for the rest of us, this cast is the same one we used as kids to keep a worm from coming off the hook. You can use it to toss extra-heavy, deep-water flies weighted with big barbell lead eyes or wound lead in the bodies. It works best for short distances, as when you drop the heaviest flies into a nearby deep mud.

Flick the fly out onto the surface about ten or fifteen feet away with a little single haul or a small roll cast. Then make a small backcast to load the rod and send the line and heavy fly zinging back behind you. Now, just as the rod loads at the end of the backcast, lob the line and fly forward in a smooth slow swinging motion. This forward lobbing cast is slow at first, then faster with no sudden stop. Lob it like a big old night crawler. For short distances, this cast will let you control a heavy fly that is competing with the weight of the fly line to be first at the target. It will help you get the fly where you want it, instead of in the back of your shoulder blade.

The Roll Cast

This cast makes too much noise for bonefishing and should only be used to free a line that has been sitting on water. The roll breaks the grip of the surface tension on the line in preparation for making a normal cast. On especially calm days, though, freeing your line this way can spook fish. Under these conditions, you can make a quieter cast by stripping your line in fast, lifting a shorter length of line directly from the water with a backcast, and then making your normal forward cast.

AIMING YOUR FLY IN BONEFISHING

The basic strategy of aiming is simple enough—you want to drop the fly inside the fish's field of vision without spooking it. In practice, however, this is a complicated judgment. Many different factors affect how a fish sees your fly and you must determine where the fish *can* and *cannot* see. You need to aim differently depending on whether the fish are feeding, cruising, or fleeing. You also have to adjust for the size and number of fish, the water depth, the current flow, the wind, and the light level. Almost every time you aim, you need to account for all of these variables.

Casting Your Fly Where the Fish Can See It

Optimized for hunting prey, bonefish see objects located anywhere from a few inches to several feet away. (They can see farther away than this, but they rely more on other senses for distant detection.) The bonefish's eyes view objects well to the front, to the side, and to the rear. They also see directly above them, giving them a hemispherical field of vision. This dome-shaped viewing window picks up objects and movements all around them as they swim.

Bonefish can also see when they tail. With their eyes perched high on their heads, they see in front of where they are eating even when vertical.

Getting Your Fly Into the Fish's Window

Where is the best place to put your fly within the fish's viewing window? It depends. If the fish swims in its normal horizontal orientation, it can see everything around it for about fifteen to twenty feet (some days more, some less, depending on conditions). But because the fish focuses more on where it is going than where it has been, it will notice a fly better if it lands in the front half of its viewing area.

When a bonefish tails, the high location of its eyes favors placing your fly on the dorsal-fin side of the fish, not on its blind or belly side.

Distance From Fish

If your fly lands too far away, a fish will not even see it. If it falls too close, the fish will spook. Unfortunately, no single distance works all the time. You must vary where you place the fly depending on the wariness of the fish. One day bonefish will jump on a fly that lands three feet away; the next day they will spook at one that drops twenty feet away from them.

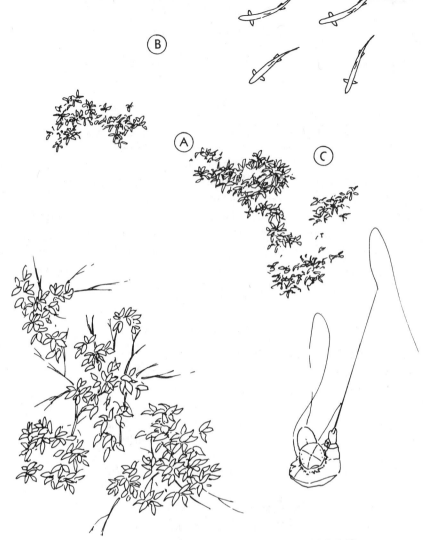

CASTING TO FISH APPROACHING AT AN ANGLE
When fish approach you at an angle, try to cast directly in front of the school (A) or on the closest side (C). Casting beyond the school (B) forces you to retrieve the fly toward the fish and makes it approach them unnaturally.

The best way to gauge the most effective fly-to-fish distance is to experiment. Just cast and watch the fish. Start each day by dropping your fly about six to eight feet in front of a school of fish. If the fish take the fly readily at six feet, try the next one at four or five feet. The closer you can lead the fish without spooking them, the better. It gives the fish less time to examine the fly or change direction. If, instead, the fish spook when you drop the fly at six feet, put the next one eight or ten feet away. After a couple of encounters, you will find the optimum distance for a given day on a given flat, depending on the mood of the fish and the conditions.

CASTING TO FISH ANGLING AWAY

When fish are angling away from you, they will see a fly dropped at either "A" or "B". At "A" the fly will appear to evade the fish naturally when stripped, while at "B" it would appear to approach the fish—an unnatural, suicidal act for most prey.

Which Side of the Fish

If a fish is going away from you at an angle or coming toward you at an angle, you should usually cast your fly to the side of the fish closest to you. While fish can see the fly on either side, you will generally spook them if you cast to the far side. When you strip the fly, it will move toward the fish, which is un-natural. Prey do not normally approach their predators—they either freeze or flee. Approaching flies either spook bonefish or turn them off.

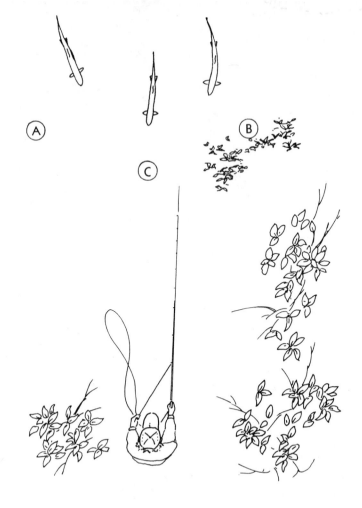

CASTING TO DIRECTLY APPROACHING FISH
When fish directly approach you, you can cast to either side in front of the school (A or B), or directly ahead of them (C).

When a fish comes straight toward you or goes straight away, you can aim to either side of it. In this orientation, the fly will appear to flee from the fish when you strip it from either side. You can also drop the fly directly in front of approaching fish, although they seem to see it better when it lands slightly to one side or the other.

If you are casting to a *school* of fish, the strategy of which side to favor with your fly is similar, but slightly more complicated, than casting to singles. Just as with solitary fish, you cast to your side of the fish as they angle toward or away from you. But with schooling fish, you must cast only to fish on the near side of the school. If you aim instead at fish on the far side of the school, the sound and sight of your fly line and leader butt will spook those on the near side of the school, and that will spook the rest. The best placement in this

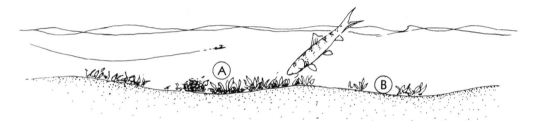

CASTING TO TAILING FISH
When casting to tailing fish, aim at the business side of the fish in front of where it is feeding (A), not on its blind or belly side (B).

situation is to drop the fly on the nearest side of the largest fish on *your side* of the school.

With schools of fish coming straight toward you or going straight away, you usually can cast to either side of the school depending on which one holds the best fish. With incoming fish, dropping the fly between the two best fish near the front will usually work well. Competing for the fly, they will hit it faster and less discriminately than usual.

Casting to Feeding, Cruising, and Fleeing Bonefish

Feeding, cruising, and fleeing bonefish each require different aiming strategies. Water depth and the speed of the fish can also affect your aim.

Feeding Fish

When fish either tail or mud, they are feeding. They should take a well-presented fly if it doesn't spook them. When fish tail in a foot or so of water, cast a light, quiet fly as close to the fish as you can get it. Favor the dorsal side of whichever fish you most want to see your fly

When fish feed this shallow they spook easily, so your fly must land quietly. If the fish are mudding in deeper water, up to three or four feet deep, they will feed more aggressively and spook less. If you can see the shape and orientation of the fish, aim to individual targets just as you would to tailing fish. But in this case, lead the fish with the fly so it sinks to the school's level by the time the fish get to it.

Aim the fly so it drops into the viewing window on the dorsal side of the fish you target. If the water is too deep or dark to see individual fish, cast to their "mud" instead. Read the mud for the areas where the water looks most intense in color and where the sediment is densest — this is where the fish should be feeding. Cast up-current of the mud so the fly is swept to it as it sinks and drifts into the active area.

Cruising Fish

When fish cruise, they may be moving from one feeding site to another. If so, they may snap up a well-presented offering if it appears naturally in their path. But cruising fish may also be sated fish. They may be leaving a flat on a falling tide after feeding for hours. These full cruisers feed discriminately, especially when they are crossing thin, sandy flats on a falling tide. They will judge your fly critically, and aiming at them is always a compromise. You want to put the fly far enough away from them so it doesn't spook them and also so it sinks to their level by the time they reach it. But you want it close enough so they don't have too much time to think about it or to turn off in another direction.

If the fish are cruising in shallow waters, up to a couple of feet deep, you can usually see their shapes or shadows well enough to judge their orientation and direction. Lead the fish by about six feet, and place your fly in front of and to your side of the target fish. If the fish spook, lengthen the lead on the next school. Fish cruising in deeper water are usually less spooky and you can drop your fly closer. You must, however, allow time for the fly to sink.

Your aiming strategy depends on both fish visibility and the depth of the water. If you can sense their direction, aim your fly to lead them. Allow about a six-foot lead for two-foot water depths, a nine-foot lead for three-foot depths, and a twelve-foot lead for four-foot depths. If the fly doesn't sink to their level

HOW LEAD DISTANCE VARIES WITH DIFFERENT WATER DEPTHS

Try to place your fly about six to eight feet in front of fish cruising in one foot of water. For fish cruising in deeper water, add two feet of lead for each additional foot of depth to give the fly time to sink to the fish's level — a typical bonefish pattern with bead-chain eyes sinks at a rate of about one foot every one and one-half seconds. Also be sure to lengthen or shorten the lead to adjust for slower or faster fish and lighter or heavier flies.

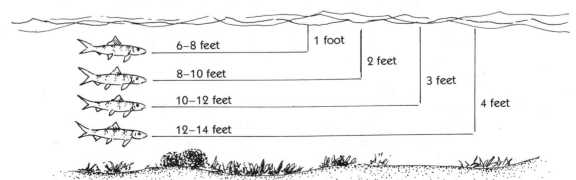

in time, lengthen the lead or use a heavier fly. When visibility is poor and you can only sense the presence of fish but not their direction, you may have to cast closer to them to get their attention and take a chance of spooking them.

Running or Spooked Fish

If fish are moving fast, they have probably been spooked—either by you or some other threat. Flushed fish seldom take a fly, but sometimes they do. If the fishing is slow, this may be the only target you see. Two different aiming strategies can work on spooked fish. If you have time to cast well ahead of them, just leave your fly in their path. Then as they reach it give it a couple of strips to get their attention. The other approach lands the fly right on top of a spooked fish. You drop the fly so hard it hits one or two feet to your side of the fish and smacks the water. In the excitement of being spooked, sometimes the noise of this presentation gets their attention. One or two times in ten it will work—the rest of the time it will spook them even more.

Aiming to Different Sizes and Mixes of Fish

Larger, more sophisticated fish swim alone or in small groups. Juveniles tend to school more. You should give larger, warier fish longer leads than you allow for small fish. They are less tolerant of both the noise and the splash of a fly on the surface. Larger fish also judge a fly's approach more critically. It should never swim up-current and it should never swim toward them—both are unnatural and larger fish know it.

Smaller, less sophisticated fish do not hunt and feed as carefully as large fish. But they make up for it by traveling in schools. They use the collective eyes of the group to alert them to danger. When one spooks, they all spook. When you aim to a school of fish, you must not only target the fish you want, you must also make sure you don't spook any other fish near it.

Sometimes, even large fish use the protective warning system of a school of smaller fish. They will travel with a school of juveniles, letting the smaller fish test new prey and watch for danger. When you cast to these larger fish, they almost always let the smaller fish take the fly first. When this happens use a bait-and-switch approach. Cast to the school, and then strip your fly toward you, fast. Let the juveniles come after it and after you draw them away, pick up your line and recast to the larger fish. (See diagram next page.)

Effect of Water Conditions on Aiming

Besides considering the movement and behavior of the fish, you must also adjust your aim to different water conditions. The deeper the water, the farther along the fish's path you must drop your fly to allow it to sink to the fish's

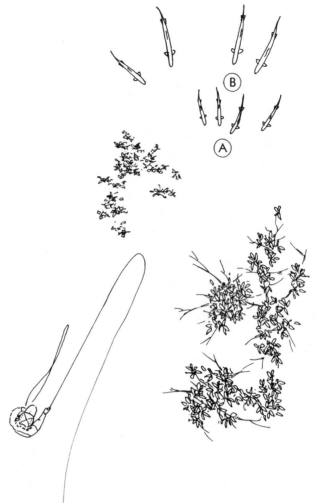

THE DRAW PLAY

Charlie Neymour of Andros uses this technique when larger bonefish hide be-hind the smaller fish in a school. Cast first to point "A" and strip very rapidly to draw away the smaller fish. Then before any of the small fish can take your fly, recast rapidly, aiming this time at "B" in front of the now unprotected larger fish. Twitch it once or twice and watch for one of the big bones to hit it.

level before the fish reaches it. If the water is quite deep, you should also switch to a heavier fly. Leading fish too far allows them to change direction before they see the fly at all. Shallow water, however, requires almost no al-lowance for sinking your fly, but you can only place it as close to the fish as they will tolerate without spooking.

Cloudy water, usually caused by feeding or wind-driven waves, also affects casting. Bonefish react to cloudy water as cover. They tend to be less spooky and more aggressive with a little sediment in the water. Their adipose eye covering allows them to see fairly well in these conditions. But you should favor closer presentations to make sure your fly is noticed amidst the muddiness and activity.

You must also account for currents and water flow when you aim. The fly should appear to reach fish looking natural and flowing with, not against, strong currents. When casting in areas such as cuts and channels or on flats with strong tidal flows, fish will normally be feeding into the current. You should aim up-current of them so your fly is carried to them naturally.

LESSONS AND PRACTICE FOR CASTING AND AIMING

If you cannot cast long and accurately, you should take lessons before you go bonefishing. You can't catch fish if you can't reach them. If you can't cast at least fifty or eighty feet through wind with accuracy, you will waste both your time and money. There are good fly-fishing schools in almost every part of the country. Orvis, L.L. Bean, and Joan Wulff all have casting schools in the East. The Fly Shop and Mel Krieger have regular classes in the West. The Saltwater Fly Fishing School in the Florida Keys offers a program taught by bonefish guides. The master of this kind of casting is Lefty Kreh, and if you get a chance to cast with him, you will find no more gifted a casting instructor. He specializes in the long-distance power casting needed in bonefishing. If you can't attend a class, try one of the good videotapes on casting. Kreh's and Krieger's are the best.

You should practice your casting before each trip to the flats. Find a playground in your town and practice forward casts, single hauls, and double hauls. If you can find a ball field with benches, stand on one and practice on top of it. You'll be about the same distance above the grass as you would be above the water in a boat. It teaches you to keep your balance and lets you practice casting from the boat stance. Also try casting to targets. Pace off sixty or seventy feet and put your hat on the ground. Practice your aim, so you can place the fly where you want it.

Practice at your destination doesn't hurt either. It gets the kinks out of your casting arm before you get into the boat. Practice downwind, crosswind, and into the wind. If you fish all the time and are a good caster, you may not need this. But you never want rusty casting to be the reason for missing a fish that you've stalked, hunted, and poled after for hours.

8

Hooking, Playing, and Releasing

The first time you hook a bonefish, you can't believe what is happening. Even an average-sized member of this species streaks off at twenty-five miles an hour. It slices across a flat so fast, your fly line kicks up rooster tails, ripping through the surface. In the first eight seconds the fish will sprint the distance of a football field. Once you've stopped it and brought it toward you, it will turn out and run again. Sometimes it will go as far the second time as it did the first—and always far enough to unnerve you. No other light-tackle fish has so much power. Or heart.

The speed of a bonefish and the length of its runs make hook-ups with this species a confrontation between the will of the fish and your angling skill. Anglers may not always agree on a single way to strip a fly, strike a fish, or wear it down. But they do all agree on one thing—the bonefish is the most challenging test of hooking and playing skills you can encounter on a fly rod.

HOOKING BONEFISH

To hook a bonefish, you must make your fly move realistically, wait until the fish takes it, and strike before the fish rejects it. To make sure you can strike anytime, you must always keep the fly line between the index finger of your rod hand and your rod when you retrieve line. As long as you strip your line across this striking finger, it will always be ready to clamp the line against the rod grip. Then you can strike the fish, either by strip-striking with your line hand or by lifting the rod.

Stripping Action

The most frequently used retrieving patterns in bonefishing are: the brisk strip; a strip-and-stop pattern; and no strip at all. Other, longer strips are sometimes used for flies that represent certain prey.

The brisk strip consists of a continuous series of six- to twelve-inch strips, one every few seconds. This pattern makes a typical weighted-eye bonefish fly move up and down through the water. This action makes the fly look like it is trying to flee from the fish. It is especially appropriate for fly patterns mimicking prey like shrimp and crabs.

The strip-and-stop retrieve is my favorite technique. It often works more effectively than the brisk strip, especially on experienced fish. While the brisk strip usually gets a lot of attention from fish, it often looks too agitated to be

One of the most effective stripping methods, the strip-and-stop retrieve, makes a fly dart and then hesitate as if it is trying to hide — just the way many natural prey do when attacked.

natural. Sophisticated fish will sometimes follow it, but most of the time they veer away after a few strips. In contrast, the strip-and-stop method makes a fly act more like natural prey. Shrimp and crabs often make one quick dash for cover at the first sign of danger and then freeze to maintain their camouflage. The more you approximate this natural escape behavior with this strip, the better it seems to work. Sometimes I make three brisk strips and then stop to watch what the fish does. Other times I will strip it only once and stop it. At times I will really speed it up to get the fish's attention. Then I'll stop it dead and the fish will hit it immediately.

No stripping at all can also be effective, especially with lively flies that have action of their own. Those made of marabou and rabbit fur work best for this method. It is used most often with spooky, tailing fish or nervous fish cruising in very thin water.

A fourth stripping technique is the classic streamer strip of twelve inches or so. It makes a fly dart like certain baitfish such as gobies, blennies, and toadfish. Depending on the depth of the water and the weight of the fly (or the line if you use a sinking tip or full-sinking model), you may vary the frequency and length of the strip to keep the fly deep.

Striking Techniques

Bonefish crack hard objects with the ceramic-like plates inside their mouths before ingesting them. Hooks should be very sharp, filed to either a triangular or diamond-shaped cross section and crimped to a non-barb or low-barb configuration to improve penetration. It takes bonefish a second or two longer than other fish to reject a fly by feel. This gives you an extra margin in striking. Normally you should wait about two seconds after the fly disappears into the fish's mouth before you strike. Many new bonefishing anglers strike fish too fast. They take the fly away from the fish before the fish has it. Others wait too long and strike after the fly has been rejected.

Anglers strike bonefish with either the rod hand or the stripping hand. Striking with the rod is probably better for beginners — it breaks off fewer fish, although it misses more of them. Strip-striking with the line hand hooks more fish, but it takes time and experience to learn how to do it.

To strike with the rod, pull some of the slack out of your line with your stripping hand and abruptly raise your rod to take up the remaining slack and to set the hook. The bend of the rod forgives the shock of the hook-up and protects your tippet, reducing break-offs. If you miss the fish, however, this method flings the fly behind you and takes it out of play. You may still interest the fish on a recast, but it is unlikely.

To hook fish by the strip-strike method, you take the slack out of the line with the stripping hand. Then you make an extra-long strip that firmly but

Knowing when to strike a bonefish is a matter of reading body language. Wait until you see the fish dart toward your fly, stop over it, or — best of all — tail on it.

gently strikes the fish. As you feel the fish, you lift the rod *into the strike* to pick up any shock of it. If the fish has not taken the fly, you resume your stripping, since the fly is still near the fish. Often the fish will hit it then.

The strip-strike, like nymph fishing, goes beyond simple skill — it is a feel, a sensing of when to transfer the strike from the line hand onto the rod, and it must happen in a smooth flow. You will break off fish learning it, but you will catch many more once you do it right.

Knowing When to Strike

Striking too early or too late probably loses more bonefish than any other single fault in the sport. Keys guide Vic Gaspeny considers it one of the two areas where bonefishermen can most improve their success (the other is learning how close to the fish you should put the fly on any given day — see Chapter 7, "Casting to Bonefish"). Even with good eyesight, the position of the bonefish's mouth makes it difficult to see if it has taken the fly.

The strip-strike is two motions: the first part is an extra-long strip that strikes the fish.

The second part of the strip-strike lifts the rod to pick up the shock of the take.

This uncommon shot of a pod of feeding bonefish shows one fish (foreground) at the exact moment it is inhaling a shrimp. The fish's tail is curled and its dorsal fin is angled to its left—a graphic display of the serpentine body language that tells an angler a bonefish has taken his fly. Note also the puffs of mud the fish has blown out under and behind its body. (Photograph by Vic Gaspeny.)

How do you know when to strike? Watch the fish. When you see the fish come in behind the fly, watch for signs that it has taken it. Usually it will quiver, or tail on the fly, or flash in the sun, or otherwise "light up," as many anglers describe it. Once you see any of these signs, count off a second or two and strike.

When the fish is too far away or visibility is poor, you may not see the take at all. In this case, you must strike the fish by touch, by watching your line, or by instinct. You will feel a slight movement or tick as the fish takes the fly into its crushing cavity. Or you may see the line hop. Count off one or two more seconds and strip-strike. If you miss, always wait a second or two and strip-strip again, then strip-strike. Fish will often chase a missed fly and hit it.

Rejections

Bonefish refuse flies for the reasons all fish refuse them: poor presentation, unnatural shape, wrong color, wrong size, or unnatural action. But in addition to these prey-imitation reasons for rejection, you should watch out for a couple of others. Bonefish have an exceptionally keen sense of smell. Flies that come in contact with gas spills in a boat, sunblock, insect repellent from your hands, or any other strong, alien scent may put off feeding fish.

Bonefish also have a refined ability to detect shine or flash, which they use to detect both prey and predators. Flies that sparkle or glitter too much may be rejected on bright days.

Line Management

In bonefishing, you either get the fish onto the reel fast or you don't get the fish at all. The bonefish runs so strong and fast that it will snap an eight- or nine-pound tippet instantly if your line jams. Once you hook a bonefish, it accelerates as rapidly as a car. Since you have to strip your line to make the fly move, you will have a reservoir of fly line lying at your feet or in the water when you strike a fish. The acceleration of the fish will rip this surplus line off the deck and pull it up through the guides in a few seconds. You must make sure it gets into the stripping guide without loops, knots, snarls or anything else that can prevent your line from going out smoothly.

Several line-handling problems cause most broken-off fish. The most common is stepping on your fly line. Others include catching loops of fly line on deck cleats and other boat hazards, or tangling them around the butt of your rod, its hook keeper, or the reel handle.

Four habits will help you prevent most of these break-off problems:

- Eliminate as many hazards on the boat as possible. Cover them with duct tape, a towel, or a jacket.
- When you hook a fish, raise your rod *immediately* to take up most of the surplus running line on the deck. Then use your line hand to guide the line into the stripping guide by forming an O with your finger and thumb around the line.
- Until the fish is on the reel, watch your surplus running line, not the fish.
- If the fish does not run immediately (sometimes it will hesitate or run directly toward you) don't grab the running line and freeze. Just grasp it firmly and take up slack until the fish turns and runs. Then loosen your grip and guide the line onto the reel.

In the beginning you may break off a few fish as you try to get them onto the reel. This is one part of this sport that requires a sense of touch to know when it's right. Only many days of flats experience will give you the coordination you need to be able to avoid almost all snags and break-offs.

PLAYING BONEFISH

Once you hook a bonefish and have it on the reel, there are three ways it can get off: by breaking off, by pulling the hook out, or by spooling you. The fish has the advantage of speed and power, but you have the advantage of a long, forgiving fly rod and about two and one-half football fields of backing. When you hold it at forty-five to sixty degrees above the horizontal, the rod acts like a shock absorber. It cushions every surging rush the fish makes. Combined with plenty of backing, it should let you wear down most fish before they can run you down to your spool.

To keep the advantage on your side, you must keep the line running free so the fish cannot pull directly against it. Keep it clear of anything that can abrade and weaken it. Also hold your rod high, almost vertical, to minimize sag and keep the line high above hazards in the water.

As in both casting and stripping, when you play fish you should stand so your lower body is as stable as possible. You will sometimes fight a large fish for fifteen minutes or more, in wind, rain, and choppy seas that often challenge your ability to keep your balance and footing.

Most bonefish run at least twice, with the first usually longest. The second is normally half to three-quarters of the first. The average speed of a sprinting fish clocks in around twenty-five miles per hour. Small fish will have slower

Most bonefish give up after a second run. But an especially hot fish may also need a couple of laps around the boat to cool it down before release.

Hooked bonefish often make a second run. Large fish will even sprint a third time — usually just as they come in close enough to sense the presence of the boat or angler.

speeds, while large fish may sprint above thirty miles per hour. Some of the very oldest fish, like older people, run slower — but they also pull harder. While initial runs can go over two hundred yards and run you out of backing, most fish will run about seventy to one hundred and fifty yards. Table 8.1 illustrates typical runs for different-sized fish.

Fish size affects how long and hard you play the fish. No fish should be played longer than necessary. Small fish can and should be brought in quickly, and most need not run a second time. Larger fish, on the other hand, must be played long enough to tire them to the point where you can handle them for release. With a really large fish, you may have to permit a third run.

Dealing with Hazards

Almost any stationary object on a flat can put enough force on your line to snap your tippet or abrade your line. Once you strike the fish, you have to keep it and your line away from mangrove roots, sandbars, coral heads, shells, and sponges. You must avoid anything that could put enough resistance on

TABLE 8.1
TYPICAL RUNS FOR DIFFERENT-SIZED BONEFISH

FISH SIZE	FIRST RUN	SECOND RUN	INITIAL SPEED	PLAYING TIME
3lb	50yds	30yds	15mph	6min
5lb	75–150yds	50yds	20mph	10min
8lb	100yds	75yds	25mph	15 min
10lb	150–200yds	100yds	30mph	20min

your line to give the fish something to pull against, or anything that can abrade your line so it weakens.

You can usually stay clear of these hazards by letting the fish go where it wants to—toward the ocean. But sometimes a fish will run across a shallow bar or coral formation that stands between you and deep water. When this happens, hold your rod as high as possible and wade or pole toward the fish until you are well over the hazard. Then you can let the fish run free again.

Sometimes a hooked fish will run off the flats through an underwater coral bed. It will zigzag your fly line from one coral formation to the next. When this happens, you should turn the drag off completely. With no pull on it, the fish will usually stop. Then, you can quickly wade to your line, free it by hand,

Underwater coral formations lace the flats at many bonefishing destinations. If a fish runs over them, holding your rod as high as possible can save your fly line.

A low spring tide reveals the formidable profile of encrusted mangrove roots, which bonefish often use to tangle fly lines and pop leader tippets.

and reel in gently until you have the line clear. Once the fish is back on the reel, give it a good tug to make sure it's still hooked, and let it run again.

If a fish starts to run into the mangroves, sometimes applying the maximum drag your tippet can tolerate will turn the fish and make it head for deep water. But if the fish persists and you are about to break it off, try the "no drag" option. Release your drag completely. The fish will often rush into the edge of the mangroves and stop. If you keep all strain off the fish, you can reel your line in gently and approach the point where the fish entered the mangrove roots. Frequently, you will be able to lead the fish back out of its refuge and onto the open flats.

Getting the Drag Right

Even experienced anglers disagree on how to set the drag in bonefishing. Many set it as light as possible, so it exerts only enough force to balance the inertia of a fast-spinning reel spool. This keeps it from over-running the line and snarling when the fish lets up or stops. With this method, the fish is worn down by the increasing drag from the friction of the line going through the

If a bonefish runs into the mangroves, releasing your drag completely and wading after the fish is sometimes the only way to keep from losing it. This one was landed.

guides and the water and as the shrinking diameter of the spool increases the drag's force on the line.

Some anglers supplement a light drag by putting additional braking force on the fish through hand-palming the spool. Others never palm the reel, believing it is too crude a method to protect the tippet.

A third technique lets the reel's drag do most of the work. You set it high enough to tire the fish fast, but not so high that the fish can jerk against it and break off the tippet.

Of all these variations, the lightest drag setting usually results in the fewest break-offs, the longest runs, and the most excitement. But too light a drag can run you out of backing. It can also wear out fish beyond their ability to recover. In some cases when fish run far, you also increase the likelihood of fouling your line on the bottom.

Combining a light drag setting with hand-applied drag lets anglers adjust drag up and down fast, but requires very sensitive hands and angling instincts to avoid frequent break-offs. Still, it is preferred by many experienced anglers.

Using heavier drag puts more responsibility on the reel and requires an extremely smooth braking action. This usually results in shorter runs, although

Lightest drag settings usually result in fewer breaks-offs while heavier drag settings reduce playing time. On large fish, however, heavy drags sometimes make fish run even harder.

some larger bonefish seem to run longer the harder you pull on them. Most of the time, though, you are less likely to run out of backing or overtire the fish with a heavier drag. But you are also more likely to give the fish a chance to break off or to loosen the hook.

Deciding which approach works best for *you* is a matter of your equipment, your experience, and your inclination. If you favor the lowest risk of a break-off, you should probably use the lightest drag settings. On the other hand, if you have a good, high-precision reel and want to tire the fish faster, you may want to let the drag system do more of the work. Some anglers also favor heavier drags when fishing near shorelines in order to slow and turn fish before they can escape into the maze-like root systems of mangrove stands.

In general, most veteran anglers favor lighter drag settings. On average, most anglers will lose fewer fish this way. I favor light drags, too. But I also believe it better for the health of the fish to play and land them as quickly as possible, especially when barracuda and sharks are on the prowl. Over time, I have come to use a hybrid approach to drag setting. I find that some fish react to drag very differently from others. With many larger fish, the harder you pull, the harder they pull back. Using a lighter drag on these fish and letting

A hooked bonefish often runs toward coral formations and mangrove stands. You may turn it from danger by increasing your drag or changing the angle of your rod. But if the fish reaches the hazard, turn your drag off. With nothing pulling on it, most fish will stop, giving you time to move in close, clear your line, and finish playing the run.

only the braking force of the water and rod guides weaken them often slows them faster than a heavy drag. Many average-sized and smaller fish, however, run less when I use a slightly heavier drag. So most of the time I leave the drag on this slightly heavier setting. Then I back it off if I find fish are running larger and making long runs. I also back it off completely when fish run to mangroves or tangle lines in coral.

Should you ever fiddle with the drag setting when you have a fish on? While many anglers never touch the drag setting during a run, I have never had any problems when *lowering* it to stop a fish running toward hazards. Adding drag, however, can be a delicate matter. The longer a fish runs, the more drag a fish will have on it. As it pulls more and more fly line through the water and the spool's diameter diminishes, the force on the line can more than double. Adding even more drag can exceed the tippet's strength. Some anglers favor this method, however, on hard-running fish, and say it works well for them.

Expert reel designer Steve Abel says that anglers can vary drag up or down on a running fish as long as they use drag systems that change smoothly. But he warns that most reels have much higher start-up drag than running drag, so if your fish stops or hesitates it will break you off when it starts to run again if you haven't lowered the drag.

TABLE 8.2
ADVANTAGES AND DISADVANTAGES OF COMMON DRAG SETTING STRATEGIES

DRAG SETTING	ADVANTAGES	DISADVANTAGES
Light	Fewest break-offs	Depletes backing; exhausts fish
Light/palming	Control	Break-offs
Heavy	Shorter runs; tires fish fast	Break-offs
Hybrid	Minimizes runs and break-offs	Requires altering drag

Turning the Fish

Turning a fish is only a problem with larger fish. Most smaller and average-sized fish will turn themselves as they get worn down from pulling against the drag. But a big fish or an especially hot fish will sometimes run without slowing down. If and when it does stop, it will buck and shake its head like a salmon or steelhead and refuse to turn.

This is the moment of truth in bonefishing. You must hold firm, keeping pressure on the fish. If it still does not move, angle your rod over to one side or the other to exert force from a slightly different direction *never once letting up on the pressure*. You must convince the fish that only turning back will relieve the pressure. Once it does, keep it moving and never let it rest. Eventually it will stop and turn back out to make a second seaward run. This usually occurs when it senses the presence of the boat or your legs in the water. In a boat, this usually happens about eighty to one hundred feet out, or just about the time you see the end of your fly line coming in to you. Some fish run almost as hard the second time as they did the first, but usually they run about half as far.

Once you have turned a fish twice, you can usually keep it coming all the way back to you. But be very careful in turning fish a second time in a long fight. Depending on the amount of drag and the length of the fight, the hook may have worn a hole in the fish's mouth or it may be bent open. You should do everything as smoothly as possible, and you must make no abrupt pulls or changes in direction.

Playing the Fish in Close

When the fish comes to you after its last run, you can sense how spent it is. If it has run itself out and comes in docilely, you can bring it to your hands and release it. Often, however, it will start to buck again when you have retrieved all of your backing and about half your fly line. If it does, lead the fish into an arc around you. Let it circle you as many times as necessary until it calms itself. Then keep reeling it into tighter circles until it is close enough to land.

As you play a fish close to a boat, a fish that is still hot can cause problems. If it dashes under the boat, throw your drag off and get into the water as quickly as possible to free the line. If you don't move fast enough you may break your rod.

RELEASING BONEFISH

Releasing bonefish is similar in most ways to reviving and releasing other fish, but it does have a couple of unique aspects as well.

You should handle the fish as little as possible. Don't keep it out of water any longer than necessary to remove the hook. If a net must be used (and I believe that they injure the fish and shouldn't be used at all), it should have a small mesh that minimizes damage to the fish's fins and gills. You can lightly cradle most small fish in one hand. For larger fish you can use one hand around the tail and one gently under the body. If you crimp the barbs on your

A bonefish must be revived completely by forcing water through its gills. Weakened bonefish become easy targets for barracuda and sharks.

hooks, you can release fish almost without touching them at all.

Bonefish spawn year-round. Be extra careful with fat-bellied fish, for they are probably females and may be carrying eggs. Also, because bonefish have hard mouths, a hook may slide back and penetrate underneath one of the grinding plates. Sometimes it will hook the fish far back in the mouth. If you try to pry it out, you will injure the fish. A pair of long-nose nippers lets you clip the hook off at the bend and gives the fish the best chance to survive. Once again, crimping barbs will virtually eliminate this problem.

Some anglers believe that any handling of bonefish is dangerous because it removes some of the fish's slime-like coating and makes it easier for sharks to detect their smell. I have found no evidence of this one way or the other, but the possibility that it may be true is another good reason to minimize handling and to use debarbed hooks.

If you do not play bonefish firmly and quickly, they may exhaust themselves by running too long. Sometimes no matter how you play them, they just burn themselves out and become weak and disoriented. I had one fish that was chased by a shark so hard it nearly killed itself. Each time I brought it to the boat it thought the big shape in the water was another shark. I finally had to step out and wade away from the boat to land the fish and revive it.

It is extremely important to revive bonefish completely. Releasing such an overtired fish where sharks, barracuda, and porpoises roam is certain death. Take the time to move the fish back and forth, forcing water through its gills until it shows positive signs of wanting to break free. Then let it return strong and vibrant to its home waters.

Wading for Bonefish

Many flats anglers prefer wading for bonefish to casting from a poled boat. Some locations such as Christmas Island have hard-bottom flats that allow anglers to fish exclusively by wading. Other areas like the Belize atolls and the Yucatan allow you to *both* wade and skiff-fish, depending on your preferences and the firmness of bottoms. Still other destinations, such as the backcountry areas of the Bahamas and the Florida Keys, usually demand that you fish by boat. Their flats are remote, and their bottoms are too unsafe to wade. Even at these destinations, however, you can find some wadable flats. And no matter where you fish, there are times when no other method but wading will let you reach fish.

Wading offers several advantages over fishing from a poled skiff. It makes less noise and fish cannot see you as well. It also lets you get closer to fish — you can make shorter casts and cast with more accuracy. You can also reach some places boats cannot go.

Wading can even increase your angling time and cut your expenses. Two people fishing in a skiff must take turns fishing. But two anglers wading can each fish full time. Locations that allow you to wade without paying boat rental and guide fees can cost you a lot less per angler.

But for all these practical advantages, most people who wade a lot like it for another reason. Wading is intimate. Being knee-deep in the water with the fish lets you see and feel more of the fish's environment. There is no better way to learn the fish's habits.

177

Wading lets you get closer to bonefish than poled-skiff angling because your profile is lower and fish cannot see you as well.

Wading presents some significant disadvantages, however. You cannot see or cast as far as you can from a boat. You stand at a lower elevation, two to three feet closer to the surface of the water than you would be on the bow deck of a skiff. A longer rod can raise your casting elevation, but nothing short of a step ladder will let you see as far as you can from a boat (I actually know an angler who uses one).

Wading also takes longer than a poled boat to cover a flat. In some places this makes fishing on foot risky, especially when fish graze selectively on only a few flats. In areas with contiguous flats, you can keep wading for miles until you find fish. But at destinations with scattered flats, you need a boat to move you from flat to flat until you find one that is productive.

One of my favorite ways of bonefishing combines the advantages of both modes of stalking fish. I drift in a skiff, giving me access to deeper flats and letting me move from one area to another. Then when tides are lower, I step out and wade in shallow areas.

READING AND SELECTING FLATS FOR WADING

Because you usually fish only one or two flats a day when you wade, you must carefully select those most likely to hold fish. Six criteria will help you choose a flat wisely: food potential, water temperature, escape routes, predator presence, fish visibility, and safety.

Food Potential

To check the food potential of a flat, look for signs of recent bonefish feeding and prey activity. Wading allows you to read prey signs and feeding signs much better than covering the flat in a skiff. You can study the bottom more closely on foot. You can also take samples from the bottom to figure out which prey live there. Look for sea-grass beds that hold prey such as shrimp and small fish. On sand flats look for the bullet-sized holes made by burrowing sea worms and clams. Or search for the small mounds made by burrowing crabs and urchins. You can also try to find small piles of debris and waste material near burrows, which indicate active prey feeding. While looking for these prey signs, watch for two- to six-inch bonefish feeding holes that indicate previous feeding. If fish have fed on a flat before, you know it holds food.

Wading has a feeling of intimacy — a sense of being in the water with the fish — that many anglers find important.

Water Temperature

If the air and water temperature have held constant within the bonefish's preferred range of sixty-eight to eighty-eight degrees, temperature will not be a
major factor in flats selection. But sometimes cold fronts, heat waves, changing water currents, and other natural events move water temperatures to the
upper or lower end of the bonefish tolerance range. When this happens, use a
thermometer to find water that is comfortable for fish. During cold spells, look
for waters warmed by the sun at midday in places with slow currents, like
small lagoons and lees. During heat waves, search the cooler-water edges of
drop-offs, deep holes, and cuts with strong flows.

Escape Routes

You can best evaluate a flat for escape routes when the tide is dead low, especially during a spring tide. Empty flats let you see the channels, cuts, and
holes bonefish use to enter and leave flats and to escape danger.

As you look for escape routes and sanctuaries, you can evaluate a flat's
fish-holding potential. Small flats completely bounded by deep water or
mangroves offer unlimited escape paths and are attractive to fish. Large, wide
flats laced with deep-water channels offer many paths of escape and also hold
fish well. But extremely shallow, wide flats provide no channels for escape
paths. They hold few fish long, and fish found on them will be nervous.

Predator Presence

Any flat that contains bonefish also attracts predators. As you search a flat for
bonefish, scan for the dark wiggling shadows of sharks and the stationary
ice-green torpedo shapes of barracuda waiting in ambush. Also keep an eye
out for the shadows of preying birds, such as osprey and frigate birds.
Bonefish may still be present even if you see any of these predators, but they
are likely to be nervous and prone to spooking.

Fish Visibility

This is a dual concern for the flats wader. You may prefer to wade flats where
you can see fish well against a plain backdrop of bare sand. But fish feel most
vulnerable there and spook more easily. You will find more fish when you
wade grass flats and along mangroves. You must develop good sighting skills
to see them here, but as a wader, you have an advantage. You can stand still
and wait to see if a suspicious-looking shape or shadow moves or not. You can
get a lot closer to a bonefish and see it better when aiming.

Safety

Wading anglers should avoid flats without firm bottoms, especially those in mangrove-rimmed swampy areas and in enclosed sounds, which often have deep and dangerously soft holes. Also, be careful on flats adjacent to large deep-water channels, narrow cuts, or windward reefs. While very productive, their deep waters and fast currents can sweep you off your feet. Wade these dangerous areas with great caution.

SEARCH STRATEGIES FOR WADING

Once you pick a flat, you must decide whether to stalk the fish or wait for them. On unfamiliar flats, stalking will usually produce best. But once you learn a flat well and know its best prey-holding areas and tide cycles, ambushing may give you better results.

Stalking

Start searching a new flat by zigzagging. Move back and forth across the areas that stand between the deep water, where the bonefish hold on low tides, and the turtle grass, mangrove stands, and coral reef areas that hold the most food. Early on a rising tide, look for fish coming onto the flats. They will cross them to feed in grass beds, mangroves, and other food-rich areas. As the tide rises

You can sneak up on tailing fish while wading if you keep a low profile and move slowly.

higher, some will even move all the way back into the mangroves, tidepools, and turtle-grass lagoons along the shoreline. By using a zigzag searching pattern, you will intercept fish or the fresh signs of their feeding.

Whenever possible try to keep both the sun and the wind at your back. You will find visibility critical when the sun sits low, early and late in the day. If wind prevents you from keeping the sun behind you, try to face north or south and fish crosswind so you at least keep the sun to your side instead of facing it. Also factor escape routes in your search plan. These are always likely places for fish to pass through. Angle your path to come upon them or along them with the sun and wind behind you.

Ambushing

Once you know a flat and where its food concentrations are, you can stake it out and wait for fish to come to you. This is an exciting form of bonefishing. You feel incredibly rewarded to see fish coming to feed when and where you predicted they would. Waiting for them on foot, you can position yourself for optimum sighting and casting advantage. You have plenty of time to target individual fish as pods come into range.

Ambushing has its risks, of course, no matter how well you know a flat. If you happen to pick a day when the water temperature just fell below sixty-eight degrees, or if the penaeid shrimp have just migrated offshore to spawn, or if the barracuda have been ripping up the flat and driving all the fish off, you may end up seeing no fish at all.

Ultimately, whether you stalk or ambush probably depends more on your nature and mood than anything else. Some days you have the patience to wait. On others you need to get out there and hunt them down.

CASTING

Wading, unlike poled-boat fishing, allows you to move and cast in any direction. Once a boat begins its drift, your path across a flat is committed and your direction is limited. As a wader, you can move against wind, currents, and tides to cast from any angle you wish. You can even walk across bars that would prevent a skiff from passing at all. This lets you circle around fish to gain a better wind angle or to see them better. Wading also allows you to position yourself inland of fish in heavy mangrove areas so a fish will be forced to run seaward when you hook it.

One major disadvantage of wading is that it limits your casting distance. If you are going to do most of your bonefishing by wading, you should consider getting a slightly longer rod than the nine-footers common for casting from a

Deep water

WADING STRATEGIES

For low-tide or bottom-of-the-tide conditions when the sea is emptying a flat or beginning to fill it again, station yourself at the places where fish enter and leave the area (indicated with an "L"). During mid-tide conditions, stake out the richest food concentrations in grass beds, on flat reefs, and coral heads (indicated with an "M"). For top-of-the-tide conditions, wait for fish along shorelines, tidepools, and mangroves (indicated with an "H").

Wading lets you reach fish in places where boats cannot go, especially at low tide.

boat. Another six or twelve inches will compensate for your lower elevation in the water.

Besides limiting your casting range, wading makes line management more difficult. You have no boat deck to provide a platform for your reservoir of shooting line. You must let your line drop into the water and drag along the surface, use a stripping basket, or hold it in your hand.

When your line lies on the water it tangles around your legs. Or it gets stuck in the surface tension of the water when you try to cast. Stripping baskets are a nuisance to wear in the heat of the tropics. Most of them do not prevent your line from tangling anyway. Holding a few loops of line in your hand will work fairly well, as long as you don't try to hold too much. Most experienced anglers end up keeping more line on the reel when they wade and make shorter casts than when they fish from a boat. Conveniently, shorter casts are usually effective when wading, because you can sneak up closer to the fish.

If you must make a long cast to a distant fish, you can always strip out the extra line you need, drape it in large loops in your hand, and then hold it gently in your mouth until you make your final forward cast. By learning to open your mouth just as you shoot the line, you'll get the extra loops to shoot up through the guides. This steelheader's technique can be effective when a big, wary fish swims just out of range and you fear spooking it by wading closer.

When you fish from a boat, you can drop spare fly line onto the deck. But when you fish on foot, you must hold your excess fly line in your hand. You can't just toss it in the water, because it will stick in the surface film and tangle around your legs. To avoid this problem, shorten your line when you wade. With only a few loops to hold, you can control your line and always be ready to shoot.

Once in a while this steelheader's technique comes in handy on the flats, By holding the line you plan to shoot loosely in your mouth, it lets you make especially long casts when wading.

SPECIAL GEAR

Flats anglers wade wet and need special footgear. Many also wear long pants to protect legs from sun, jellyfish, and microscopic organisms that cause some people to break out in a skin rash. A pair of thick-soled boat shoes will give you minimal foot protection, but a pair of special flats wading shoes made of neoprene with thick bottoms and tightly zippered tops will make your flats wading much more comfortable. The bottoms resist puncture and the tops

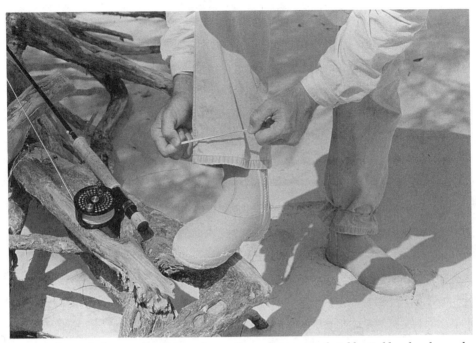

A pair of special shoes makes flats-wading safer and more comfortable. Rubber bands can be fastened around pants cuffs to help keep out fine-grained sand and mud.

protect your feet from the coral dust, sand, and mud you kick up when wading. If you wear long pants to protect your legs, fasten them tight against the outside of your wading shoes with rubber bands to keep the sand out.

Inconspicuous clothing will allow you to approach fish without their spotting you. I prefer unobtrusive colors such as light khaki or pale blue, which seem to work well. Long-sleeved shirts will help protect you from sun. You can always roll up your sleeves if it gets too warm.

A belt pack, chest pack, or small knapsack will carry your spare gear, water, lunch, and raingear. A collapsible wading staff that you can wear folded up on your hip makes an effective prod for rays and sharks and lets you test soft-looking bottoms before you step on them.

WADING DANGERS

The greatest danger most anglers experience on saltwater flats is a foot blister from too much coral dust in their wading shoes. Most creatures on the flats want nothing more than to avoid anglers. As long as you move slowly and deliberately, they leave you alone. But rays, sharks, barracuda, and a few others are dangerous and can injure you. A hooked bonefish that is struggling on your line acts like bait. It attracts predatory fish, and you may need to scare them off. Usually kicking up water with your feet or slapping the surface with your hand will frighten them.

One precaution has served me particularly well when wading: I never wade more than mid-thigh deep. Just remember that you are the intruder here. It pays to be sensible and alert.

Other common dangers for waders are soft bottoms and strong tides. Any place that experiences little current or tidal flow can contain deep, soft sediment. Sinking crotch-deep into muck is no joke. Early on, I once started to step over the side of a skiff to wade after a school of tailing fish in a back-country sound. Fortunately, my guide stopped me. He stood his push-pole on end and sank it almost five feet to show me what I almost did to myself.

Tides can be hazardous, too, if you neglect the dynamics of tidal flow. Cuts and channels can run deeper and faster on spring tides and become treacherous. They can wash you off your feet when you wade too deep. Also, flats with steep gradients can trap you on high tides when water fills channels or holes between you and the shore.

If you are new to wading, wade with a friend, wade shallow, and get to know one flat at a time. Never underestimate the sea, its creatures, and your own vulnerability.

Stingrays indicate a healthy, prey-rich flat. But be alert for them buried in the mud and avoid their dangerous tails. Shuffling your feet will scare them off, although this usually alarms bonefish as well. Instead, wade slowly and watch where you step. Like sharks, to whom they are related, most rays sense your presence in the water and swim away long before you reach them.

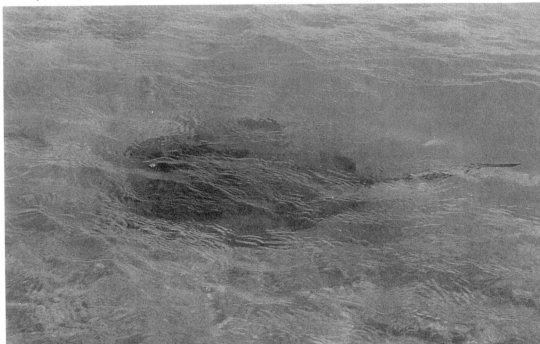

10

Fly-Fishing Equipment

Bonefishing demands more of fly fishing equipment than just about any other light-tackle angling. You cast only occasionally, but when you do, you must punch line fast, far, accurately, and against the wind. Reels have to withstand runs so fast that their spools must have counter-balances. Rods need to cast efficiently and throw tight loops. They must have the backbone to cut through wind and to turn a streaking fish before you run out of line.

Even components like rod guides become critical — they should be smooth to reduce drag and strong to withstand the tendon-popping forces on them. Your lines and leaders must not soften in the sun and tangle. They should have enough stiffness to shoot well and turn over heavy flies. They should glide through the guides quietly.

In addition, all your equipment has to stand up to daily doses of saltwater spray, sand, and coral grit as well as the jackhammer-like pounding they get in boat racks. Everything must always perform flawlessly when called upon, and it should all travel well and get to your destination with you.

A decade ago many of these features and capabilities did not exist at any price. Today, they are not only available, but they also come in a choice of quality and price ranges.

In choosing your tackle there is one general consideration to keep in mind from the outset: equipment specs change, needs don't. A decade ago, the Sage rod company was an unknown enterprise and Abel reels did not exist. A decade from now all the current brand names may have changed. But the basic

Bonefishing demands more of fly-fishing equipment than most other light-tackle angling.

requirements that bonefishing demands of equipment will stay the same. If you understand the *criteria* used to judge bonefishing rods, reels, lines, and leaders, then you can select the best gear offered today or ten years from now. You can match your needs whether you are a beginner or an experienced flats fisherman — and whether you are looking for a bargain or can spend top dollar.

BONEFISHING RODS

Any rod you use in bonefishing must punch against wind, cast far, and turn fish. To do all this best, it should be matched to the type of bonefishing you will do most. The size of fish you pursue and the flies you cast will determine your choice of line weight. Whether you fish mostly on foot or in boats should dictate your choice of rod length. If you frequently travel by air — as most of us do — you should also consider a rod's pack length. Other rod considerations

Casting opportunities in bonefishing are sometimes hours apart, leaving no room for marginal tackle that fails just when you need it.

such as fittings, grips, and butts are also critical in bonefishing rods. They affect both durability and your ability to handle fish well.

Rod Action

Don't let this mysterious area of rod design confuse you. All rods designed by major rod makers for bonefishing today are made out of the same basic material — graphite — and they all have acceptable tapers, actions, and casting dynamics.

Much technical jargon surrounds this area of fly fishing and you should probably be at least a little familiar with it. You will hear, for example, that bonefishing rods must have heavy butts and high hoop strength to turn fish. They should have fairly quick action to drive tight loops at high line speeds. You will also hear about single-plane tracking — the tendency of the rod to stay in a flat plane — which increases accuracy. Fast damping, another important characteristic, describes a rod's inclination to minimize vibration and makes casting smoother and more efficient.

If you are technically oriented, you may want to examine such design criteria and specifications as part of your rod selection. But for most anglers, this is unnecessary. Rod design today is so good that any fairly good-quality, stiff "saltwater-action" graphite rod from a major rod maker will do the job. You will probably end up with a better solution to your casting needs if you focus more on matching a rod's line weight, length, fittings, grips, and other features to the type of bonefishing you plan to do.

Line Weights

The size of fish and flies you will encounter should determine your choice of line weight. Most bonefishing anglers today use nine-foot graphite rods for 7-, 8-, and 9-weight lines. But some, who toss #8 or #10 flies to small fish on calm days, use a lighter 5- or 6-weight rod. Others prefer big 10- or 11-weight rods to deliver large-profile flies to heavy fish, such as those of the Florida Keys.

You can buy a different-weight rod for each of these situations if you can afford to and are so inclined. But, if you want only one rod, those for 7-, 8-, or 9-weight weight-forward lines are most versatile.

Rod Length

A rod length of nine feet should meet the needs of most anglers, especially those who do most of their bonefishing from a poled boat. But those who wade may prefer the slightly higher elevation that a 9 1/2- or ten-foot rod gives to their casts. There is a trade-off, however. Every additional inch added to the rod makes it more difficult to control and turn fish. So although you will be able to cast farther with a longer rod, you will give up some fish-handling abilities.

Pack Length

One additional and increasingly important rod consideration is pack length. If you frequently fly to bonefishing destinations, a travel rod can do a lot for your peace of mind.

Two-piece rods usually break down to a pack length of about 52 to 54 inches. Most airlines require you to check anything this long as shipped baggage, where it can be lost, stolen, or damaged. But if you carry a travel model, with a pack length as short as 29 to 38 inches, you can keep your rod with you as carry-on baggage. You will be sure it arrives when and where you do.

Some anglers reject travel rods because of the poor reputation of earlier models. The stiff ferrules of many of the older designs deadened these rods' casting actions. But today's sleeve-over joints, internal-spigot ferrules, and other techniques used in graphite blanks have eliminated most flat spots, especially in the stiffer models used in bonefishing. Sophisticated casters *will* notice some difference in performance, and you *do* have to check a couple more ferrules for tightness and make sure your line guides are aligned. But getting your rod to the flats on time and intact easily offsets these small disadvantages.

The first time you arrive at a fishing destination without your rods because they've been lost or broken, you will learn the wisdom of travel rods as no other experience can teach it to you. One of my good fishing friends spent an entire bonefishing trip to Andros on the phone trying to track down his rod bag. It not only had all his two-piece rods in it, but also his reels. The bag ultimately turned up—it had gone to Puerto Rico—but not until three days after he returned home.

Three- and four-piece travel rods break down to lengths between twenty-eight and forty-two inches — short enough to qualify as carry-on baggage on a commercial airline. But two-piece rods have pack lengths of about sixty inches and must travel as checked-in luggage with much greater risk of loss or breakage.

Fittings, Grips, and Butts

Features like fittings, grips, and butts may seem mundane considerations when compared to rod weight and length. But they can dramatically affect your casting and fish-handling abilities, as well as determine how well your rod holds up to the brutal world of salt water.

Many anglers choose a reel seat of corrosion-resistant metal — usually aluminum — on their bonefish rod, as opposed to the hardwood-and-metal seats found on freshwater rods. The all-metal seat provides a stable and dependable bond between your reel and your rod, keeping the reel from wobbling or twisting under stress.

The stripping guide, which is the rod's lowest line guide, funnels your line when getting a fish onto the reel during a high-speed hook-up. A guide lined with a tough, slick, ceramic-like material like silicon carbide works best to prevent tangles. You also want upper guides made of high-quality, polished, heavy-gauge material.

Rod grips are important since they transfer the energy from your casting hand into the rod. You need one that fills your hand and gives your thumb ample area to fully transmit thrust and punch tight loops. Meaty grips with a raised front end, such as the full-wells shape, do this best.

A fighting butt that hooks under your forearm, or braces against your chest or belly, gives you leverage during a long fight. You do not need a large butt — one or two inches is long enough. But select a rod with a fixed butt, which is more reliable than a removable or retractable one. It's always there when you need it.

Manufacturers

The majority of rods on the flats today are made by Sage, G. Loomis, Orvis, Winston, Fisher, Scott, and Powell. Major manufacturers like these usually lead the rest in implementing the latest generation of graphite. They offer the most rod models and provide good-quality reel seats, line guides, and other accessory fittings. Smaller suppliers often use the same rod blanks as the major rod makers. Some add high-quality fittings and finishings to make luxury models; others use economical finishing and fittings to provide lower-priced rods for economy-conscious anglers.

Each year manufacturers offer new rods using new generations of graphite that deliver greater stiffness (faster line speed, longer casts) at lower rod weight (less wind resistance, more energy transmitted to the fly line). Anglers often question whether their fishing needs require this very latest graphite and can justify its premium prices. But in bonefishing, which puts so much demand on casting performance, anglers need the very best rod they can

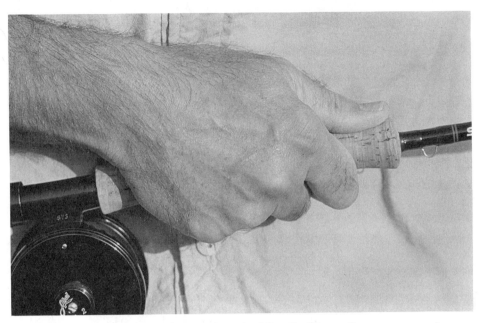

A meaty grip with a raised front edge, such as the full-wells design, allows you to put the most casting energy into a fly rod.

A short fixed fighting butt gives you leverage during the long run of a bonefish.

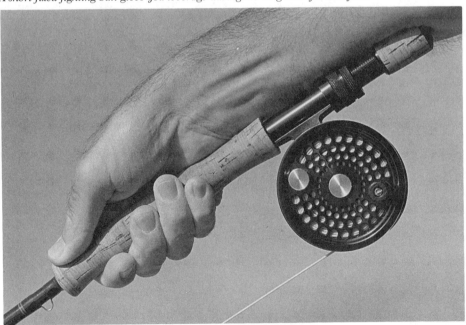

afford. On the other hand, even if you decide on an economy rod, it will probably cast better than any rod you could have bought ten years ago.

When selecting a rod manufacturer, one area that anglers should consider is the warranty. A few manufacturers will repair or replace a rod if it gets broken. Some guarantee the first 25 years of use, others cover the lifetime of ownership. Given the high cost of rods and the high risk of rod damage, such a warranty should factor into your purchase decision, as it could be worth several hundred dollars.

Rod Models

Anglers can choose from so many well-designed and well-built rods today that you should have no problem finding a model that meets the criteria you consider most important. Excellent models from major rod makers like Sage, G. Loomis, Scott, Winston, Orvis, and many smaller suppliers all work well. House brands from companies like L.L. Bean and Cabela's often use similar (and sometimes the same) rod blanks and may be a good value.

Probably the best bargains in bonefishing rods come from companies like Sage, Orvis, and Fisher, which offer beginner or economy models. Often made from blanks used in earlier generations of rods, companies sell these models that once topped their product line at almost half the price of their newest rods. They offer a lot of performance at a very attractive price.

Tables 10.1 and 10.2 list several of the most popular rod models seen today across a variety of price ranges.

What Rod Should You Pick?

If you are fairly sure you are going to stay with bonefishing and want one rod you can use everywhere, I would buy a three- or four-piece 8-weight model with a stiff action, full wells grip, fixed rod butt, and aluminum reel seat, from any of the top manufacturers. If I knew I were only going to fish Ascension Bay, I would buy a 5- or 6-weight. If I fished only the Florida Keys, I would buy at least a 9-weight, or possibly a 10-weight.

If you want to spend as little as possible, or if you are not sure whether you will stay with the sport, I would buy one of the four-piece beginner or economy models. Later, if I upgraded to a top-line model, I'd keep the first one as a back-up rod.

Realistically, you should always carry a back-up rod in bonefishing. The risks of damage en route, in boat racks, and during fishing are high, and at most destinations your chances of getting a replacement rod are zero.

TABLE 10.1

TWO-PIECE BONEFISHING RODS (9-FOOT, 8-WEIGHT)

MANUFACTURER	MODEL	GRIP	FIGHTING BUTT	PRICE[1]
Standard Models				
G. Loomis	FR1088 IMX	Full wells	1 1/4" fixed	$355
Orvis	HLS Powerhouse	Full wells	1 1/2" removable	$350
Powell	Legacy 989	Full wells	2" removable	$354
Sage	GFL 890-RPL-X	Full wells	1 1/2" fixed	$355
Scott	G908T	Western	5/8" fixed	$400
Winston	W908 IM6-XD	Half wells	1 1/2" fixed	$395
Economy Models				
Fisher	FGT27808	Full wells	2" fixed	$270
Orvis Rocky Mountain	Western B & B	Full wells	2" removable	$235
Sage Discovery	GFL 890DS	Full wells	1 1/2" fixed	$175

[1] 1992 suggested retail price

TABLE 10.2

TRAVEL BONEFISHING RODS (9-FOOT, 8-WEIGHT)

MANUFACTURER	MODEL	GRIP	FIGHTING BUTT	PRICE[1]	PACK LENGTH	NO. PIECES
Standard Models						
Fisher	FD47808	Full wells	2" fixed	$350	29"	4
G. Loomis	FR1088-4 IMX	Full wells	1 1/4" fixed	$395	32"	4
Orvis	HLS Powerhouse	Full wells	1 1/2" removable	$410	29"	4
Sage	GFL890-3RPL-X	Full wells	1 1/2" fixed	$400	38"	3
Scott	G908/4T GBF	Western	1 1/2" fixed	$475	30"	4
Winston	W908/3IM6XD	Half wells	1 1/2" fixed	$400	38"	3
Economy Models						
Fisher	F47808	Western	None	$260	29"	4
Orvis Rocky Mountain	4-Pc 9-by-9	Full wells	2" removable	$265	29"	4
Sage Discovery	890-4-DS	Full wells	1 1/2" fixed	$215	30"	4

[1] 1992 suggested retail price

BONEFISHING REELS

Unless you also fly fish for other saltwater species such as tarpon, permit, sail-fish, or marlin, you probably never viewed a fly reel as a critical consideration in buying a fly-fishing outfit. Aesthetics aside, you can handle most trout, salmon, bass, and steelhead on a simple, inexpensive reel with a click-and-pawl drag like that used in the classic Medalist.

But a bonefish runs one hundred yards or more at a burst speed of twenty to thirty miles per hour. The forces and stresses it exerts on a reel require a whole different level of strength, balance, capacity, precision, and drag quality. According to reel maker Steve Abel, if a bonefish runs at twenty-five miles per hour, your reel spins at over 10,000 revolutions per minute as you reach the end of your backing—almost 1 1/2 times faster than the speed of the crankshaft in high-performance cars!

Drag

The drag system in a good bonefish reel should apply a smooth, continuous braking force on the line as the fish pulls on it. The reel should not hesitate or

Many fly-fishing reels meet the strenuous requirements of bonefishing. Left to right, top row: STH Eliseo, Valentine 95; bottom row: Scientific Anglers 89, Abel 2, and Stream Line 3N.

sputter when the fish first starts pulling line off the reel. Nor should it falter when the reel's body heats up as the fish runs. The fish must never get an opportunity to leverage even a slight amount of its weight and speed against the tensile strength of the tippet. Anything that causes the reel to halt or slow for an instant will let the fish use its momentum and velocity to snap the tippet immediately.

Compressed-disc drags and caliper-and-disc drags dominate bonefish reel design today. Occasionally you will see the older, simpler click-and-pawl designs on the flats; sometimes an entirely new design will appear. But if you understand the disc and the caliper drag designs, you should be able to evaluate most of the bonefish reels available and choose the one that matches your needs.

Concentric Compressed-Disc Drag Design

Many better bonefishing reels such as the Abel, Billy Pate, and even some of the economy reels such as the Valentine, use this drag design. Each of these reels uses some arrangement of flat, washer-shaped rings of cork, Teflon, nylon, stainless, or other materials that are stacked concentrically on one or both ends of the reel's spindle.

Typically, a thin sheet of cork or other material that has predictable and durable friction characteristics covers one of these washer-shaped rings. This ring, called the "drag disc," has machined teeth around its edge or some other mechanical arrangement that allows it to turn one way and not the other. When you tighten the drag knob, you compress the stack of rings, forcing the braking material on the drag disc against the side of the reel's spool or against

Two drag systems dominate bonefish reel design, the concentric-compressed-disc design shown in the Abel 2 (left), and the caliper-and-disc design shown in the Scientific Angler 89 (right).

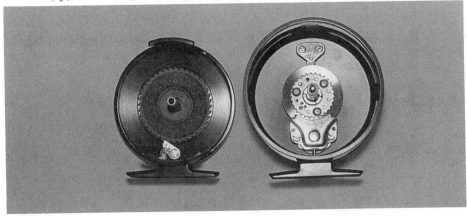

an intermediate braking disc attached to the spool. When you retrieve line, the spool and drag-disc move together and turn easily. But when the spool turns the other way, allowing line to go out, teeth engage the drag disc and the spool must turn against the friction of the braking material pressed against it.

Reliable and smooth, most concentric compressed-disc drag reels have few parts and seldom jam up. They last for years with minimal maintenance — you must only clean salt out after a trip and rub pure neat's-foot oil into cork pads once or twice a year. The major disadvantages anglers encounter in reels of this design are expense and difficulty in converting from right- to left-hand use.

Off-Center Compressed-Disc Drag Design
The off-center version of the disc drag, used by Orvis in its DXR reels, moves the drag disc off to the side of the spindle. Like the concentric designs, it consists of a sandwich of discs that provides friction (Rulon and other synthetic materials are used in the Orvis reels), and transmits the drag to the spool through a flat little gearbox of sprockets. The gearbox engages the spool when it turns in the outgoing direction and lets it turn drag-free in the retrieve direction. This design produces a smooth, continuous drag at a reasonable price. All gear boxes, however, are susceptible to dirt and debris, causing jam-ups if you don't keep them clean.

Caliper-and-Disc Drag Design
Scientific Anglers, Lamson, Marryat, and several others use this design, which presses a pair of shoes or "calipers" around a braking disc. This stops turning much the way you clamp your hand around the cover of a jar to put enough force on it to twist it open. Like the concentric compressed-disc drag, this design stacks the braking disc and spool on the reel's spindle along with a flat, sealed ratchet-and-pawl assembly that lets the spool turn drag-free in the retrieving direction. But when the spool turns to let line out, the ratchet-and-pawl assembly engages the braking disc and makes it turn against the pinching force of the calipers. This drag design usually requires less expensive machinery and parts than compressed-disc drags and is found in many reels in the moderate-price range. Corrosion and grit can jam its gearbox, but if you clean your equipment regularly, you can get good reel performance from this design.

Precision

A well-made reel with fine tolerances and a minimum of parts will turn smoothly, seize less, and cause little unintentional drag. Hard polished finishes reduce corrosion and last longer. But precision machining and finishing are expensive, which is why most well-made high-performance reels cost so much.

Capacity and Weight

The more backing you can store on your spool, the more time you have to wear down a big fish. But larger spools and more backing increase the weight you carry on the rod butt. With today's light reels, however, this is not a bad trade-off. Most reels can hold between one hundred fifty and three hundred yards of twenty-pound backing and weigh a comfortable eight to ten ounces — less than many top-line salmon reels that are designed to be cast hundreds of times a day.

Some anglers prefer thirty-pound backing for handling big bonefish. But this extra margin of safety against abrasion reduces your backing capacity by about twenty percent. If you feel the need for it, you should consider a larger-capacity reel, which will add one to two ounces to your outfit. Table 10.3 shows the weights and capacities of most of the reels available today.

Direct-Drive versus Anti-Reverse Reels

Just as some car owners like manual transmissions and others prefer automatics, some bonefishing anglers choose direct-drive reels while others use anti-reverse models.

If you are not familiar with these two types of reel designs, you can easily tell them apart. When you pull line off a direct-drive reel, its handle turns. An anti-reverse reel lets you pull line off its spool without the handle turning. This lets you keep your hand on the reel handle even when the fish is running.

Because direct-drive reels require you to let go of the reel handle each time the fish runs, you must be experienced enough to anticipate when the fish is getting ready to sprint. When the fish stops, you grab the handle and start cranking; when it runs, you take your hand off and let the fish go. Most of the classic freshwater trout reels, from Medalists to Hardys, have this direct-drive design.

Anti-reverse reels, like automatic transmissions, require less of the operator. They let you just keep cranking whether the fish is running or not. And, like automatics, they work less efficiently. You do not get one turn of line retrieved for every turn you make on the crank.

At first, it would seem that most bonefishermen would choose anti-reverse reels. When a bonefish runs at twenty-five miles per hour, a reel's spool and handle spin at about five thousand revolutions per minutes at half spool. As

TABLE 10.3
SELECTED BONEFISH REELS

MANUFACTURER	MODEL	WEIGHT	CAPACITY (WF 8F, 20#)	TYPE	DRAG[1]	PRICE[2]
Precision Models						
Abel	2	7.8oz	250yds	DD	CCD	$490
Abel	3	10.0oz	300yds[3]	DD	CCD	$545
Billy Pate	Bonefish	10.0oz	300yds	AR	CCD	$425
Billy Pate	Bonefish	10.0oz	300yds	DD	CCD	$425
Standard Models						
Orvis	D-XR 7/8 AR	7.0oz	160yds	AR	OCCD	$260
STH	CBR08	6.5oz	220yds	AR	CCD	$295
STH	ELR08	6.5oz	220yds	DD	CCD	$295
Stream Line	3N	6.9oz	250yds	DD	CCD	$375
Economy Models						
Lamson	LP-3.5	8.0oz	200yds	DD	C&D	$168
Marryat	8.5	5.0oz	235yds	DD	C&D	$208
Scientific Anglers	89	8.2oz	240yds	DD	C&D	$175
Valentine	95	6.8oz	200 yds	DD	CCD	$129

[1] CCD: Concentric Compressed-Disc; OCCD: Off-Center Compressed-Disc; C&D: Caliper and Disc
[2] 1992 suggested retail prices
[3] 30#

Some reels like these two Billy Pate models come in both an anti-reverse version (left) and a direct-drive version (right). Each design has its advocates.

you reach the bottom of your spool, rpm will double. An ill-timed attempt to grab your reel's spinning handle can result in a bruised knuckle, snapped tippet, and lost fish. A non-spinning handle would seem to be a big advantage.

But the additional parts required to make a reel anti-reverse often make many of them heavier and more prone to jamming and slippage. The simpler designs of direct-drive models usually weigh less, pick up line more efficiently, and jam less often. They *do*, however, require you to sense the pulse of the fish and take your hand off the reel.

Most experienced bonefish anglers I know use direct-drive reels. They do not mind reading the fish closely: in fact, many consider this an essential part of the fishing experience. They also prefer the better line pick-up performance and reliability of direct drives. Many anglers, however, like the ease and safety of anti-reverse reels. While I have a slight preference for direct-drive, I find either is satisfactory as long as it is well made. Both designs come in models of excellent quality for about the same price, so the choice is ultimately a matter of personal style and preference.

Right-Hand or Left-Hand Wind

Some anglers wind a reel with their dominant or strongest hand and prefer to play the fish with their secondary hand. Others favor playing the fish with the strongest hand, using their weakest to do the cranking on the reel handle.

Like choosing between direct-drive and anti-reverse reels, the choice between right- and left-hand reels has strong advocates and critics on both sides. Some emphasize winding needs. They choose reels that wind with the same hand they use for casting. If they are right-handed, they cast with their right hand, switch the rod to their left to play the fish, and wind the reel with their right hand. They reason that the winding demands the strength of their best hand.

Right-handed anglers of the other school of thought use left-hand reels. They do not have to switch hands in the middle of hooking fish and they use their strongest hand to control the rod. I have used both methods and I prefer playing fish with my strong hand. But this is not an area I can get too excited about — they both work just fine.

Reel Models

As you can see in Table 10.3, the reels currently used in bonefishing span a price range from about $130 to $550, and offer line capacities from one hundred and sixty to three hundred yards.

Many veterans end up with Abels or Pates. Both have highly reliable concentric compressed-disc drags and both are flawlessly made mechanical masterpieces. They also command prices consistent with their precision machining and finishing.

The bargain end of bonefishing reels includes the Valentine, with a disc drag, and Scientific Angler, Lamson, and Marryat models, with caliper drags. They range from about $130 to $200. Orvis, STH, and Stream Line models fill the middle $250 to $375 range.

First Reels, Back-Up Reels, and Ultimate Reels

Knowing what I do today, I would buy only top-line reels at the outset and be done with it. But I say that after buying eleven bonefishing reels in the last fifteen years. Clearly, I did not follow my own advice.

One way to outfit yourself is to start with one of the better inexpensive models. You can later upgrade, keeping the first one for a back-up. This makes more sense than it might seem at first. There are many ways a reel can be damaged, jammed, or lost on a trip to the flats. You will eventually end up wanting two reels if you do much bonefishing.

FLY LINES FOR BONEFISHING

A perfect fly line for bonefishing would do all of the following:

- cast both weighted and unweighted flies in sizes from 10 to 1 a distance of fifty to eighty feet or more comfortably, consistently, and in wind
- turn over big flies easily
- cast quietly, land softly on the water, and be visible to the angler but invisible to the fish
- pick up and recast easily
- deliver both weighted and unweighted flies to the bottom as fast as possible
- resist coiling, tangling, snagging, and sticking to itself — even lying on a deck in the hot sun
- resist abrasion when pulled across as much as six hundred feet of coral flat by a fish

To determine which fly lines best match this ideal, you must consider size, finish, stiffness, color, taper, and density of those available.

Line Size

Flies, wind, and size of fish determine line size. By far, 7-, 8-, and 9-weight lines shoot more bonefish flies across more flats to more fish each year than any other weight class. In destinations where the fish and the flies are small, a 6-weight system may be adequate. On the other hand, if you are after large fish and often use bushy #2 flies, you may lean toward a 9-weight or even heavier system. Heavier lines, however, offer much larger profiles and greater resistance for casting in the wind. They also tend to splash when they land.

Line Finish, Stiffness, and Color

In general the stiffer and slicker the line, the better it shoots through the guides of your rod. Stiffness and slickness also reduce line tangling, improving the odds of getting your line onto the reel quickly and cleanly during a hook-up. As you can see from Table 10.4, most bonefishing lines commonly in use today have stiff designs and tough, slick finishes — as long as you clean the salt and scum from them regularly.

Line color allows you to see your line to track your fly. At the same time, you want your line to be invisible to the fish so it doesn't spook them. Although shallow-water fish like bonefish can see most of the colors humans can, there is no research yet that tells us which colors bonefish see most or least, so we are left to speculate.

In my experience, fish do not notice colors such as pale white, ivory, mint-green, tan, and light gray as much as others. Clear or translucent lines spook fish least of all, but *you* will not be able to see them in the water either. (But if your eyes can follow a fly without a visible line to guide them, you may want to consider one of these.) Anglers can see high-visibility lines like coral, yellow, dark green, and dark gray best of all; unfortunately, so can the fish. I used a bright red model once that spooked fish every time I dropped it to them. Now I favor pale colors that I can see, such as light green, tan, and beige, which do not seem to affect the fish overly.

Line Taper

Most bonefish anglers use weight-forward fly lines. By concentrating most of their weight near the tip of the line, these models allow anglers to cast quickly with little false-casting. But not all weight-forward models are tapered the same. Some models have special saltwater or bonefish tapers that push the line's weight even closer to the front end than the conventional weight-forward lines.

The trade-off anglers must consider in choosing among these models is

Bonefishing equipment and lines work better and last longer if rinsed down with fresh water after each day of fishing.

speed of loading the rod versus presentation and splashdown impact. I prefer standard weight-forwards, which load well and cast fast enough for me. These also turn over my fly better and make less noise when I use them. Some anglers have a strong preference for the fast-loading saltwater tapers and find their presentation and turnover satisfactory with their style of casting. Table 10.4 illustrates popular models with both of these tapers.

Line Density

Many anglers use floating lines almost exclusively for bonefishing, because they pick up and recast fast. Sinking-tip and slow-sinking intermediate lines have advantages for deeper water and windy conditions, however. Most experienced anglers on the flats today carry both types with them. Full-sinking lines and shooting heads probably have more disadvantages than advantages in bonefishing.

Floating Lines

Most bonefishermen prefer floating lines above all other line types for the flats. They land fairly quietly, lift quickly from the water, and are easy to recast when fish change direction or when you miscast. They also perform well during hook-ups and runs: floating lines stay on top while sinking models belly down, increasing the likelihood they will abrade or snag on underwater hazards. With nine- to fifteen-foot or longer leaders, floating lines also let you get weighted flies down to fish fast, as long as the water is no more than three to four feet deep. They do not work well for deeper water, or for cutting through wind.

Sinking-Tip Lines

Sinking tips pull unweighted and bulky flies to the bottom fast. They cast well in the wind. They also give you a more direct line to the fly for hook-ups. Some do not land quietly, however, and sinking tips can snag underwater during runs more than floating lines do. Sinking tips also take longer to lift and recast; you must strip the line closer to you before you can lift its weighted tip to cast again. Most anglers find these trade-offs manageable, however.

Intermediate Lines

Some anglers prefer slow-sinking intermediate lines for most deep-water bonefishing. Intermediate models increase the sinking rate of flies, look nearly invisible, and cast well in wind. They prevent choppy water from transmitting unnatural action to a fly, and they provide a direct pull on the hook for striking. Intermediate lines are particularly effective on deep-cruising fish and on fish swarming in large schools just under the surface. As with all sinking lines, they are more difficult to lift and recast than are floating lines.

Full-Sink Lines

Full-sink lines deliver flies to prescribed depths at predictable rates. When bonefish leave the flats in hot weather for cooler, deeper water, full-sink lines can reach them faster than other methods. Full-sinking lines do not lift well, however, and recasting is slow. But this kind of deep-water bonefishing often involves more of a fishing-the-water technique, which requires less recasting than shallow-water sight-casting.

What Fly Line to Use

I usually rig two outfits for most bonefishing destinations — one floating and one sinking. For the floating outfit, I use a fairly stiff pale-colored weight-forward floating line, and this is the rod I use eighty to ninety percent of the time. The second outfit I rig with a sinking-tip (or sometimes intermediate) line and I use this to get down to fish holding deep in hot weather or feeding deep on high tides.

You may also want to consider fly action in choosing fly lines. Since most

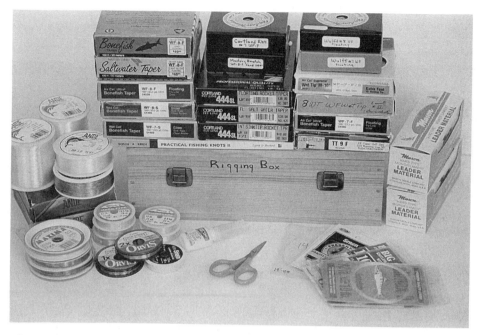

Selecting different fly lines and leaders lets anglers adapt to different bonefishing needs and casting styles. Fly line choice should evaluate taper and outer finish for casting dynamics, density for sink rate, and color for visibility to both angler and fish. Leader selection should emphasize stiffness for turning over heavy flies, abrasion resistance for preventing break-offs, and colorless, invisible profiles for wary fish.

flies in use today emulate shrimp, which make jumping-and-diving actions, floating lines have been very effective. They tend to pull the fly up to the surface on stripping. But patterns that require other actions like those representing baitfish, crabs, and worms, may appear more realistic with lines that sink more and either swim then or drag them across the bottom.

LEADERS AND TIPPETS

Leaders for bonefishing should have heavy butt sections that transfer casting energy and turn over weighted flies. They must look invisible to fish and withstand abrasion from coral, shells, and barnacle-encrusted mangrove shoots. For sinking lines, most anglers use shorter three- or four-foot leaders because they keep the flies closer to the sinking section of the line. Deep-cruising fish

TABLE 10.4
FLY LINES (8-WEIGHT)

MANUFACTURER/MODEL	LENGTH (FEET)					COLOR	STIFFNESS
	TOTAL	TIP	FRONT TAPER	BELLY	REAR TAPER		
Floating Lines							
Cortland 444SL	105	1	10	32	6	Mint green	Stiff
Scientific Anglers Mastery WF	100	1	10	29	14	Mint green	Stiff
Cortland 444SL Salt Water Taper	105	.5	6	20	6	Mint green	Stiff
Scientific Anglers Mastery Bonefish	100	1	5.5	26.5	10	Sand	Very stiff
Scientific Anglers Mastery Salt Taper	100	1	5.5	26.5	10	Pale yellow	Stiff
Lee Wulff Bonefish Taper	90		35*		3	Pale green	Moderate
Intermediate Lines							
Cortland 444SL Intermediate Sink	105	.5	6	20	6	Transparent white	Stiff
Scientific Anglers Mastery Bonefish Sinking Line	100	1	5.5	26.5	10	Clear	Stiff
Sinking-Tip Lines							
Cortland 444SL Intermediate Sink Tip	105	.5	10	22	6	Mint/ice blue	Stiff
Scientific Anglers Wet Tip I Air Cel Ultra	90	10	3	19	7	Buckskin/green	Moderate
Scientific Anglers Wet Tip Air Cel Ultra Intermediate Tip	90	10	4	17	10	Buckskin/green	Moderate

* The Wulff line has one continuous front taper that includes the tip, front taper, and belly sections.

feed aggressively and seldom spook at sunken lines and leader butts. Floating lines, however, require much longer leaders of nine to fifteen feet, depending on the difficulty of the fish and the conditions.

Tips to Improve

Your

Bonefishing

Preface

Bonefish are creatures of the flats. They respond to the primordial rhythms of the tides, charging and retreating over beds of bright sand and blankets of turtle grass. They are sleek and slender, shy and suspicious. They blend in perfectly with the turquoise waters and the shimmering bottom; their silver sides reflecting all giving them the ability to seemingly change color.

Bonefishing combines the best of hunting and fishing. You must have the visual concentration and patience to find the fish and a hunter's stalking ability to get within casting range. Your cast must then deliver the fly quietly and precisely. You must entice the fish, with a proper retrieve, to accept and eat your fly. You must develop a feel for the hookset. In bonefishing rarely is blind luck rewarded. Usually, the fisherman with the most skills catches the most fish.

The reward for all this concentration and applied technique is the hookup. The magical moment when that ghostly shadow is attached to your casting arm. The run is explosive and blazing. You struggle for control; your line rattling through the guides in a demonstration of pure power 50, 100, then 150 yards of backing evaporate into the mix of sizzling tropical heat and turquoise gin clear water.

This is bonefishing. For many anglers, after all the trout, salmon, tarpon, and sailfish, the bonefish is still the ultimate quarry. The bonefish, *albula vulpes*, the white fox brings anglers back to flats time and time again, year after year. Many words have been written about why we do it but its really just "damn good fun".

What follows are a few hints to improve your bonefishing. If you are an expert we invite your suggestions and additions. If you are a novice we will be happy to clarify any of these recommendations.

Here's to bonefish tails shimmering and twinkling in the sunlight, delicate casts and screaming runs.

Tips to Improve Your Bonefishing
Preparing to Cast

■ The majority of bonefishing is done with a weight forward floating line. These lines lift easily off the water without spooking the fish and rarely get hung up on the bottom. Use a neutral or pale colored fly line, gray or sand is best. Very bright lines, especially fluorescent colors, can be as easy for the fish to see as it is for you. If you use bright fly lines make sure your leader is long enough to compensate for the line's increased visibility.

■ Throw a wet towel over any obstructions on the casting deck of your boat. Cleats and handles can easily snare your fly line and ruin a cast or worse, break off a fish.

■ Don't strip out more line than you need to make your cast. Make a practice cast, then leave that measured amount of the line trailing in the water (if you are wading,) or stacked carefully on deck (if you are casting from a boat.) This will minimize the amount of line that can tangle on your feet or form knots. Do not pull line off your reel and stack it on the deck of the boat. If you do, the forward portion of your line is underneath the pile, then when you cast with the line stacked in this way you will end up with a tangled bird's nest. Make sure you make a practice cast, then stack your line.

■ If you are casting from the deck of a boat take off your shoes. This will allow you to feel the fly line stacked on the deck and you can avoid stepping on it.

■ If you are using a monofilament butt section nail knotted to your flyline, for loop-to-loop connection to leader, use .025 or heavier medium to medium limp mono on an 8 weight. This will transfer the energy from your cast to the leader. A butt section of less than .025 causes the cast to die as the energy is transferred from line to leader.

■ Using loop-to-loop connections allows you to change leaders quickly. Attach a two foot butt section to your fly line, as mentioned above, then tie a loop in the end. Then depending on conditions, you can use a pre-looped 7 foot leader if its windy or up to a 15 foot leader if it is calm.

■ A ten pound clear mono tippet works well on bonefish. Check your leader regularly for abrasion and re-tie your fly after each fish. Test your knot every time you tie on a new tippet.

Flies

■ The most important aspect of fly selection is sink rate. When tying or purchasing bonefish flies vary the sink rate of your assortment through no eyes (lightest), to pearl eyes, to bead chain eyes, to lead barbell eyes (heaviest). This allows you to fish different depths of water and to fish tailing (cast close with light fly) and fast cruising fish (cast well ahead with quick sinking fly), effectively.

■ Bonefish have a powerful sense of smell. They can smell shrimp and crabs they cannot see. They can also smell insect repellent, sun block, gasoline and after-shave. Keeping your hands clean will help keep your fly clean.

■ As a general rule, use light colored flies on light (sand) bottom and dark colored flies on dark (turtlegrass, coral) bottoms. In nature, overt visibility can make any animal prey. Most prey on bonefish flats are well camouflaged. Try smaller flies (6,8) to fish that are spooky or are tailing on clear shallow flats in clam weather conditions. On deeper flats, or in windy conditions larger flies (2,4) work well on larger fish or fish that are cruising very fast. Larger flies should be cast further away from bonefish.

■ Subtle earth tone flies, (tan, brown, olive, green, gold, yellow) work best on sunny, bright days in shallow water when bonefish are spooky. Bright flies, (pink orange, chartreuse) work best on cloudy or darker days in deeper water or later in the day especially at sunset.

Seeing and Being Seen

■ Polarized sunglasses are absolutely essential for spotting bonefish. Brown or gray lenses work best on bright days; yellow or amber work best on cloudy, low light days. Side shields will eliminate peripheral light. Make sure you use an eyeglass retainer strap to avoid losing your expensive glasses.

■ Wade quietly and slowly. Bonefish can "feel" water being pushed by your legs. Use your eyes; scan constantly, you are hunting as much as fishing. You are pitted against an animal with an incredible array of sensory organs.

■ Bonefish have an acute sense of vision enabling them to see colors well and in a wide variety of light conditions. They can see motion in muddy or clear water and when they are stationary or traveling at top speed. That mango Hawaiian shirt looks well in pictures - but tan and pale blue will allow you to spook fewer fish. Remember to remove shiny jewelry. Also, don't hesitate to cast from your knees or to crouch if fish come in very close.

2

■ Use the wind and sun to your advantage. If possible, wade a flat with the wind behind you. If there is little or no wind, have the sun behind you. Also often, after spotting fish, you have time to navigate upwind of the fish, but wade slowly until you are in place.

■ A hat with a long bill will protect your face from the sun but will also improve your vision especially if the bill's underside is dark. The dark underside absorbs reflected light.

■ Scan the water constantly, you can look for surface disturbances (nervous water) but to consistently spot bonefish you must imagine the water does not exist, looking through it to the bottom.

When The Excitement Starts

■ False cast away from the fish, especially with slow moving or tailing fish. This will keep the fly line from spooking the fish. Cast away at a 45° to 90° angle to the direction that the fish are heading.

■ If it is windy, make your false cast holding your rod as parallel as possible to the plane of the water. The wind's friction with the water lessens its velocity in the area 3 to 4 feet above the water's level. This casting technique makes it harder for the fish to see the fly line and allows for a very quiet presentation since the fly does not drop from much height.

■ Never cast too early or begin to cast when the bonefish is out of your range. Be patient, know your comfortable casting range. If you try to make too long a cast and your fly falls short, it will take too long to cast again and the bonefish will have moved on.

■ It is better to cast too short and hope the fish sees the fly, than to cast too long and spook the fish. In nature, prey never moves toward a predator. Never place a fly so that when retrieved it moves toward a bonefish. Predators chase their prey, they expect their prey to be moving away from them. When confronted with an approaching fly, a bonefish will change roles, from predator to prey, and flee. Few fish can leave a flat as quickly as a bonefish.

■ Generally, a tailing fish has his head tipped down and is already occupied; consequently, the fly must be dropped very close to him. In contrast, cruising fish can see a fly from a much greater distance and the fly can be presented further away.

■ Learn to strip strike .... Trout fishermen, (there are lots of us,) usually raise the rod tip to strike a fish. This technique when used on a bonefish will quickly remove the fly from its field of vision if he has not eaten the fly. The strip strike keeps the fly in the bonefish strike zone and will give you a second chance. A 1 to 3 foot strip strike done firmly by the hand not holding the rod accomplishes the strip strike.

■ When retrieving your fly point your rod tip directly at the fly. Th allows the fly to be imparted with the proper action.

■ Lift your fly line quietly and slowly off the water to initiate another cast. DO NOT use the initiation of the back cast to load the rod tip. Many beginning anglers do this to allow themselves to make longer casts o to cast into the wind - this noisy lift off will almost always spook bonefish.

■ Do your homework before going fishing. Learn to cast accurately and quickly. Do not false cast excessively. Learn to make 2-3 false casts playing out line with each cast then shooting your line accurately to the fis on your last cast. As well as wasting valuable time. Repeatedly false casting over a fish in an effort to "measure" distance and accuracy often spooks fis as they repeatedly see the fly line whipping in the air.

The Hookset and After

■ When a bonefish follows a fly he will almost always take it. Other clues that a fish has taken your fly are: his dorsal fin or tail flutter or quive he flashes his side in the sun, the fish races a second fish to a spot or the fis scurries to another spot leaving his companion or school behind and most important if he tips down and his tail comes out of the water. If any of the occur, chances are he has your fly. Count off one or two seconds and strip strike. Sometimes if you can't see the fish, you can feel your line vibrate o jump. In that case strip strike again.

■ If a fish follows closely but does not take your fly change your retrieve, speed up, slow down or stop entirely. This change will often elici a strike.

■ A bonefish can travel 26 m.p.h. for several hundred feet in six inches of water. Set your drag <u>before </u>you cast to a fish, and once hooked, let all the spare line safely out through the guides. Always fight a bonefish on the reel; to do otherwise invites disaster. Until the fish is on the reel, watch your line , not the fish.

■ After getting the line on the reel hold your rod high. This will create a steeper angle and help the line get over coral and mangrove shoots, resulting in fewer break offs.

■ The harder you fight a bonefish, the harder he will pull back. If a fish gets tangled around a mangrove or in the weeds or coral, take all the pressure off the fish. Bonefish will usually stop. You can untangle your line and resume the fight.

■ Handle a landed fish as little as possible. Pinch the barbs on your hooks. Hemostats will often allow you not to have to touch the fish at all.

When Day is Done.

■ To avoid corrosion, rinse your reel and rod with fresh water at the end of each day.

■ After you start to head home, trail your fly line behind the boat without a fly to remove kinks and twists. As you reel in the fly line, pass it through a cloth soaked with fly line cleaner and you will be ready for the next day.

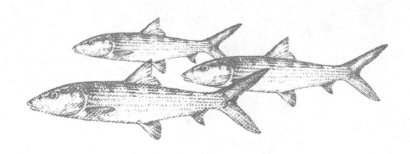

Commercial Leaders for Floating Lines

The standard leaders sold for floating lines in bonefishing are nine- to twelve-footers with a heavy butt and a tippet with a tensile strength of about eight to twelve pounds. You should find many good leaders with these characteristics from companies like Climax, Orvis, Umpqua, and others. The growing popularity of saltwater, salmon, and steelhead fishing has produced an abundance of these well-tapered, heavy-duty leaders with thick butts to transmit casting energy from the end of the fly line all the way to the fly. Among these, those with the heaviest butts (.024 inches or greater in diameter) transfer this energy more effectively and turn over the fly the best. You should choose the clearest leaders you can find. Pale green is an adequate second choice, but avoid those dyed tea color, blue, or green entirely — they are far too visible on saltwater flats.

As good as many of these packaged leaders are, you may want to modify them in a couple of ways. You can improve their ability to stand up to mangrove roots and coral by replacing their tippets with heavy-diameter, abrasion-resistant material like Maxima, Rio, Climax, Stren, or Ande. I usually replace the last one or two feet of a commercial leader with a three-foot tippet of one of these materials. In addition to reducing break-offs, this also increases the original length of the leader by a foot or two.

You may, however, want to lengthen your leaders by much more than a foot or two. Many anglers use very long leaders for calm days, thin water, and sophisticated fish. Guides in the Florida Keys often recommend leaders of fourteen to fifteen feet on a regular basis for their large, experienced fish.

Most anglers who use these long leaders design and build their own. But you can modify a commercial leader to do the job as well. To convert a nine- or twelve-foot leader into a fourteen- or fifteen-footer, you must lengthen the butt end. Adding this much length to the tippet would give you a wimpy performance that would not turn over your fly. But you should have no turnover problems if you extend the leader at its butt end with heavy-diameter, hard butt material. Use material with a diameter that falls between that of your fly line and that of the leader. I often use thirty-two-pound hard Mason mono of .028-inch diameter, for example, as a butt extension between a .025-inch diameter Climax leader butt and a .038-inch diameter 8-weight fly line tip.

Tying Your Own Leaders

Some anglers like to tie their own leaders because it lets them control taper better and tailor the leader's turnover to their own casting style. It also allows them to adjust leader length to their fishing circumstances. Tying your own leaders will let you vary the mix of hard and soft materials to further fine-tune it. You can, for example, combine a butt of very hard material such as Mason with more pliable tapered sections of Stren or Ande.

The taper in traditional leaders that anglers tie for other kinds of fishing often consists of about sixty percent butt, twenty percent midsection, and twenty percent tippet. But the dilemma in bonefishing is that you always want leaders that are one hundred percent butt for turnover and one hundred percent tippet for deceiving wary fish.

Anglers who tie their own leaders constantly search for ways to balance these two opposing goals. Bob Nauheim, for example, ties twelve- to fourteen-foot leaders that are two-thirds to three-quarters butt material (twenty-five- to thirty-pound mono) and one-third to one-quarter tippet (eight to ten pounds). Angler Jim O'Neill tapers a ten-foot leader out of five segments of hard Mason (thirty-two to twelve-pound) and then adds a tippet, sometimes using softer material like Maxima for the last section. He follows a thirty-percent butt, forty-percent midsection, thirty-percent tippet design. Keys guide Vic Gaspeny ties fourteen-foot leaders out of clear (not fluorescent blue) Stren using 4 1/2 feet of thirty-pound for a butt, 4 1/2 feet of twenty-pound for a midsection, and four to five feet of ten-pound for a tippet. Learning to throw long leaders like these can mean making some adjustments in your casting, but sometimes only very long leaders with very long tippets will allow you to interest fish at all.

Leaders for Sinking Lines

Because most sinking fly lines are less visible to fish, you can use shorter leaders with them. But with the clear water typical of the flats and the sharp close-in sight of bonefish, you should still put three to four feet between your line and the fly. You can tie a leader for sinking lines using about thirty inches of heavy butt material and eighteen inches of tippet. Or, as Lefty Kreh has been recommending for years, you can just attach a three- to four-foot-long tippet directly to the fly line.

RIGGING

The best rigging for a bonefish outfit gives you the maximum amount of backing with a smooth connection between all the elements to prevent snags and break-offs during high-speed sprints. Markers in your backing, made with different-colored splices or permanent marking pens, can also be useful if you want to accurately estimate lengths of runs, fish speed, and the amount of line you have left.

Micron or Dacron backing is connected to the reel with an arbor knot. The

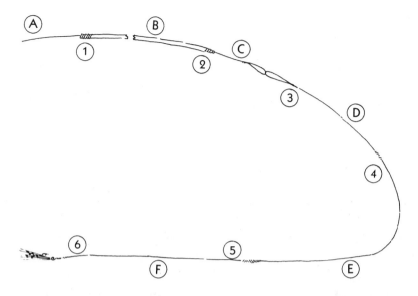

RIGGING

You can attach your backing (A) to your fly line (B) with a nail knot (1). Less pretty, but still effective: whip a loop on the tail of the fly line, tie a triple surgeon's loop in your backing and join them with a loop-to-loop connection. At the front of your fly line, use a leader butt extension (C) to keep the tip of your line from getting eaten up by leader changes. It should be one to two feet long and at least two-thirds the diameter of your fly line's tip (e.g., .025 or heavier for a .038 8-weight standard weight-forward floating taper). Attach the leader butt extension to your fly line with a nail knot, needle knot, or whipped loop connection (2). Join the leader's butt (D) to the leader-butt extension (C) using surgeon's loops (3) and connect the leader segments (D) through (F) with surgeon's knots or blood knots (4 and 5). The Trilene or improved clinch knots are effective for tying on your fly (6).

easiest backing-to-fly-line connection is a loop-to-loop using a surgeon's loop on the backing and a whipped loop on the fly line. You can also nail-knot the Micron or Dacron to the fly line for a cleaner connection.

Leaders can be connected to fly lines using a nail knot or loop-to-loop joint. You can whip a loop directly onto the end of your fly line or you can nail-knot a one- or two-foot extension onto the tip of your fly line using heavy leader butt material. Put a surgeon's loop at the end of this extension. Then tie a surgeon's loop in the butt of your leader and loop the two surgeons together to join the leader to the fly line's tip.

For tying leader sections and tippets together, both the blood knot and the surgeon's knot hold up equally well for me, if I've tied them well. For the tip-

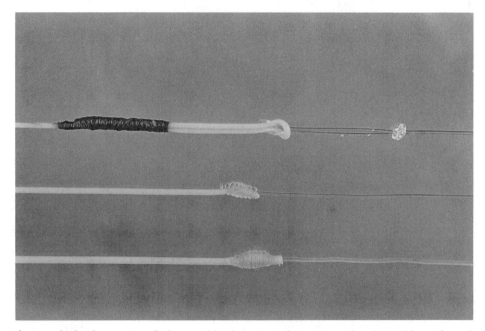

Three methods of connecting fly lines and leaders, top to bottom, are: the whipped loop, the nail knot, and the needle knot. Of these, the nail knot, which provides a clean, low-profile, secure bond between fly line and heavy-butt leaders, has become the favorite of most experienced bonefishing anglers.

pet to fly, I prefer the Trilene knot over the improved clinch knot and use it almost exclusively now for bonefishing. Angler Ben Estes uses the improved-improved clinch knot he learned from Keys guide Capt. Eddie Wightman. It is identical to the improved clinch, except that you start the knot by going through the hook eye twice and snugging down the resulting loop onto the eye before proceeding with the normal five turns of the improved clinch. The rest of the tying sequence is the same as the ordinary improved clinch.

Diagram 10.1 shows the elements that make up the rigging and knots for a typical system. If you are new to fly fishing or just not technical about rigging, you can have your reel and line rigged by any good tackle shop. Or you can assemble it yourself. But there is no black magic in rigging. Any angler can learn the basic knots and techniques needed using Lefty Kreh and Mark Sosin's *Practical Fishing Knots II*, the best handbook around for anglers' knots.

11

Personal Gear, Clothing, and Other Tackle

Most gear, clothing, and miscellaneous tackle you use for other fishing will serve you well in bonefishing. But fishing the flats also requires several special items like polarized glasses, long-brimmed hats, protective footgear, and sunblock. Other items such as tackle packs, boat bags, and fast-drying clothing, while not essential, can make life on the flats a lot more comfortable and productive.

PERSONAL GEAR

Polarized Glasses

In bonefishing, good-quality polarized sunglasses are as critical to your success as a rod and reel. They let you see through the surface glare to spot fish. Without them, you are blind. The polarizing layer of your fishing glasses must filter out reflected light and cut glare. You can test how well glasses do this by looking at reflections on a car's windshield or on a body of water. The lenses should allow you to pierce through the glare and see details behind it.

Bonefishing lenses should also contain a tinted layer to reduce the harshness of intense tropical sunlight. Amber hues are best for the flats because they exaggerate contrast, making it easier to distinguish the shapes of fish.

Fishing the flats requires a number of specialized personal items including polarized glasses, long-brimmed hats, and fast-drying clothes.

Yellow, the lightest member of the amber family, lets you see well in low light. Medium brown or amber work well for cloudy bright conditions. For the harshest midday sun, dark brown glasses will shield your eyes but still enhance contrast. Veteran flats anglers often carry two or three pairs of polarized glasses with different tints and vary them as brightness changes. That may sound compulsive, but it isn't. Your ability to catch bonefish depends on how well you can see them.

Tight-fitting side shields on your glasses will further enhance fish-seeing ability. They prevent sunlight from creeping in around the edges of your lenses. By shading your eyes, your pupils stay open and you see more.

You should also check lenses for optical quality. Look at straight-line patterns like floor tiles or window blinds for wiggling or bending. Also make sure the frames fit well and will stay on when you jump in and out of boats or stumble your way through a coral bed. Curved ear pieces and Croakie-type retainer straps also help.

Because you must protect your eyes from sun damage, make sure your glasses block both Type A and B ultraviolet wavelengths. These dangerous high-energy rays burn corneas and retinas, and they cause cataracts that permanently damage eyes. Most good-quality fishing glasses have a 99% UV A and B rating, which will sufficiently protect you on the flats. But make sure you don't end up with glasses designed for less-demanding general outdoor use that provide only 95% UV protection. Read labels closely.

Scratch-resistance may seem a mundane concern, but the crystalized salt, dust, and coral grit of the flats can destroy glasses. Most lenses sold today are plastic with coatings that resist scratching. If you are careful and wet-clean your glasses with fresh water, plastic lenses will hold up well. But if you often wipe your glasses with the inside of your shirt sleeve, as I do, you should consider glass lenses. They are much heavier but the glass is virtually scratch-proof. While some anglers hate heavy glasses and prefer to take the time necessary to clean plastic lenses carefully, I am hard on eyewear and prefer to put up with the weight of glass, rather that ruin a pair of plastics every year.

If you wear corrective lenses, you can order polarized fishing glasses ground to your prescription. Eyeglass manufacturers such as Action Optics or Specialized Eyewear supply many tackle shops. Orvis also carries a wide assortment of glasses. One model, called the Ultimate Fisherman's Glasses, has highly effective leather side shields. I have had excellent experience with this model, which comes in both single and bifocal prescription versions. You can also have an optometrist make glasses for you. If you do, make sure the frames have adequate side protection.

Polarized clip-on lenses that attach over your prescription glasses are adequate for emergencies. They do not, however, work well for long-term use. The two layers of lenses collect crystalized salt spray between them and magnify reflections, making it hard to see.

Sunblock

Most bonefish anglers use sunblock to shield their skin against sunburn and protect against skin cancer. But most anglers do not know which sunblock SPF rating to pick to shield themselves fully. The SPF (Skin Protection Factor) system for rating sunblock is quite simple. Everyone has a natural level of skin protection provided by the amount of melanin in their skin. Lightest-skinned people have the least melanin while darker-skinned people have the most. In the bright sun typical of Miami, a very light-skinned person has only enough melanin to shield them naturally for about twelve minutes. A fair-skinned person would have about eighteen minutes of natural protection. Average complexions would be safe for about thirty-five minutes, and so on.

The SPF rating tells you how much a sunblock product increases this normal safe period. With a sunblock rated at fifteen SPF, a person with an average complexion can increase their safe period from thirty-five minutes to almost nine hours (fifteen times thirty-five minutes). A very light-skinned

Sunblock should be applied everywhere your skin is exposed, especially under your chin and on your ears and nose. Be sure you pick a high enough SPF number to protect you, based on your skin type and melanin level.

angler with a twelve-minute safe period would require a much higher SPF rating of forty-five to stay safe for the same period.

I have fair skin with a safe period of about eighteen minutes. Most of the time I use SPF-30 sunblock, which protects me for nine hours. This is plenty of protection for a full day of fishing. My wife, who is very light-skinned, needs an SPF-45 product for a full day on the flats.

All sunblock protects best when it has penetrated the skin surface. Put it on early, before you go out for a full day's fishing. Also, be sure to put it everywhere that's exposed — under your chin, behind your earlobes, and on top of your ears. If you do much wading or have your hands in and out of the water much, use waterproof sunblock. If you have sensitive skin, avoid sunblock with para-aminobenzoic compounds (PABA) — they irritate and cause skin rash.

I cannot over-emphasize how important it is to be fully protected with sunblock. Many years ago I forgot to put sunblock on the back of my right hand one morning. By about ten o'clock, I noticed a burning sensation on my hand and put sunblock over it. By noon the hand looked like steak tartar and I had to stop fishing. I ended up losing the better part of two days fishing to that mistake.

TABLE 11.1

SUNBURN-FREE SAFE PERIOD (HOURS) YIELDED BY VARIOUS SPF RATINGS

SPF RATING	LIGHT-SKINNED (12 MIN. SP)	FAIR-SKINNED (18 MIN. SP)	AVER. SKINNED (35 MIN. SP)
15	3.0 hours	4.5 hours	8.7 hours
20	4.0	6.0	11.7
25	5.0	7.5	14.6
30	6.0	9.0	17.5
35	7.0	10.5	20.4
40	8.0	12.0	23.3
45	9.0	13.5	26.2

CLOTHING

Headgear

A wide-brimmed hat gives you a protective canopy that shields light from above your eyes. Dark underbrims are best. Together with polarized glasses and side shields, they shelter your eyes. This allows your pupils to collect as much light as possible from underwater images, boosting your ability to see detail and spot fish. A rear hat brim will protect the tops of your ears and the back of your neck from burning.

Get a hat with a chin strap if you do much fishing in boats. It keeps the hat on your head and prevents the wind from blowing it into the water. I find retainer cords that clip your hat to your collar useless. While they keep you from losing a hat overboard, they do nothing to keep it on your head when you are fishing in the wind.

Footgear

The perfect footgear for bonefishing would protect your feet, provide comfort while wading, and grip a slippery boat deck. Unfortunately, no shoe available does all of this.

For boat fishing, the classic Sperry Topsider-type boat sole is sure and comfortable. Laced canvas models give you the best arch support and stay on your feet better than the moccasin models. You can also wade in the canvas models, but they quickly fill with sand and mud.

For wading, the neoprene hard-soled flats shoes made by Orvis, L.L. Bean, Cabela's, and others are tall enough, tight enough, and impenetrable enough

For boat fishing, the sole of a boat shoe such as the Sperry-Topsider (left) is sure, safe, and comfortable. For wading, specialized flats shoes protect feet from coral and other hazards and keep out irritating mud and grit.

to keep out sand and coral grit. Their heavy-walled sides and thick soles protect feet from most wading hazards. But the tread designs on their bottoms do not grip a boat deck. In fact, most of them are downright treacherous in a wet boat. So if you alternate your bonefishing between boating and wading as I do, you must either switch back and forth between boat shoes and wading shoes, or put up with a shoe that is not totally up to the job. If I'm in and out of the boat a lot, I just keep on my canvas boat shoes — and tolerate the grit.

Shirts and Pants

Bonefishermen need clothing that protects them, keeps them comfortable, and doesn't alert or spook fish.

Long-sleeved shirts and long pants let you cover or uncover yourself as sun and temperature conditions change. Cotton stays reasonably cool and rinses out well. Newer materials, such as Supplex used in specialized tropical clothing, dry faster than cotton. Supplex breathes well and helps keep you cool. Light colors also help you stay cool, and pale shades of blue, khaki, and green are less noticeable to fish than some of the hot pink, fuchsia, and chartreuse hues in catalogs.

One simple item that can increase your comfort is socks. Whether you stand on a boat deck all day or wade the flats, you are on your feet for long hours. For boat fishing, a pair of medium-weight cotton socks will cushion your feet against the constant rocking-and-rolling adjustments you must make to keep your balance. Socks also reduce the chafing common in some of the special wading shoes.

Gear for Rain, Wind, and Cold

Many anglers leave for bonefishing trips when their homes are covered in snow. Spellbound by the prospect of standing on a boat deck in seventy-five-to eighty-five-degree sunshine, they forget that it is also winter on the flats in Florida, the Bahamas, Belize, and the Yucatan peninsula. Only Christmas Island in the equatorial latitudes escapes some form of winter. While you may find the weather balmy for weeks at a time in January, February, or March, a sudden cold front can rapidly drop temperatures twenty degrees and dump cold rains. Most fishermen expect such changes in the mountains and on the rivers of the north, but they are surprised when it happens in the tropics.

To stay dry in tropical rainstorms, you need heavy-duty but breathable protection. PVC rainwear is weatherproof but does not breathe. You get as wet from sweat as you would from rain. Chemically treated windbreakers allow airflow, but they provide little rain protection from a tropical downpour. Gortex garments, if double-layered, are both waterproof and breathable. They provide the added benefit of warming for early morning breezes and chilly days.

If you fish subtropical areas like Florida and the Bahamas in the coldest months of December through March, you should also carry along a light polar fleece-type jacket or pullover. You may feel silly packing winter gear into a bag headed south, but you will be grateful when wind, clouds, or a cold front chill you to the point of chattering.

OTHER TACKLE AND GEAR

The Boat Bag

One of the most useful items for poled-boat anglers is a good boat bag. It need not be fancy, and it should not cost you too much—none of them last very long under the constant attack of salt water, sun, gasoline, and general knocking around.

A good boat bag has plenty of room and organizes everything from flies, lines, and tippet material to a thermos and lunch.

It should have a plastic zipper and fittings, a shoulder strap, and carry handles. Plastic-lined bags are also an advantage on wet decks. But you can get the same protection by putting raingear in the bottom of a cloth bag. Most important, make sure your bag has enough pockets and dividers to keep the following types of items handy, organized, and protected:

- four or five boxes of flies
- four to six tippet spools
- spare leaders
- nippers
- hook sharpener
- thermometer
- crimping pliers
- spare floating fly line
- spare sink-tip fly line
- spare intermediate fly line
- sunblock
- insect repellent
- monocular or binocular

- tape measure
- Swiss Army knife
- thermos or water bottle
- camera double-wrapped in plastic
- spare hat
- spare glasses
- rain jacket
- lunch or snack

The Wader's Pack

When you go to destinations such as Christmas Island or Los Roques, where punt boats, vans, or water taxis drop you off to wade for the day, you must carry enough gear and tackle to be self-sufficient while wading. Some anglers find belt packs, chest packs, or small day-hiker type knapsacks useful. Like the boat bag, the arrangement of pockets and dividers should help you organize things so you can find them.

Whichever style of pack you consider, try wearing it while you walk and cast. Be sure it leaves your arms and shoulders free to move and that it doesn't snag the reservoir of fly line you carry in your hands. I find that most of these gear packs just get in my way too much. They are also uncomfortable in the tropical heat. I usually just wear a fishing shirt with big enough pockets to carry tippets, flies, sunblock, and other items I consider essential.

12

Tying Bonefish Flies

Compared to delicate trout flies, elegant salmon patterns, and elaborate deer-hair bass bugs, bonefish flies look deceptively simple. They appear easy to tie and uncomplicated in design. But the need to cast these flies far, punch them through wind, and get them down to the fish quickly and quietly creates some of the most complex challenges fly tiers encounter.

In addition, flats anglers are just beginning to investigate the enormous variety of prey bonefish eat — one of the most diverse assortments of animal life on earth. As fly tiers investigate this richness and experiment with patterns that suggest or imitate them, a whole new world of bonefish patterns is emerging. Tying bonefish flies has suddenly become one of the most exciting areas in fly design.

But all of this is very new. We must remember that bonefishing with flies began only a few decades ago. Tiers of trout, salmon, and bass patterns have fiddled with their designs for centuries. They have fine-tuned every nuance of both their form and function. In contrast, during the early period of bonefish flies, tiers concentrated on just getting flies that worked well — patterns that sank and didn't snag. Only today, after a handful of pioneers have worked out the functional problems of bonefish flies, are designers free to focus on the niceties of imitation.

A BRIEF HISTORY OF BONEFISH FLY DESIGN

Not until Capt. Bill Smith plucked the hackle off the back end of an Islamorada chicken, tied it onto a hook, and took his now-famous 1939 bonefish had anyone ever designed a fly pattern specifically for *Albula vulpes*. But bonefish fly tying, like the sport of bonefishing with flies itself, didn't really get started until even later when Joe Brooks and a few others began popularizing the sport after World War II. Two of the most important early contributions to bonefish fly design occurred during this early period, and they both came from two of Brooks' closest friends and fishing partners. The first addressed the very important need of getting the fly down to the level of the fish.

George Phillips and the Variable-Sink-Rate Pink Shrimp

George Phillips headed the Pennsylvania-based Phillips Fly and Tackle Company that supplied Joe Brooks and many others with bonefish flies. He created a pattern for Brooks that he called the Pink Shrimp. This novel pattern allowed anglers to vary sink rate. By using different amounts of deer hair in the carapace and tying it on different hook sizes (#2, #4, and #6), Phillips varied the sink rate for different levels of water. This ingenious little fly became Brooks' favorite for bonefish and it still appears in catalogs today — a testimony to its effectiveness.

The Pink Shrimp had one major problem, however, that plagued anglers when they fished it on the bottom. In snagged badly in coral and grass. Phillips had tried to make it weed- and coral-proof by palmering the body with stiff hackle. But another technique would prove far more effective.

Pete Perinchief and the Reverse-Wing Horror

Pete Perinchief, director of the Bermuda Fishing Information Bureau for twenty-one years, conceived what was probably the most innovative of all early bonefish patterns, the Horror. He designed it after a frustrating fishing trip in the Florida Keys with Joe and Mary Brooks.

The three anglers were fishing for deep-cruising bones. Perinchief says Brooks kept telling him to let the fly sink to the bottom and wait for the fish to come onto it. But every time he did, his fly snagged in the turtle grass. Finding no flies that worked, he went home and started experimenting with weed-proof designs.

Finally, he woke up one night with an idea based on a weedless freshwater fly he had seen. He got up and tied a fly with the wing on the reverse side and

Older bonefish flies used in the Florida Keys include: a version of the Frankee Belle tied by Captain Cecil Keith (1), a gray squirrel tail fly tied by Captain Bill Smith (2), two early bonefish flies tied by angler Ben Estes over forty years ago (3, 5), and a Captain Bill Smith pattern used by Bonnie Smith to catch permit (4).

dropped it in his bathtub to test the way it landed. It flipped over on its back as it fell and settled to the bottom hook point up. The Horror, a spartan red-headed fly with a brown bucktail wing and yellow chenille body, changed bonefishing flies forever.

The wing of the Horror was tied on the underside of the shank, so its ends covered the hook point. The bucktail worked like a rudder, turning the fly over on its descent. It also served as a weed guard to prevent the point from snagging.

This reverse-wing design became so successful, it was the standard technique for winging almost all bonefish flies for thirty years. Even today, the Horror remains an effective fly. Reel-maker Steve Abel says it is still one of his best producers for Christmas island. The Horror also stimulated several generations of similar upside-down-wing shrimp and crab patterns. Innovative tiers like Chico Fernandez have designed whole families of reverse-wings that suggest the colors and patterns of mantis, snapping, grass, and other shrimp species. Lefty Kreh ties a heavily dressed chartreuse version, the Shallow-H_2O fly that is one of his favorite flies.

Along with sink-rate control and snag-proofing, early bonefish fly tiers also sought faster ways to sink flies and better ways to achieve fly action. The most influential event in this search came from a California angler who wanted to mimic a small baitfish he had seen on the flats in the Bahamas. He ended up creating the most popular bonefish pattern of all time.

Bob Nauheim and the Fast-Sinking Charlie

On a trip to Andros in the late 1970's, Bob Nauheim had watched large bonefish chase small glass minnows across the flats. Drawing from his steelhead fly-tying experience, he tied a pair of metal bead-chain eyes on a silver-bodied fly, overwrapped it with transparent mono, added two splayed

Five classic bonefish patterns: the Pink Shrimp (1), the Horror (2), the Nasty Charlie (3), the Mini-Puff (4), and the Bonefish Special (5).

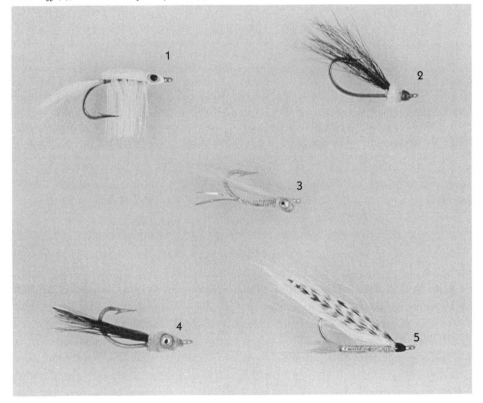

These five flies show the evolution of the Crazy Charlie pattern. Bob Nauheim tied the original Nasty Charlie (3) in Andros in the late 1970s. It had a body of 15-pound-test Mason mono over silver tinsel, a tail of a few tinsel strands, and a wing comprised of two off-white hackle tips tied in so they curved outward and away from each other. A later version tied by Bob's wife Helena (1) used wings twice as long as the original, and other versions followed. One that used hair instead of hackle (4) was tied by Jan Isley for the Florida Keys. Nauheim himself tied another version (2) that substituted pearlescent Flashabou for silver tinsel for use at Andros. But best known of all these derivative patterns was the Crazy Charlie (5) popularized by Orvis' Leigh Perkins after his company adopted the Nauheim prototype as one of its most successful saltwater fly patterns.

white saddle hackles, and changed bonefish fly tying forever. The Nasty Charlie, as the fly was first named, became the prototype for an endless series of fast-sinking metal-eyed patterns.

The Nasty Charlie was later modified into the Crazy Charlie and popularized by the Orvis Company. It became such a sensation in bonefishing that it flooded the flats with bead-chain eye patterns for a decade. The weighted eyes sank Charlie patterns to the bottom fast. The weight of the eyes also flipped the fly over so it landed with the hook facing up, further weed-proofing the pattern. Equally important, the weight of the eyes made Charlies move with a realistic up-and-down action when stripped. Combined with a reverse-tied wing, all these features resulted in a fly that dived to the fish's level quickly and moved naturally without snagging.

The Charlie style succeeded so well, it inspired an endless series of derivative styles that combined metal eyes with many different kinds of body, wing, and tail materials. Experimental anglers, guides, and tiers such as Lefty Kreh, Jan Isley, Jim McVay, Ben Estes, and many others have made the Charlie-type patterns the most diverse family of flies in bonefishing.

Nat Ragland's Permit Puff and the Mini-Puff Derivatives

As popular as the Crazy Charlies became, their metal eyes sometimes spooked fish by splashing too loudly. Another archetypal pattern, the Mini-Puff, illustrates how creative tiers learned to avoid this spooking problem by cushioning the noise and impact.

The Puff, a popular permit pattern conceived by Nat Ragland for the Florida Keys, uses a heavily dressed chenille head and body to quiet the impact of its large beady eyes. The design worked so effectively that it spawned a series of Mini-Puffs for bonefishing. These smaller versions with bare shanks, reverse wings, and bead-chain eyes were wrapped in puffy little heads of pink, yellow, or orange chenille. A duller as well as quieter fly than the Charlies, the Mini-Puff became a favorite alternative for calm water and bright days, when the Charlie's splashy landings and flashy bodies sometimes spooked fish. Mini-Puffs are still a popular and effective pattern in the Bahamas.

BONEFISH FLY TYING TODAY — SOME NEW TRENDS AND TECHNIQUES

Today's bonefish fly designers are free to concentrate on form and prey imitation because early designers solved most of the critical problems governing sink rate, action, and snag-proofing. But some designers continue to experiment in these functional areas as well, seeking even better control of sinking and snagging characteristics. Most designers, however, now concentrate on better ways to suggest the look and action of prey.

Some of today's trends in bonefish fly tying have resulted from anglers learning more about bonefish eating habits and the prey bonefish eat in different locations. But many others have emerged as tiers have applied new materials or techniques learned in other areas of fly fishing to bonefishing.

Many of today's newer bonefish patterns experiment with both shape and action to better represent prey and entice fish. Pictured (in boxes) are Jim's Golden Eye Shrimp, the Rubber Band Worm, the Clouser Deep Minnow, the Gotcha, and the Beady Crab (in vise and boxes).

Tim Borski, for example, is using spun deer-hair heads and bodies to "push" water and vibrate in Muddler fashion to attract fish. Jeffrey Cardenas' Bunny Bone designs incorporate the soft, subtle live action of rabbit fur so successful in Zonker styles. Carl Richards is experimenting with the intriguing possibilities of extruded latex bodies to better depict prey species, yet retain lively movement.

Still other trends reflect experimentation with prey size. Large shrimp patterns like Jim Orthwein's big Golden Eye Shrimp and small flies like Craig Mathews' Turneffe Crab patterns push the size barriers at both ends. A few other innovations come from just seeing things in a fresh way. Patterns like Jack Gartside's Piggy Back Shrimp, J.G. Chiton, and Sand Flea capture the look of prey forms in a whole new way. They symbolize the excitement and creative thinking occurring in bonefish fly tying today.

Larger Flies, Smaller Flies

Larger bonefish often eat large and aggressive prey such as gobies, mantis shrimp, snapping shrimp, and large crab species. Many bonefish fly designers today are tying flies on #2, #1, and even larger hooks. Ben Estes' Epoxy Shrimp, Tim Borski's Slider, Bonefish Short, and Chernobyl Crab, Bob Clouser's Deep Minnow, Jim McVay's Gotcha, and Jim Orthwein's Golden Eye all successfully take fish in large sizes. Ahead of his time in bonefishing as well as baseball, Ted Williams has fished the Islamorada area for years with a big deer-hair pattern tied on a 1/0 hook!

Other anglers have explored areas where bonefish survive by consuming smaller prey in very large quantities. They tie patterns on tiny hooks down to #14 to mimic these diminutive species. Craig Mathews' Turneffe Crab and his Bonefish Soft Hackle typify this trend. Ben Estes ties his Ben's Epoxy fly down to #8 for the bonefish of Ascension Bay. Anglers Jim O'Neill and Bill Tapply have also reported success with small patterns on Belize's skinny atoll flats.

Tying Flies that Mimic Specific Prey

Bonefish anglers and fly designers have just begun to explore the enormous diversity of prey that bonefish eat. As they fish in more and more destinations, they are discovering scores of shrimp, crab, worm, urchin, eel, and forage fish species that are consumed by bonefish. This rich variety of prey forms is stimulating a parade of new patterns that suggest novel prey shape, color, and action characteristics.

Carl Richards, Craig Mathews, and Jack Gartside are three of the most innovative tiers today mining this rich new vein of bonefish prey. All three have explored new materials and novel tying techniques, as well as traditional approaches to produce effective new patterns that mimic shrimp, crabs, urchins, and baitfish. Carl uses latex compounds to form realistic (in action and appearance) bodies, legs, tails, and antennae for mantis shrimp, mud and swimming crabs, common and grass shrimp, and numerous other prey commonly eaten by inshore gamefish from snook and redfish to tarpon and bonefish. Craig combines traditional and new materials (round rubber legs, Zelon, etc.) to design swimming crabs, urchins, and other prey imitators for the large cruising bonefish in Belize. Jack uses many ordinary materials as well as a few synthetics and combines them in novel ways. In addition to shrimp, his suggestive patterns portray many other prey types, such as sea urchins, eels, baitfish, worms, and even smaller mollusks such as the chiton.

Tying for Total Control of Sink Rate

Bonefish anglers commonly vary the sink rate of flies into at least three or four categories for changing depths of water. They use eyes or lead strips of different densities to sink the flies at varying rates. But more recently, tiers have begun controlling sink rate more subtly. They vary the ratio of heavy elements such as hooks, metal eyes, and lead strips to bulky elements such as wool and deer-hair bodies to achieve sink rates just below the neutral density point. This lets anglers "float" flies down to different levels and hang them in the water column. Ben Estes' Styrofoam-eyed epoxy models, Jeffrey Cardenas' plastic-eyed Bunny Bones, and several of Jack Gartside's patterns like the Glimmer, Black Sea Urchin, and Cockbone function this way. They extend the range of places in the water column that anglers can connect with fish.

Tying Flies to Blend with Different Habitats

Many garish-colored "attractor" patterns take bonefish in many situations. But flies that look more natural are growing increasingly popular. These new patterns look camouflaged. They blend into the surrounding habitat like many of the natural prey they emulate. Tiers design them in drab earth tones with materials that have mottled or barred patterns to break up light and blend well. The Cardenas Bunny Bone Natural, Mathews Bonefish Soft Hackle, and Clouser Deep Minnow are all examples. Many of Carl Richards' new latex patterns also capture the camouflaged look of the species they depict, as do patterns such as Jim Orthwein's Golden Eye Shrimp and Jack Gartside's Saltwater Sparrow, Elver, and Sand Flea. Other new styles of flies employ transparency and reflectivity for disguise. The mirror-like McVay Gotcha, the Ben's Epoxy, and the Borski Bonefish Short all illustrate this alternative camouflage technique.

Tying Flies for Lifelike Movement

Many bonefish flies jump and dive to represent the movements of crabs, shrimp, and other prey. Lead weight or heavy eyes placed at the front or tail give flies this jig-like action. Off-center elements like the asymmetric tail on the Golden Eye Shrimp deflect water flow and make a fly wiggle. Materials like rabbit and marabou ripple and pulsate in water in patterns such as the Soft Hackle Streamer, Bunny Bone, and Wiggle Shrimp. The tail in the Orthwein Rubber Band Worm swims and vibrates when stripped.

Tying On Different Hooks

For years, picking a hook for bonefish flies meant choosing which size Mustad 34007 or 3407 to use. These two Mustad models, one stainless steel, the other tinned carbon steel, still serve as the standard. But tiers now also use Tiemco's 800S, the Eagle Claw D67, and the Partridge Sea Prince series as well.

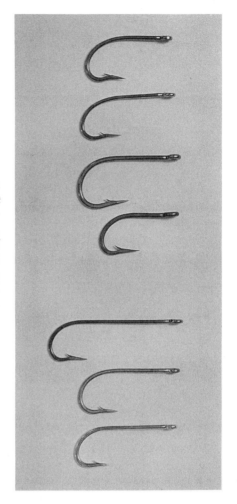

Hooks with standard-length shanks are used in many traditional bonefish patterns, but longer-shanked hooks provide better profiles for patterns suggesting mantis shrimp, polychaetes, and other elongated prey. Top to bottom, standard shanks: Partridge Sea Prince, Mustad 34007, TMC 800S, and Eagle Claw 254SS. Long shanks: Mustad 34011, TMC 811S, and Eagle Claw D67. All hooks are size #4.

Today's tiers also experiment with longer shank lengths to reflect the profiles of some prey; they tie in many more sizes from #14 to #1.

Tying with New Materials

Tiers today are also experimenting with both new synthetic materials and many of the livelier natural materials popular in freshwater flies. Craft Fur, dolls hair, FisHair, and Polar Hair are used to give a translucent quality to wings. Pearlescent diamond braid, Mylar tubing, Krystal Flash, and many other reflective materials liven bodies, tails, and wings. Eyes of unweighted plastic, medium-weighted bead chain, and heavy-weighted lead barbells in a wide variety of sizes allow tiers to achieve any sink rate desired. Soft materials such as marabou, after-shaft feathers, and rabbit fur — as in Cardenas' Bunny Bones — give lifelike action to patterns. Wool, in patterns such as the Borski Wool Crab, gives bulk yet holds water for slow sink rates. Latex bodies, rubber legs, and synthetic tails in Carl Richards' and Craig Mathews' lifelike patterns portray new shapes and convey lively movement.

Tying Flies to Make Less Noise

Many different materials are being used to reduce splashdown impact. Soft, water-absorbing or water-holding materials such as rabbit, marabou, chenille, and wool dampen fly splashdown noise. Spun deer hair in big patterns like the Chernobyl Crab tends to reduce noise if the hair is loosely packed, in contrast to tightly packed deer-hair crab patterns trimmed flat that belly-flop and spook fish. Palmered hackle and collars on patterns such as the Saltwater Sparrow, Golden Eye Shrimp, and Orange Annelid also reduce noise and splash.

BONEFISH FLY PATTERNS

Almost all of the fly samples that appear in the color plates of this book and in the material lists below were supplied by the pattern's originator. In the half dozen cases where flies were either supplied by a third party such as Umpqua or bought commercially, I have attempted to verify the pattern materials.

Many tiers and anglers make minor variations to flies — especially when tying saltwater patterns. You are free to do the same — but you should at least know the creator's original pattern at the start. Then, if you choose to change it, vary it with purpose. I have seen at least nine different versions of the Andros killer fly, the McVay Gotcha, in the past year. All were billed as the authentic pattern — and not one of them matched Jim McVay's original. The listing that follows contains the patterns as the originators designed them. To facilitate tying, I have tried to follow the convention of listing material in the order it is applied to the hook or to the pattern.

☐ *A. K. Bonefish Fly (A. K. Best pattern):*
   HOOK: Mustad 3407, #4
   THREAD: Tan Monocord 3/0
   TAIL: Tan bleached grizzly
   EYES: Glass eyes, 3 mm
   BODY: Dyed plastic dip over template plastic wrapped in cream single-strand floss

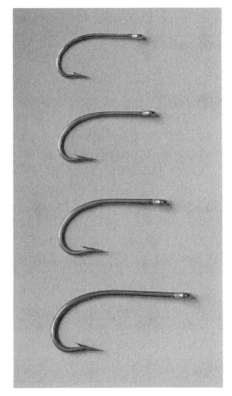

Partridge's Sea Prince saltwater hooks are one of the newer designs gaining popularity with bonefish fly tiers. Top to bottom: #8, #6, #4, #2.

COMMENTS: Sandwich hook and eyes between two 1/4" x 5/16" kite-shaped pieces of .002" template plastic. Cut plastic with serrated edges, wrap with floss, and coat with plastic dip dyed with Humbolt model paint; color: Unbleached Linen.

□ *Apricot Charlie (Bill Hunter pattern):*
HOOK: Mustad 34007, or AC #3406B, #4, #6, #8
THREAD: Orange 6/0
EYES: Gold bead chain
TAIL: Eight to ten strands of pearlescent orange Flashabou
BODY: Pearlescent orange Flashabou with V-rib over
UNDERWING: Pinkish-orange calftail
OVERWING: Cree hackle tips, one each side
COMMENTS: Bill Hunter says the pearlescent orange Flashabou is getting hard to find, so he substitutes a blend of pearlescent orange and pearlescent pink Krystal Flash. Also, if you don't have pinkish-orange calftail, blend pink calf with orange calf.
       Bill's sample of this pattern arrived after the book's color photogra-

phy sessions. The fly that appears in the color plates was tied by the author using pearlescent orange Mylar tubing in the tail — a personal modification.

☐ *Barber Pole Shrimp (Craig Mathews pattern):*
HOOK: TMC 800S or Mustad 34007, #8
THREAD: White 6/0 or Monocord 3/0
LEGS: White Spandex or Sili legs
WEED/CORAL GUARD: White deer hair
BODY: Red chenille ribbing and white chenille underbody
WEIGHT: .020 lead (optional)

☐ *Beady Crab, tan (Author's pattern):*
HOOK: Mustad 34007 or Partridge Sea Prince CS-52, #2, #4, #6
THREAD: Tan Monocord 3/0
UNDERBODY: Two strands of small bead chain (four beads each), fig-ure-eighted perpendicular to hook shank
LEGS: Four pairs tan Sili rubber legs
CLAWS: Cree or tan grizzly saddle tips tied in at eyes
BODY/CARAPACE: Mottled tan chenille wound through legs and around underbody
EYES: Exposed ends of bead chain
COMMENTS: Tied inverse; if mottled chenille is not available, use black or brown Pantone pen to make mottling pattern on body. Also tied in green, gray, or other colors, selecting chenille and leg color to blend with bottom colors or match local prey.

☐ *Beady Crab, white Spider (Author's pattern):*
HOOK: Mustad 34007 or Partridge Sea Prince CS-52, #2, #4, #6
THREAD: White Monocord 3/0
UNDERBODY: Two strands of small bead chain (four beads each), fig-ure-eighted perpendicular to hook shank
LEGS: Five pairs white rubber Sili legs
BODY/CARAPACE: White wool (or chenille) wound through legs and around underbody
EYES: Exposed ends of bead chain
COMMENTS: Tied inverse. Also tied in other colors to match bottom and lo-cal prey.

☐ *Ben's Epoxy (Ben Estes pattern):*
HOOK: Mustad 3407, #1 to #8
THREAD: White, tan, or pink 6/0

TAIL: Two cree, grizzly, furnace, or badger saddle hackles, flared outward, over dyed Arctic fox over two to four sprigs of Krystal Flash and two to four strands of Flashabou

EYES: Vary from small Styrofoam beads (joined by mono) to 1/50- and 1/32-ounce lead eyes to alter sink rate

BODY: 5-Minute Devcon epoxy over Mylar Christmas tree tinsel (may also use pearlescent-colored Mylar tinsel or Flashabou) wrapped length of body and figure-eighted around eyes

HACKLE: Cree, grizzly, furnace, or badger palmered forward before epoxy dries and trimmed top and sides

WEED GUARD: 12- or 15-pound Mason hard mono inserted in front of eyes before epoxy dries

COMMENTS: Can substitute Craft Fur, calftail, or marabou for Artic fox. Ben varies color of tail and body: tan, pink, and lime.

☐ *Big-Clawed Snapping Shrimp (Carl Richards pattern):*
HOOK: Mustad 34011, #1, #2, #4, #6, #8
THREAD: White Monocord 3/0
FRONT LEGS: Tan Spectra Hair
ANTENNAE: White boar's bristles or moose mane hairs
CLAWS: Rub-R-mold liquid latex
EYES: Burnt mono
BODY: Spectra Hair or polar bear for large sizes; FisHair or Fish Fuzz for small sizes; over belly of white mohair yarn
REAR LEGS: Tan or white webby hen hackle, palmered
TAIL: Spectra Hair, polar bear, FisHair, or Fish Fuzz
COLORING: Sharpie or Pantone waterproof pens
COMMENTS: Using a photo or drawing of the prey species as a template, Carl lays down a layer of hobbyist liquid latex from a syringe to form the shape of claws (and the belly plate on crabs) and lets dry seventy-two hours to form a pliable and realistic replica that is tied into the body.

☐ *Black Sea Urchin (Jack Gartside pattern):*
HOOK: Mustad 34007, #2
THREAD: Black 6/0
TAIL: Black deer body hair (spiky)
BODY: Stiff black saddle or neck hackle, palmered full

☐ *Black-Tipped Mud Crab (Carl Richards pattern):*
HOOK: Mustad 34007, or AC 3406B, #2, #4, #6, #8
THREAD: White Monocord 3/0

BODY/CARAPACE: White egg-fly yarn spun Muddler fashion and clipped to desired carapace shape

LEGS/UNDERSIDE: Cement Rub-R-Mold leg and claw assembly under the body (liquid latex flexible mold compound from a craft shop; see comments under Big-Clawed Snapping Shrimp)

EYES: Burnt mono 40- to 80-pound

FEELERS: Cream boar's bristle

COLOR: Sharpie waterproof or Pantone pens

□ *Blue Crab, Juvenile (Carl Richards pattern):*
HOOK: Mustad 34007, or AC 3406B, #2, #4, #6, #8

THREAD: White Monocord 3/0

BODY/CARAPACE: White egg-fly yarn spun Muddler fashion and clipped to desired carapace shape

LEGS/UNDERSIDE: Cement Rub-R-Mold leg and claw assembly under the body (liquid latex flexible mold compound from a craft shop; see comments under Big-Clawed Snapping Shrimp)

EYES: Burnt mono 40- to 80-pound

FEELERS: Cream boar's bristle

COLOR: Sharpie waterproof or Pantone pens

□ *Bonefish G.P. (Author's pattern):*
HOOK: Mustad 34007, #4, #6, #8

THREAD: Hot orange 6/0 or Monocord 3/0

BODY: Orange rug wool or dyed seal fur dubbing

HACKLE: Orange or orange grizzly saddle hackle

ANTENNAE: Golden pheasant tippet feather and orange Krystal Flash

CARAPACE: Golden pheasant breast feathers

□ *Bonefish Short (Tim Borski pattern):*
HOOK: Mustad 34007, #2

THREAD: Tan Monocord 3/0

TAIL: Tan calftail with Krystal Flash

WING: Palmered tan hackle with two grizzly hackle tips

EYES: Glass beads strung on burnt mono

HEAD/BODY: Five-minute epoxy over gold Mylar

□ *Bonefish Soft Hackle (Craig Mathews pattern):*
HOOK: Mustad 3407 or TMC 800S, #4, #6, #8; Mustad 3906, #10, #12, #14

THREAD: Tan 6/0 or 3/0 Monocord

BODY: Chenille in tan, apple green, white, or olive

HACKLE: Hungarian partridge, pheasant, blue or ruffed grouse, one or two turns

WEED GUARD: Deer hair tied short and clipped at eye (optional)

☐ *Bonefish Special (Chico Fernandez pattern):*
HOOK: Mustad 34007, #4
THREAD: Black Monocord 3/0
TAIL: Orange marabou
BODY: Flat gold tinsel overwrapped with gold or clear mono
WING: White bucktail flanked by two grizzly saddle hackles

☐ *Borski No Name Shrimp (Tim Borski pattern):*
HOOK: Mustad 34007, #2
THREAD: Beige Monocord 3/0
TAIL: Craft Fur barred with Pantone 462-M and topped with Krystal Flash
EYES: Lead, black pupil on yellow, vary size for sink rate; tied under shank so fly hangs upright
BODY: Wide tan or badger hackle, palmered, trimmed on top and sides
WEED GUARD: 15-pound Mason hard mono

☐ *Borski Wool Crab (Tim Borski pattern):*
HOOK: Mustad 34007, #1, #2, #4
THREAD: Beige Monocord 3/0
EYES: Burnt mono overwrapped with Krystal chenille
LEGS: Wide webby palmered hackle
BODY: White wool, packed, trimmed flat and weighted with lead eyes under and just behind hook eye
WEED GUARD: 15-pound hard Mason (optional)
COMMENTS: For tailing fish, tie on a #4 hook with no weight

☐ *Bunny Bone Grizzly (Jeffrey Cardenas pattern):*
HOOK: Partridge Sea Prince, #4
THREAD: Black Monocord 3/0
EYES: 1/50-ounce nickel-plated lead
FAN TAIL: Grizzly rabbit, two strands black Krystal Flash
BODY: Tightly wrapped rabbit
COMMENTS: Sinks fast for deep-cruising fish

☐ *Bunny Bone Natural (Jeffrey Cardenas pattern):*
HOOK: Partridge Sea Prince, #4
THREAD: Tan Monocord 3/0

EYES: Plastic shrimp eyes
FAN TAIL: Natural tan rabbit, two strands copper Krystal Flash
BODY: Tan Aunt Lydia's rug yarn
COMMENTS: Eyes maintain profile but add no weight

☐ *Charlie Bunny Bone (Jeffrey Cardenas pattern):*
HOOK: Partridge Sea Prince, #4
THREAD: White Monocord 3/0
EYES: Stainless bead chain
FAN TAIL: White rabbit; two strands pearl Krystal Flash
BODY: Silver tinsel

☐ *Chernobyl Crab (Tim Borski pattern):*
HOOK: Mustad 34007, #1 or 1/0
THREAD: Tan Monocord 3/0
TAIL: Calftail, cree hackle tips (splayed outward), Krystal Flash
BODY: Spun deer hair with wide tan or badger hackle palmered forward
       through it, clipped across top and bottom
EYES: Lead eyes, vary for sink rate

☐ *Clouser Deep Minnow (Bob Clouser pattern):*
HOOK: Mustad 34007, #2
THREAD: Tan or chartreuse Monocord 3/0
EYES: Lead, 1/50- and 1/36-ounce, vary for sink rate
WING/BODY: Khaki and white or chartreuse and white bucktail

☐ *Cockbone (Jack Gartside pattern):*
HOOK: Mustad 34007, #4, #6
THREAD: Orange 6/0
EYES: Silver bead chain
TAIL/WING: Grizzly saddles, splayed three to a side
BODY: Fluorescent orange Antron, dubbed
COLLAR: Coon or brown bucktail

☐ *Common Shore Shrimp (Carl Richards pattern):*
HOOK: Mustad 34011, #2, #4, #6, #8
THREAD: White Monocord 3/0
FRONT LEGS: FisHair or Fish Fuzz
EYES: Artificial flower stamens
ANTENNAE: White boar's bristles
ROSTRUM: Clipped cock hackle segment

The endless sand and grass flats of Andros Island, rimmed with coral shores, mangroves, and beaches, typify the world where the bonefish hunts and is hunted.

Anglers stalk bonefish on shallow, saltwater flats where this nomadic predator comes to search for shrimp, crabs, worms, juvenile fish, and clams.

Bonefish also feed in food-rich mangrove areas when high tides give them access to this nutritious shoreline habitat.

When bonefish feed in shallow water, they sometimes splash and make audible slapping sounds as their tails smack the surface — one of the easiest signs of fish presence anglers encounter.

Bonefish tails, such as these three glistening in the afternoon sunlight, allow anglers to spot this otherwise well-camouflaged fish at well over one hundred feet.

Surface water disturbances such as nervous water, finning, and bulging can indicate fish cruising or feeding in the shallows.

A brief flash of sunlight reflects off a bonefish's side and gill plate, revealing an otherwise well-disguised body.

On bright days over clear sand, the distinctive shadow of a bonefish can reveal a fish even more than its prominent caudal fin and barred back.

Swimming over turtle grass, the black dorsal bars of a lone bonefish blend almost invisibly with its mottled environment.

The bonefish reflects the world around it. Even up close it is virtually impossible to see for more than a few seconds — like this eight-pounder swimming through turtle grass.

A school of sixty or seventy bonefish graze next to the decaying hull of a partially submerged native fishing boat. As they zigzag across the sand flat, they are momentarily silhouetted against its pale ochre bottom.

Bonefish that graze over light sand for long periods of time can appear white against the stark bottom.

While easily visible from below, this fish cruising in three feet of water would disappear completely when viewed from above. *Photo by Jay Morgan.*

This close-up of the head of a bonefish found on a grass flat shows how some fish darken or change hue to blend into a habitat when they feed there for long periods. Also notice the transparent, canopy-like adipose covering on the eyes.

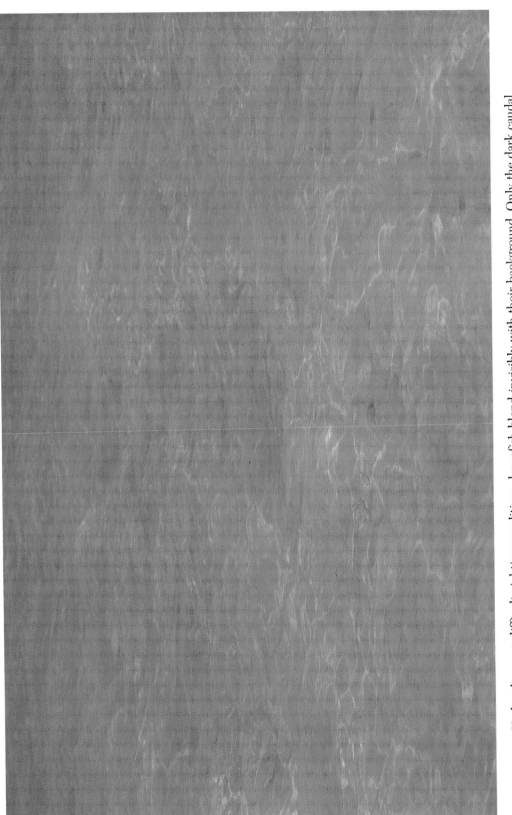

Under the most difficult sighting conditions, bonefish blend invisibly with their background. Only the dark caudal fin (right of center) and black eye (left of center) of this fish are visible to an angler.

Many species of bottom-feeding sharks frequent the saltwater flats, but they are easily distinguished from bonefish by their size, dark color, and undulating motion.

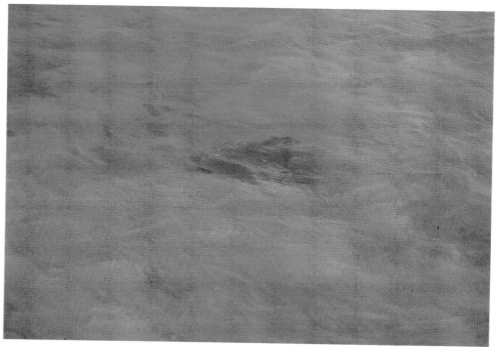

Rays frequently cause muds when they graze on the flats, but are easily identified by their dark flat shape. Bonefish often feed on the leftovers in their wake.

A pod of three feeding bonefish made this small chalky mud that measures about four feet across.

Half a dozen or more bonefish, feeding on the bottom, created a car-sized, mud cloud that tracks the entire school.

This large thirty-foot mud along a coral shoreline indicates an actively feeding school of fish in deep water. The whitish-gray color comes from disturbed bottom sediment and contrasts starkly to the natural clear, pale-green color of surrounding water.

Old bonefish feeding holes, like these three interspersed among bullet-sized prey burrows, lose their distinct shape and color, as tides slowly wash sediment back into them.

Recent bonefish feeding holes, like this one in the center, have distinctive, hard-edged shapes and fresh dark sediment around them.

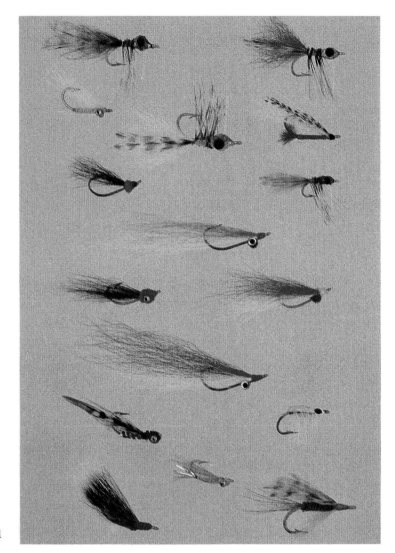

PLATE 1

Top line: Ben's Epoxy, Styrofoam eye (Ben Estes pattern)   Ben's Epoxy, bead-chain eye (Ben Estes pattern)

Second line: Crazy Charlie (Bob Nauheim derivative)   Ben's Epoxy, 1/36-ounce lead eye (Ben Estes pattern — slightly below)   Bonefish Special (Chico Fernandez pattern)

Third line: Horror (Pete Perinchief pattern)   Ben's Epoxy, plastic eye (Ben Estes pattern)

Fourth line: Clouser Deep Minnow, tan/white (Bob Clouser pattern)

Fifth line: Mini-Puff (Nat Ragland derivative)   Shallow-H$_2$O Fly (Lefty Kreh pattern)

Sixth line: Clouser Deep Minnow, chartreuse (Bob Clouser pattern)

Seventh line: Dr. Taylor Special (Phil Taylor pattern)   Pink Shrimp (George Phillips pattern)

Bottom line: Bill Smith Bonefish Fly (Bill Smith pattern)   Nasty Charlie (Bob Nauheim pattern — slightly above the other two patterns in this line)   Frankee-Belle   (Frankee Albright, Belle Mathers pattern)

Each of these flies was tied by its originator except for the Clouser Deep Minnow (tied by Lefty Kreh), the Mini-Puff and Bonefish Special (tied by the author), the Pink Shrimp (purchased from Orvis), and the Frankee-Belle (tied by Capt. Cecil Keith, Jr.).

PLATE 2

Top fly: Rusty Bunny Bone (Jeffrey Cardenas pattern)

Second line: Bunny Bone Natural (Jeffrey Cardenas pattern)   Charlie Bunny Bone   (Jeffrey Cardenas pattern)

Third line: Bunny Bone Grizzly (Jeffrey Cardenas pattern)

Fourth line: Rubber Band Worm (Jim Orthwein pattern)   Jim's Golden Eye Shrimp (Jim Orthwein pattern)

Fifth line: Turneffe Crab (Craig Mathews pattern)   Diamond Bitters (Craig Mathews pattern)   Winston's Urchin (Craig Mathews pattern)

Sixth line: Sea Lice (Craig Mathews pattern)   Pops' Bonefish Bitters (Craig Mathews pattern)   Flash Urchin (Craig Mathews pattern)

Seventh line: Punta Squid (Craig Mathews pattern)   Barber Pole Shrimp (Craig Mathews pattern)   Bonefish Soft Hackle (Craig Mathews pattern)

Each of these flies was tied by its originator.

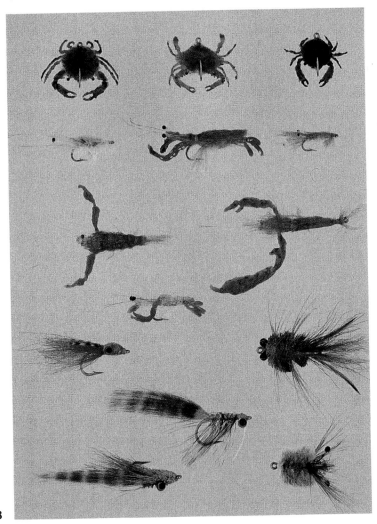

PLATE 3

Top line: Green Reef Crab (Carl Richards pattern)   Blue Crab, Juvenile (Carl Richards pattern) Black-Tipped Mud Crab (Carl Richards pattern)

Second line: Common Shore Shrimp (Carl Richards pattern)   Mantis Shrimp (Carl Richards pattern) Grass Shrimp (Carl Richards pattern)

Third line: Flat-Browed Snapping Shrimp (Carl Richards pattern)   Big-Clawed Snapping Shrimp (Carl Richards pattern)

Fourth line: False Mantis (Carl Richards pattern)

Fifth line: Bonefish Short (Tim Borski pattern)   Chernobyl Crab (Tim Borski pattern)

Sixth line: Borski No Name Shrimp (Tim Borski pattern)

Bottom line: Slider (Tim Borski pattern)   Borski Wool Crab (Tim Borski pattern)

Each of these flies was tied by its originator.

PLATE 4

Top line: Cockbone (Jack Gartside pattern)   Soft Hackle Streamer (Jack Gartside pattern)

Second line: Magic Minnow (Jack Gartside pattern)   Glimmer (Jack Gartside pattern)

Third line: Black Sea Urchin (Jack Gartside pattern)   Peacock Angel (Jack Gartside pattern) Saltwater Sparrow (Jack Gartside pattern)

Fourth line: Piggy Back Shrimp (Jack Gartside pattern)   Elver (Jack Gartside pattern)   Sand Flea or Amphipod (Jack Gartside pattern)

Bottom line: Orange Annelid or Bristle Worm (Jack Gartside pattern)   J.G. Chiton (Jack Gartside pattern)   Hover Bugger (Jack Gartside pattern)

Each of these flies was tied by its originator.

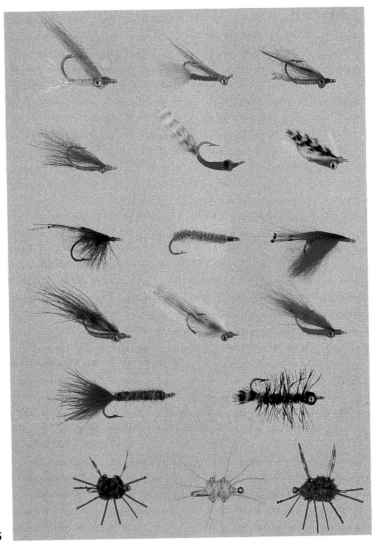

PLATE 5

Top line: Gotcha (Jim McVay pattern)   Yucatan Charlie (Jan Isley pattern)   Apricot Charlie (Bill Hunter pattern)

Second line: Orange Buck Bone (Bill and Kate Howe pattern)   A.K. Bonefish Fly (A.K. Best pattern)   Madonna Pink (George Hommell pattern)

Third line: Bonefish G.P. (Author's pattern)   Pink Polly (Author's pattern)   Hare Trigger (Author's pattern)

Fourth line: Wiggle Shrimp, brown (Author's pattern)   Wiggle Shrimp, pink (Author's pattern)   Wiggle Shrimp, green (Author's pattern)

Fifth line: Dick's Fanworm (Author's pattern)   Goby Bugger (Author's pattern)

Bottom line: Beady Crab, green (Author's pattern)   Beady Crab, Spider, white (Author's pattern)   Beady Crab, brown (Author's pattern)

Each of these flies was tied by its originator except the Yucatan Charlie (tied by Bob Nauheim) and the Apricot Charlie (tied by the author).

SWIMMING LEGS: White hen hackle
BODY: FisHair or Fish Fuzz
TAIL: FisHair or Fish Fuzz

☐ *Crazy Charlie (Bob Nauheim derivative):*
HOOK: Mustad 34007, #4, #6
THREAD: White Monocord 3/0
EYES: Silver 3/16" bead chain
BODY: Plastic body wrap over pearlescent Mylar
WING: White calftail

☐ *Del Brown's Permit Fly or Del's Merkin (Del Brown pattern):*
HOOK: Mustad 34007, #2, #4
THREAD: Fluorescent green thread
TAIL: Sparse pearl Flashabou over which are four to six ginger variant hackle tips curving out
LEGS: White rubber hackle with red tips
BODY: Alternating strands of tan and brown yarn, tied along the shank using fluorescent green thread
EYES: Chrome lead dumbbell eyes
COMMENTS: This pattern, received too late to appear in the color plates, is included in the pattern listing to provide readers with the ingredients necessary to tie it.

☐ *Diamond Bitters (Craig Mathews pattern):*
HOOK: TMC 800S or Mustad 3407, #6, #8
BODY: Diamond hot glue blanks
THREAD: White 6/0 or Monocord 3/0
LEGS: Spandex or Sili legs to match diamond color
WEED/CORAL GUARD: Natural deer hair tied short to hook point

☐ *Dick's Fanworm (Author's pattern):*
HOOK: Mustad 34011, #4
THREAD: Tan 6/0
TAIL: Dark brown marabou
BODY: Tan chenille
EYES: None

☐ *Elver (Jack Gartside pattern):*
HOOK: Mustad 34011, #6, #8
THREAD: Tan 6/0

TAIL: Short tan marabou
BODY: Dubbed or wound tan marabou (very slender)
EYES: Tan with black pupil

☐ *False Mantis (Carl Richards pattern):*
HOOK: Mustad 34011, #1, #2, #4, #6, #8
THREAD: White Monocord 3/0
FRONT LEGS: Same as body
ANTENNAE: White boar's bristles
EYES: Burnt mono
CLAWS: Rub-R-Mold liquid latex
BELLY: White mohair yarn
SWIMMING LEGS: White hen hackle
BODY/ABDOMEN: Spectra Streamer Hair or polar bear in large sizes and FisHair or Fish Fuzz in small sizes
TAIL: Same as body

☐ *Flash Urchin (Craig Mathews pattern):*
HOOK: Mustad 3407 or TMC 800S, #6, #8
THREAD: White 6/0 or Monocord 3/0
SPINES: Krystal Flash in lime, olive, copper, and peacock

☐ *Flat-Browed Snapping Shrimp (Carl Richards pattern):*
HOOK: Mustad 34011, #1, #2, #4, #6, #8
THREAD: White Monocord 3/0
FRONT LEGS: Same as body material
ANTENNAE: White boar's bristle
EYES: Burnt mono
CLAWS: Rub-R-Mold liquid latex
BELLY: White mohair yarn
REAR LEGS: White hen hackle
BODY: Spectra Hair or polar bear for large sizes; FisHair or Fish Fuzz for small sizes
TAIL: Spectra Hair, polar bear, FisHair, or Fish Fuzz
COLORING: Sharpie or Pantone waterproof pens

☐ *Flats Master (Mike Wolverton Pattern):*
HOOK: TMC 811S, #2, #4, #6, #8
THREAD: Fluorescent orange 6/0 or other bright orange thread
EYES: Smallest silver bead chain
TAIL: Hot orange marabou
BODY: Thread, same color as head

WING: Tan acrylic hair or Craft Fur

COLLAR: Natural grizzly hackle, two turns

COMMENTS: This pattern, received too late to appear in the color plates, is included in the pattern listing to provide readers with the ingredients necessary to tie it.

☐ *Glimmer (Jack Gartside pattern):*

HOOK: Mustad 34007, 1/0, #2, #4

THREAD: White 6/0 or Monocord 3/0

TAIL: Glimmer

BODY: Glimmer

COLLAR: Glimmer

EYES: Lacquered eye (optional)

☐ *Goby Bugger (Author's pattern):*

HOOK: Mustad 34011, #4

THREAD: 6/0 black

EYES: Medium silver bead chain

TAIL: Grizzly marabou or after-shafts

BODY: Gray and green medium chenille

HACKLE: Grizzly

☐ *Gotcha (Jim McVay pattern):*

HOOK: Mustad 3407, #2, #4

THREAD: Pink flat nylon 3/0

EYES: Bead chain, sized for desired sink rate

TAIL: Pearl Mylar tubing, as long shank

BODY: Pearlescent diamond braid

WING: Beige doll hair or Craft Fur, four to six strands of Krystal Flash

COMMENTS: Jim sometimes ties the Gotcha with an orange Craft Fur wing for dark flats. He also ties another variation with a tapered underbody of pink thread built up to about five layers and overwrapped with swannundaze plastic body wrap. All other elements remain the same.

☐ *Grass Shrimp (Carl Richards pattern):*

HOOK: Mustad 34011, #2, #4, #6, #8

THREAD: White Monocord 3/0

FRONT LEGS: Same as body

EYES: Burnt mono

ANTENNAE: White boar's bristles

CARAPACE/ROSTRUM: Clipped cock hackle segment

BODY: FisHair or Fish Fuzz
SWIMMING LEGS: White hen hackle
TAIL: Same as body

☐ *Green Reef Crab (Carl Richards pattern):*
HOOK: Mustad 34007, or AC 3406B, #2, #4, #6, #8
THREAD: White Monocord 3/0
BODY/CARAPACE: White egg-fly yarn spun Muddler fashion and clipped to desired carapace shape
LEGS/UNDERSIDE: Cement Rub-R-Mold leg and claw assembly under the body (liquid latex flexible mold compound from a craft shop; see comments under Big-Clawed Snapping Shrimp)
EYES: Burnt mono 40- to 80-pound
ANTENNAE: Cream boar's bristles
COLORING: Sharpie waterproof or Pantone pen

☐ *Hare Trigger (Author's pattern):*
HOOK: Mustad 34007, #4
THREAD: Chartreuse 6/0
EYES: Burnt 40-pound mono
BODY/LEGS: Dyed olive rabbit fur strip wound palmered style
ANTENNAE: Golden pheasant tippet feather and pearlescent Krystal Flash
CARAPACE: Golden pheasant breast feather

☐ *Horror (Pete Perinchief pattern):*
HOOK: Mustad 34007, #4
THREAD: Red 6/0 or Monocord 3/0
WING: Natural brown bucktail
BODY: Yellow chenille in a small ball covering only the forward one-third of the shank
COMMENTS: Pete says that when he first fished this fly with Joe Brooks in the 1950s, they often tied it on #1 and 1/0 hooks. Today he puts in a sprig or two of flash material like Krystal Flash and he crimps the barb down on all hooks.

☐ *Hover Bugger (Jack Gartside pattern):*
HOOK: Mustad 34007, #2, #4, #6
THREAD: Tan or brown Monocord 3/0
TAIL: Grizzly marabou shorts
BODY/CARAPACE: Closed-cell foam (e.g., Orvis Fly Foam)
RIB/LEGS: Grizzly, dyed tan or rusty brown
COLOR: Pantone or other waterproof pen (red-brown or tan)

☐ *J.G. Chiton (Jack Gartside pattern):*
Hook: Mustad 34007, #2, #4, #6
Thread: Tan, brown, gray 6/0
Tag: Orange poly dubbing (optional)
Body: Trimmed deer hair over bead chain
Rib: Dyed or natural grizzly over deer hair and trimmed top and bottom

☐ *Jim's Golden Eye Shrimp (Jim Orthwein pattern):*
Hook: Mustad 9674, #4; Dai-Riki 700, #4
Thread: Beige Monocord 3/0
Antennae: Peccary hair
Eyes: Gold bead chain, vary size for sink rate
Head/face: Ends of FisHair carapace and gold Mylar tubing underbody trimmed and brushed out
Body: Clear swannundaze over gold Mylar tubing
Legs: Brown saddle hackle palmered and clipped top and sides
Carapace: Strands of nugget gold FisHair (which were tied in for face) are twisted into a rope and pulled over back to form carapace
Tail: End of FisHair is doubled back on one side of body
Comments: Hook is bronze-finish freshwater model. Bend both ends down from the middle of the shank after fly is tied so FisHair back lies flush along curved body. Apply plenty of head varnish to back and head.

☐ *Madonna Pink (George Hommell pattern):*
Hook: Mustad 3407, #4
Thread: White 6/0
Eyes: Silver bead chain
Wing/tail: Two grizzly saddles over white calftail with four sprigs of Krystal Flash
Body: Pink-dyed, 5-Minute epoxy over mono framework
Weed guard: 15-pound hard Mason
Comments: Body formed by tying tips of two strands of mono in at the eyes with the trailing sections pointing forward of the fly. Two trailing ends are then doubled back on the body and tied in at the bend of the hook forming a Valentine-shaped framework that encloses the eyes. Pink-dyed epoxy is dripped into the framework and allowed to dry overnight.

☐ *Magic Minnow (Jack Gartside pattern):*
Hook: Mustad 34007 or 34011, #4, #6
Thread: White or gray 6/0

WING: Mallard flank folded, over two strands of flat Mylar, doubled

□ *Mantis Shrimp (Carl Richards pattern):*
HOOK: Mustad 34011, #1, #2, #4
THREAD: White Monocord 3/0
FRONT LEGS: Same as body
ANTENNAE: White boar's bristles
EYES: Burnt mono
CLAWS: Rub-R-Mold liquid latex (see comment on Big-Clawed Snapping Shrimp)
SWIMMING LEGS: White hen hackle
CARAPACE/BODY: FisHair or Fish Fuzz; belly is white mohair yarn
TAIL: Same as body

□ *Mini-Puff (Nat Ragland derivative):*
HOOK: Mustad 34007, #4, #6, #8
THREAD: Tan
EYES: Silver bead chain
WING: Dark brown or orange grizzly saddle over red fox squirrel tail
BODY: Tan chenille figure-eight style around eyes only, hook shank left bare

□ *Nasty Charlie (Bob Nauheim pattern):*
HOOK: Mustad 3407, #4, #6
THREAD: White Monocord 3/0
EYES: Silver 3/16" bead chain
BODY: Wrap 15-pound Mason tippet mono over silver flat tinsel (later modified to silver Flashabou)
WING: Two white saddle hackles, splayed and curving out

□ *Orange Annelid or Bristle Worm (Jack Gartside pattern):*
HOOK: Mustad 34011, #4
THREAD: Orange 6/0
BODY: Orange Mylar chenille
HACKLE: Grizzly palmered along body

□ *Orange Buck Bone (Bill and Kate Howe pattern):*
HOOK: Mustad 3407, #4, #6, #8
THREAD: White Monocord 3/0
EYES: Mini gold bead chain
TAIL: Fluorescent orange saddle hackle tip

BODY: Hot pink Lite-Brite coated with Hot Stuff acrylic glue, then sprayed with Kick It accelerator

WING: Fluorescent orange bucktail

OVERWING: Ten strands of Lite Brite

☐ *Peacock Angel (Jack Gartside pattern):*
HOOK: Mustad 34007, #4, #6, #8
THREAD: Red 6/0
EYES: Silver bead chain (optional)
TAIL: Glimmer (optional)
BODY: Pearl Glimmer
WING: Peacock swords

☐ *Piggy Back Shrimp (Jack Gartside pattern):*
HOOK: Mustad 34007, #2, #4, #6
THREAD: Tan, gray, pink, etc. 6/0
BACK BEADS: Bead chain along top of shank (small or large, three or four, to vary sink rate)
TAIL: Grizzly marabou short
BODY: Grizzly saddle feathers (use marabou on butt), palmered along shank and trimmed to shape

☐ *Pink Polly (Author's pattern):*
HOOK: Mustad 34011 or Partridge CS 11GRS, #4
THREAD: Fluorescent-orange Monocord 3/0
TAIL: Tan or white marabou short
BODY: Pink chenille
HACKLE: Brown grizzly or white palmered, trim top and bottom
COMMENTS: Hook bent slightly at one-third segments along shank to give it the shape of a wiggling sea worm.

☐ *Pink Shrimp (George Phillips pattern):*
HOOK: Mustad 34007, #1, #2, #4, #6
THREAD: Gray 6/0 or Monocord 3/0
TAIL: Pink bucktail
BODY: Flat silver tinsel wrapped with tightly palmered pink hackle (clipped on top) for legs; finished with an oversized head
CARAPACE: Pink bucktail
EYES: Painted eyes on both sides

☐ *Pops' Bonefish Bitters (Craig Mathews pattern)*
HOOK: Tears-of-the-Keys blank with bead eye (lime, gold, amber, white, or orange), on a TMC 800S or Mustad 3407, #6, #8

THREAD: White 6/0
LEGS: Sili legs to match body color
UNDERWING: Zelon to match body color and add flash
WEED/CORAL GUARD: Deer hair tied in as an overwing

☐ *Punta Squid (Craig Mathews pattern):*
HOOK: Diamond Head blank on Mustad 3407 or TMC 800S, #6, #8
THREAD: White 6/0
LEGS/TENTACLES: White Spandex
WEED/CORAL GUARD: Red over white deer hair

☐ *Rubber Band Worm (Jim Orthwein pattern):*
HOOK: Mustad 3407 or TMC with shank 3/4" to 1" long, #4, #6
THREAD: Beige Monocord 3/0
EYES: Gold bead chain in three sizes, vary to control sink rate
TAIL: Beige rubber band, same width as body and two times as long as hook shank; trim to a point
BODY: Beige wool or chenille

☐ *Rusty Bunny Bone (Jeffrey Cardenas pattern):*
HOOK: Partridge Sea Prince, #4
THREAD: Beige Monocord 3/0
EYES: Black plastic shrimp eyes
FAN TAIL: Rust-colored rabbit with two strands of copper Krystal Flash
BODY: Beige Aunt Lydia's rug yarn
COMMENTS: Shallow-water tailing fly

☐ *Saltwater Sparrow (Jack Gartside pattern):*
HOOK: Mustad 34007 or 34011, #4, #6
THREAD: Tan 6/0
TAIL: Grizzly rump marabou (short)
BODY: Dubbed Polyfur or rabbit/Antron
HACKLE: Pheasant rump with long barbules that extend at least to tip of tail
EYES: Gold or silver bead chain
HEAD: Pheasant after-shaft hackle wound behind, over, and in front of eyes

☐ *Sand Flea or Amphipod (Jack Gartside pattern):*
HOOK: Mustad 34007, #6, #8
THREAD: Tan 6/0
TAIL: None
BODY: Three or four beads on chain tied on top of shank over which is wound dubbed fox/Antron mix with legs picked out from body

☐ *Sea Lice (Craig Mathews pattern):*
   HOOK: Mustad 3407 or TMC 800S, #6, #8
   THREAD: White or cream 6/0
   ABDOMEN: Fine white chenille
   RIB: White or grizzly saddle palmered and trimmed flat, top and bottom
   THORAX: Chartreuse dubbing, picked out

☐ *Shallow-H$_2$O Fly (Lefty Kreh pattern):*
   HOOK: Mustad 34007, #4
   THREAD: White Monocord 3/0 or flat waxed nylon
   WING: Chartreuse bucktail, heavy — twice normal-size wing
   BODY: One-third White chenille, two-thirds chartreuse

☐ *Slider (Tim Borski pattern):*
   HOOK: Mustad 34007, #2
   THREAD: Beige Monocord 3/0
   TAIL: Craft Fur barred with permanent marker (Pantone 462-M), and orange Krystal Flash
   HACKLE: Palmered long soft grizzly hackle back half of body, trimmed on underside
   BODY: Spun deer hair (natural), trimmed to finger-tip shape
   EYES: Lead barbell, vary size for sink rate

☐ *Soft Hackle Streamer (Jack Gartside pattern):*
   HOOK: Mustad 34007, 3406, #2, #4, #6
   THREAD: White 6/0
   TINSEL: Flat Mylar
   WING: Tan, pink, and white marabou bloods stripped one side and wound soft-hackle fashion
   COLLAR: One barred mallard, teal, or pheasant flank feather
   HEAD: White
   EYES: Lacquered or painted (optional)

☐ *Dr. Taylor Special (Phil Taylor pattern):*
   HOOK: Mustad 34007, #4
   THREAD: Fluorescent-orange Monocord 3/0
   EYES: Silver bead chain or nickel-plated lead to vary sink rate
   BODY: Silver Mylar tinsel ribbed with brown-orange body glass or Larva Lace
   WING: Badger saddle over grizzly underwing
   HEAD: Fluorescent red-orange chenille

☐ *Turneffe Crab (Craig Mathews pattern)*:
HOOK: Mustad 3407 or TMC 800S, #6, #8
THREAD: White or cream 6/0
WEIGHT: None to six wraps .020" lead wire
LEGS: Sili or round rubber legs to match body color
BODY: Olive, lime, or tan chenille
WEED/CORAL GUARD: Natural mottled deer hair over Zelon underwing (color to match body)

☐ *Ultra Shrimp (Bob Popovics pattern)*:
HOOK: TMC 811S, #4, #6, #8
THREAD: Tan or cream 6/0
TAIL: Tan Ocean Hair with copper Krystal Flash
EYES: Burnt monofilament; tie eyes at tail area
HACKLE: Ginger, palmered through body
BODY: Pale ginger yarn or dubbing
BACK: Tan Ocean Hair (leave tuft protruding over hook eye), topped with 5 Minute epoxy or Soft Coat; pinch rear of back to shape just before epoxy sets up
COMMENTS: This pattern, received too late to appear in the color plates, is included in the pattern listing to provide readers with the ingredients necessary to tie it.

☐ *Victor's Candy (Bill Hunter pattern)*:
HOOK: Mustad 34007 or equivalent, #4, #6
THREAD: Brown 6/0
TAIL: Short tuft of orange marabou
BODY: Fine tan chenille (four turns of lead at front of hook, just rear of head)
WING: A mix of golden pheasant tippet strands and black tipped neck or throat from an elk, and two strands of Krystal Flash
HEAD: Dark brown thread
EYES: Place black dot on each side of body at rear of hook to represent eyes of shrimp with waterproof marking pen
COMMENTS: Bill says he tied this fly to mimic a tan shrimp that looked more lively than the pattern he had been fishing in the Keys. It was first field-tested by a group fishing Boca Paila where it outperformed all other flies in camp and was named by field-tester Bud Olin for his guide, who was smitten by the pattern. Although received too late to appear in the color plates, it is included in the pattern listing to provide readers with the ingredients necessary to tie it.

☐ *Wiggle Shrimp (Author's pattern):*
HOOK: Partridge Sea Prince CS-52, #2, #4
THREAD: Monocord 3/0, color to match body
EYES: Bead chain or lead; vary for sink rate
BODY: Rug yarn (tan, cream, brown, apple green, or chartreuse)
WING: Tan, cream, etc. marabou to match body. Flanked by two cree
    saddle hackles with three or four sprigs of Krystal Flash

☐ *Winston's Urchin (Craig Mathews pattern):*
BODY/HOOK: Hot glue bubble head on Mustad 3407 or TMC 800S, #6, #8
THREAD: White or cream 6/0
SPINES/LEGS: Spandex or Sili rubber legs to match color of body bubble
WEED/CORAL GUARD: Dyed deer hair to match body

☐ *Woolly Bugger (Russell Blessing pattern):*
HOOK: Musted 34011, #2, #4
THREAD: Black 6/0
WEIGHT: Can vary with lead wraps or metal eyes for desired sink rate
TAIL: Black marabou blood
BODY: Olive chenille
HACKLE: Black saddle, palmered
COMMENTS: Also in orange or flesh-colored body and white marabou and
    saddle hackle for polychaete seaworm imitator

☐ *Yucatan Charlie (Jan Isley pattern):*
HOOK: Mustad 34007, #4
THREAD: Chartreuse Monocord 3/0
EYES: Silver bead chain
TAIL: Bushy pink yarn or marabou
BODY: Chartreuse Amnesia mono
WING: White calftail

13

Bonefishing Destinations

Bonefish inhabit most of the world's tropical zones. But only a few of these warm-water areas qualify as fly-fishing destinations. As the map on the next page shows, most of the places where you can pursue bonefish with fly rods are located in the Atlantic Ocean — the Bahamas, the Florida Keys, Belize, Mexico's Yucatan coast, and along the northern coast of Venezuela. The Pacific Ocean presently offers anglers only one developed bonefishing area — Christmas Island.

Fishing can differ substantially among these many destinations, just as it can vary from one trout stream to another. An angler who wades for five-pound bonefish on the hard, glistening flats at Christmas Island has one experience; an angler who drifts the marly cuts of Andros for ten-pound trophies has quite another.

But bonefishing destinations differ in more than just the quality of fishing. The type of accommodations and the cost of a trip can vary greatly too. Some destinations are first-class resorts that have luxurious rooms and offer activities like tennis or diving for non-fishing companions. Others are strictly fishing camps that provide comfortable quarters but no amenities. Trip costs at these destinations can vary a great deal — more than many anglers realize. You will pay almost twice as much to fish at some destinations as you will at others.

Which of these destinations best matches your requirements depends on your preferences, personal needs, and circumstances. Do you like wading or poled-skiff fishing? How skilled are you at finding and seeing fish? Do you

250

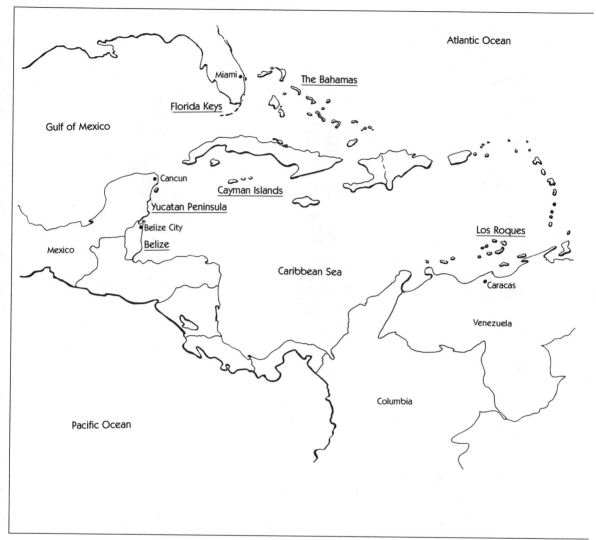

MAJOR BONEFISHING DESTINATIONS

In the Atlantic, the most popular bonefishing destinations lie in a crescent extending from the Bahamas and Florida, west to Mexico's Yucatan peninsula and Belize, then south to Los Roques in Venezuela. A few Pacific locations, including Christmas Island, have bonefishing, although they are remote for most eastern U.S. anglers.

prefer large fish or lots of fish? Do you want to fish for other species as well? When do you intend to travel? How much do you want to spend? Will you travel with a spouse or partner? Is the quality of the accommodations or the availability of non-fishing activities important?

Some bonefishing destinations such as Andros, Los Roques, and Christmas Island attract serious, well-outfitted anglers and offer few non-fishing activities for non-angling travel companions.

QUALITY OF THE FISHING

Angling quality depends on the size, number, and sophistication of the fish at a destination. It also varies with the type and number of flats, the quality of guides, the weather, and the fishing pressure.

Size, Number, and Sophistication of Bonefish

Anglers who seek big trophy bonefish should focus on either Key Biscayne and Islamorada in the Florida Keys or on Bimini in the Bahamas. More world records have been set in these three areas than any other. You may not see as many bonefish at these destinations as you would at some areas, but those that you do see are likely to be large and experienced. Fishing for these trophies can be extremely challenging, however, especially on the flats that are most heavily fished.

White, hard-bottomed sand flats, excellent for both wading and visibility, are common at destinations like Los Roques and Christmas Island.

If you prefer large numbers of smaller fish you should consider destinations such as Ascension Bay and Boca Paila/Pez Maya, in Mexico's Yucatan area, or Ambergris Caye in Belize. Schools run very large at these locations and anglers often have ten- and twenty-bonefish days.

For large numbers of medium-sized fish, you might consider Christmas Island, Los Roques, and many of the Bahamian out islands. Schools here are smaller than the Yucatan's, but the fish are bigger. You will also find some really large trophy-sized fish in most of these areas, though not to the extent Florida and Bimini hold them.

Type and Number of Flats

Most of the bonefishing flats in the Atlantic grew as extensions of the continental shelf. Typified by the flats of the Bahamas and the Florida Keys, these areas contain coral beds and mangrove stands that have slowly collected sediment and built up over tens of thousands of years.

But three of these bonefishing destinations — Venezuela's Los Roques, Belize's Turneffe Islands, and little Glover's Reef — are high-atoll-type areas, more like the Pacific's Christmas Island. Atolls consist of rings of coral heads on high plateaus that rise abruptly from the ocean floor and rim large open expanses of shallow lagoons.

Continental-shelf flats such as those found in Florida, the Bahamas, and the Yucatan contain more variety than atolls. Small islands, keys, and cuts lace these areas. Large stands of mangroves provide shelter for anglers in wind. Continental-shelf flats also usually contain more grass bottoms, a greater diversity of prey, and a larger variety of fishing experiences than atoll flats.

If you prefer the intimacy of stalking bonefish on foot, you should consider the open-ocean atoll-type flats found at Christmas Island and Los Roques. These destinations contain endless miles of white sandy bottom ideal for safe wading and excellent fish-spotting visibility. All bonefishing is on foot.

If you dislike wading and prefer drifting flats in a skiff, you will find no place with more boats, guides, and driftable waters than the Florida Keys. Ambergris Caye in Belize is also a good poled-boat fishing destination. In fact, Ambergris has virtually no wadable flats. The Florida Keys area does offer limited wading, but this is incidental to its attraction as a poled-boat fishing destination.

Anglers who like to alternate wading with poled-boat fishing will find that most Bahamas destinations give them ample opportunities to use both methods. The terrain of the Bahamas offers a greater variety of wadeable bottom than most atoll areas. In addition, the large population of native guides here

Good bonefishing skiffs, like these 16-foot Dolphins, have shallow drafts, clean upper decks for casting, ample rod racks for stowage, and plenty of room for two anglers, gear, and a guide.

TABLE 13.1
COMPARISON OF FISHING AT VARIOUS BONEFISHING DESTINATIONS

	BONEFISH		MODE OF FISHING	PERMIT/ TARPON	BEST FISHING
	AVER SIZE	AVER NO			
Bahamas					
Abacos	med-lge	med	wade/boat	–	Apr-June; Oct-Jan
Deep Water Cay	med-lge	med	wade/boat	permit	Apr-June; Oct-Jan
Bimini	med-trophy	few-med	wade/boat	–	Apr-June; Oct-Jan
Berry Islands	med-lge	med	wade/boat	permit	Apr-June; Oct-Jan
N. Eleuthera/ Harbour Island	med-lge	med	wade/boat	–	Apr-June; Oct-Jan
Andros	med-lge	med	wade/boat	permit, tarpon	Apr-June; Oct-Jan
Exumas	med-lge	med	wade/boat	–	Apr-June; Oct-Jan
Long Island	med-lge	med	wade/boat	permit	Apr-June; Oct-Jan
Florida					
Biscayne Bay	med-trophy	few-med	boat	–	Apr-June; Oct-Dec
Keys	med-trophy	few-med	boat	permit, tarpon	Apr-June; Oct-Dec
Mexico					
Rio Area	small-med	med-lge	wade/boat	permit, tarpon	Apr-June; Oct-Nov
Ascension Bay	small-med	med-lge	wade/boat	permit, tarpon	Apr-June; Oct-Nov
Belize					
Mainland	small-med	med-lge	boat	tarpon	Apr-June; Oct-Nov
Ambergris	small-med	med-lge	boat	permit, tarpon	Apr-June; Oct-Nov
Turneffe Island	med-lge	med	wade/boat	permit, tarpon	Apr-June; Oct-Nov
Caymans					
Little Cayman	small-med	med	wade/boat	tarpon	Apr-June; Oct-Nov
Venezuela					
Los Roques	med-lge	med	wade	–	Apr-Aug; Nov
Pacific					
Christmas Is.	med-lge	med	wade	–	March-Nov

offers anglers good availability of poled skiffs. Other destinations that allow you to fish both methods are the Turneffe Islands in Belize and most of the Yucatan peninsula areas in Mexico. And Turneffe offers some especially good wading for large experienced fish.

Quality and Experience of Guides

The most sophisticated bonefishing guides work in the Florida Keys and the Bahamas, where a rich tradition of guiding experienced anglers dates back to Zane Grey, Van Campen Heilner, and Joe Brooks. Early Florida guides such as Bill Smith and Jimmie Albright pioneered bonefishing with flies. Today, many of Florida's flats guides design flies, develop tackle, and practice leading-edge fishing strategies on what may be the most sophisticated population of bonefish in the world. They include Sandy Moret, Steve Huff, Rick Ruoff, Stu Apte, Harry Spear, Vic Gaspeny, Al Polofsky, Eddie Wightman, Bill Curtis, Dick Williams, George Hommell, Tim Borski, Randy Towe, and Jeffrey Cardenas. Many have also captained some of America's major fishing celebrities from Ted Williams to Jack Nicklaus to George Bush.

Some extremely gifted guides have also evolved in the Bahamas. These entrepreneurial native Bahamians often display legendary fishing instincts and

The quality of bonefishing guides varies considerably from place to place. Some like the legendary Joe Cleare of Harbour Island have guided anglers for over forty years and can always seem to find fish no matter what conditions exist.

vision; among them are Joe Cleare on Harbour Island, Rudy Dames on Bimini, and Charlie Smith, Rupert Leadon, Charlie Neymour on Andros, and Percy Darville and Franklin Pigstock in the Berry Islands. Other highly experienced guides outside the United States include Winston "Pops" Cabral and William Taku Johnson of Turneffe Flats and Moanafua T. Kofe of Christmas Island.

Guide Selection

You cannot select the guide you will fish with at all destinations. Most larger developed clubs will rotate you among several guides during a week's stay. Other places will try to match your skill and needs to whichever guides they have available. But other destinations — especially in the Bahamas and Florida Keys — will require you to find your own guide and make your own arrangements. I am often asked by anglers for advice on what to look for in a guide. Here are a few guidelines:

- Boat handling — If you are going to fly fish from a poled boat, your guide must be able to handle the boat and postion it for you to cast and retrieve. He or she should be able to position you to see fish with the wind and sun quartered to the rear and be able to hold the boat steady during the retrieve so you know what your fly is doing.
- Sighting ability–The more a guide sees, the more he can help you. He should not only be able to see fish, but also your fly and the fish's reaction to it, so he can direct your aim and retrieve.
- Local prey knowledge–A guide should know local bonefish feeding preferences — by flat and by season — so he can advise you on pattern, color, and size strategies in fly selection.
- Finding fish–Finding a nomadic spooky fish like *Albula vulpes* — especially in heavily fished areas — is not a trivial task. It takes experience and knowing the location of prey concentrations and fish routes, as well as a constant awareness of the effects of changing tides, temperatures, and seasons. It also takes tenacity.
- Attitude–Finding bonefish is hard work and a good guide deserves the respect of his fishermen. Bonefish *angling* can also be tough — an angler who is serious and trying hard should be respected by his guide. Don't accept anything less.

Weather Conditions

Weather conditions have a lot to do with how productive or unproductive a bonefishing trip will be. Temperature determines whether fish will be actively

Outside the United States the quality of fishing guides and equipment varies, but lodges such as those on Deep Water Cay, Walker's Cay, and Andros provide their own skiffs and experienced guides.

feeding on the flats or holed-up offshore. Wind not only affects fish availability, but also how well you can see and cast to fish.

If you can choose when to take your bonefishing trip, April through June and October through November are the best months overall for temperature and wind conditions (see Table 13.2). If you want to bonefish other months, fortunately there is enough diversity in bonefishing destinations that you can usually find at least one place where temperatures are moderate and wind is appropriate for your casting skill level.

Cold temperatures and strong winds make popular places like Florida and the Bahamas unpredictable in the winter. If you want to bonefish in December and January, you will find Christmas Island, nearly on the equator, a more reliable choice. Even when winter winds blow at this Pacific location, at least the temperatures remain warm.

The flats at Ascension Bay in Mexico offer another good winter alternative. In latitude, they lie about halfway between Christmas Island and the northern-most Bahamian locations. Sheltered inside the caye-studded bay, anglers find protection from cold winter winds that make fishing unproductive in more exposed areas.

TABLE 13.2

AVERAGE MONTHLY TEMPERATURE AND WIND
CONDITIONS AT POPULAR BONEFISHING DESTINATIONS

	J	F	M	A	M	J	J	A	S	O	N	D
Bahamas												
Temperature	G	G	G	E	E	G	P	P	P	G	E	E
Wind	G	P	P	G	E	E	E	P	P	G	G	G
Florida												
Temperature	P	P	G	E	E	E	P	P	P	G	E	G
Wind	G	P	P	G	E	E	E	P	P	G	G	G
Mexico												
Temperature	G	G	G	E	E	G	P	P	P	G	E	E
Wind	P	P	P	G	E	E	E	G	G	G	G	P
Belize												
Temperature	G	G	G	E	E	G	P	P	P	G	E	E
Wind	P	P	P	G	E	E	E	G	G	G	G	P
Venezuela												
Temperature	P	P	G	E	E	E	G	G	P	P	G	G
Wind	P	P	P	G	E	E	E	E	G	G	G	P
Christmas I.												
Temperature	E	E	E	E	E	E	E	E	E	E	E	E
Wind	P	P	G	G	G	E	E	E	G	G	G	P

E   Excellent; G   Good; P   Poor

For summer fishing in July and August, both Christmas Island and Los Roques offer good bonefishing. Winds are moderate to low at both destinations, and temperatures are favorable.

If wind conditions are a primary consideration, you should plan your bonefishing in the spring and summer when most destinations have gentler winds. If you must fish in the colder months, avoid destinations such as the atoll areas that offer little protection from prevailing winds and temporary storms.

Fishing Pressure

Some anglers like the society of fishing near many other fishermen and the challenge of pursuing sophisticated fish that see many anglers and flies. Others prefer seeing no other anglers where they fish. They want to stalk wild fish alone on remote flats.

Of all the bonefishing areas in the world today, Florida's Biscayne Bay and the Keys receive the heaviest pressure. In spite of hundreds of square miles of fishable flats, the bonefish in Florida see many fishermen, boats, and water-sports activity. They are sophisticated, spooky, and often difficult to take. The Keys guides have had to develop highly refined techniques, and some anglers find this the most challenging and rewarding place of all to bonefish.

Occupying the other end of the fishing pressure spectrum, remote places like Christmas Island, Los Roques, and Andros offer enormous expanses of solitary flats. A guide at Andros once told me that he seldom fishes the same flat more than once every two months. And when he does, he gets bored. Bonefish in these areas are more willing to take your fly. You can also fish all day without ever seeing another fisherman.

Some of the most interesting bonefishing occurs at places that offer both solitude and sophisticated fish. The Bahamian out islands and Belize have plenty of medium- and large-sized experienced fish. These fish see moderate fishing pressure from experienced anglers who return regularly to fish them each year. But pressure is kept down by sparse accommodations and a limited number of guides. Fish at these locations are often fairly selective and challenging.

Availability of Other Fishing

Many bonefishing destinations offer other fishing, both on the flats and off-shore. The Florida Keys, for example, have some of the finest sight-casting for permit and tarpon in the world. Christmas Island contains three different types of trevally, ranging from the fifteen-pound blue to the one hundred-pound giant trevally. Atlantic atoll-type areas, including the Turneffe Islands and Glover's Reef off Belize, hold reef fish including barracuda, snapper, and grouper. Virtually all locations offer some offshore fishing for species such as tuna, wahoo, and marlin.

TRIP COST

A week of bonefishing will cost you twice as much in some areas as others. Many locations let you control one of the largest costs — accommodations — by offering several places to stay with different price ranges. Others have only one choice for lodging and offer a single package price for fishing.

The total you can pay for accommodations, guides, meals, transportation, and incidentals can range from relatively economical to expensive. The prices used in the following section are accurate in 1992 and they typically increase about five percent each year, tracking the average rate of inflation.

Cost of Accommodations

Accommodations account for one of the largest and one of the most variable cost components of a bonefishing trip. In a place like Florida there are hundreds of accommodations from which to choose. Price-conscious anglers can find inexpensive rooms at places like the Shoreline Motel in Islamorada or the Fairfield Inn-by Marriott in Miami for about $55 to $65 a night. For anglers who want luxury accommodations, Cheeca Lodge in Islamorada has accommodations from $200 to $800 a night, and Hawk's Cay, just north of Marathon, rents rooms and suites from $210 to $615 a night.

The Bahamas contain fewer accommodations, but most of the larger resorts offer rooms in a range of prices. At the Bimini Big Game Fishing Club, for example, rooms range from about $140 to $295 a night.

In contrast, most bonefishing *lodges* located in remote areas, such as those at Casa Blanca, Deep Water Cay, and Christmas Island price all rooms the same and include them in a single package price. Although captive pricing is necessary to cover the costs of developing these remote areas, this allows you no control over accommodation costs.

Cost of Guides

Guide rates usually cost anglers more than any other daily bonefishing expense and rates vary substantially from location to location. In Florida, guides typically charge $275 to $350 a day for up to two anglers per boat. In most places in the Bahamas, guides charge $200 a day, although at some places they are as low as $180 and at others as high as $300. In Belize and Mexico, guides are generally less expensive, often $150 or $200 for a full day's fishing. If you fish on your own, boats rent for about $50 to $150 a day. If you wade on your own, you can fish for the lowest day rate of all — for free.

Transportation Costs

Airfare to the major city nearest a bonefishing destination usually accounts for most of the travel expense of a fishing trip. But local travel costs can sometimes surprise you. Two anglers fishing the Florida Keys will each pay $100 to $200 a week to share a rental car. Bahamian destinations require $100 to $200 per person for a round-trip local flight from Florida or Nassau to your final destination. Some especially remote locations like Mexico's Casa Blanca on Ascension Bay have long second-leg local flights. Round-trip airfare to Casa Blanca from Cancun costs about $300 per person. The longest trek of all, Christmas Island, requires a two-hour, forty-five-minute local plane trip once you get to Honolulu. Its cost, bundled into the weekly bonefishing rate, is one of the factors that places Christmas Island among the most expensive of all bonefishing destinations.

Miscellaneous Costs

Even minor items can sometimes inflate the cost of one destination over another. Meals, for example, can cost a little or a lot in a place like Florida, where you have a variety of options. Full-service luxury resorts outside the United States offer fewer alternatives and cost about twenty percent more. Meals at the most exclusive resorts may cost twice as much. Over a week's time they can add up to enough to pay for another day's fishing. Taxes, though a small cost, vary considerably from place to place. In the Bahamas, an eight-percent tax is added to room charges. In Florida, plan on an eleven-percent tax added to room charges plus a seven-percent tax added to meals.

Some Examples

Considered as a whole, the above costs combine in some interesting, and not always predictable, ways to determine how much a week of bonefishing might cost. For example, in Florida, guides may cost more than most other places, but this is offset by the availability of inexpensive accommodations and meals. As a result, Florida offers some of the most economical guided bonefishing available.

But if you fish the Florida Keys from one of their luxury resorts, Florida bonefishing can be among the most expensive. Table 13.3 estimates what a week-long bonefishing trip costs for one person at several different destinations. Costs are based on *double occupancy*. Except for incidentals like tips and beverages, they include everything but airfare from an angler's home to the major airport nearest the final destination. Based on 1992 rates, you can approximate rates in later years by allowing a five percent annual increase for inflation. (See Table 13.3.)

Going off-season can reduce the cost of accommodations and airfare by twenty-five to thirty-five percent. Destinations where you can wade on your own can also lower the cost of a trip by hundreds of dollars.

QUALITY OF ACCOMMODATIONS

Anglers with a family or a non-fishing partner may want better accommodations than those traveling alone to fish. They often want non-fishing activities such as diving, golf, snorkeling, or sailing available.

Many bonefishing destinations offer first-class accommodations, as well as other sports and leisure activities. Some of the best include the Hawk's Cay Resort and Marina on Duck Key and Cheeca Lodge at Islamorada in the Florida Keys, the Green Turtle Club on Abaco, the Bimini Big Game Fishing Club, and both the Romora Bay Club and the Dunmore Beach Club on Harbour Island in the Bahamian out islands. Each of these destinations functions as a full resort with all amenities such as dining room, diving, tennis, and swimming on site or close by.

Some destinations do not have many non-fishing activities. They offer excellent fishing and good-quality accommodations — a major consideration for bonefishing couples — but little else. Fishing lodges in this category include Cargill Creek Lodge on Andros, Casa Blanca at Ascension Bay, and Deep Water Cay Club on the east end of Grand Bahama Island.

THE BAHAMAS

With over seven hundred islands and 2400 islets, the five-hundred-mile-long chain of the Bahamas contains the largest array of bonefish flats in the world. They offer great variety of bonefish size and habitats. With a long, rich tradition of bonefishing, anglers can find guides on almost every island. Even small, family-oriented resorts are usually sensitive to the needs of fishing guests. The Bahamas have large schools of small fish and small schools of medium-sized fish. They also offer a fairly large population of singles, doubles, and triples in the trophy range. Bahamas fish average a healthy five pounds. Several world-record fish have been taken at Bimini, and anglers regularly report seeing fish in the ten- to fifteen-pound range at Bimini, Andros, and the Berry Islands.

People inhabit only about thirty of the hundreds of Bahamian islands. Most of the others offer endless stretches of uninhabited pink and white beaches, mangrove-rimmed cays, and turquoise water. This is easily one of the most beautiful and productive bonefishing areas in the world. Bahamas resorts tend to be luxurious and seldom offer economy rates. A few of them have developed as strictly fishing destinations. But most function as family resorts that offer diving, snorkeling, sunbathing, boating, tennis, and sometimes golf.

The major drawbacks of Bahamas bonefishing are unpredictable weather and varied guide experience. The location of these islands at the northern edge of the bonefish's tropical range, like Florida, makes them susceptible to bone-chilling cold fronts in the winter months. In February, you should expect one or two days of every ten fished to be cold enough to keep the fish off the flats — or windy enough to make fishing challenging.

TABLE 13.3

TYPICAL COSTS FOR A WEEK OF BONEFISHING IN 1992

LOCATION	LODGE/RESORT/ MOTEL	COST[1]	COMMENTS[2]
Bimini, Bahamas	Bimini Big Game Fishing Club	$1,285–$2,021	For total trip cost add airfare from your home airport to Bimini, plus any gratuities.
Islamorada, Florida	Shoreline Motel	$1,289–$1,512	For total trip cost add airfare from your home airport to Miami, plus any gratuities.
Ambergris Caye, Belize	El Pescador	$1,300	For total trip cost add airfare from your home airport to Belize City, plus any gratuities.
Exuma, Bahamas	Peace & Plenty	$1,313–$1,463	For total trip cost add airfare from your home airport to Georgetown, Exuma, plus any gratuities.
Harbour Island, Bahamas	Romora Bay Club	$1,331–$1,576	For total trip cost add airfare from your home airport to North Eleuthera, Bahamas, plus any gratuities.
Key West, Florida	Comfort Inn	$1,449–$1,773	For total trip cost add airfare from your home airport to Miami, plus any gratuities.
Abaco, Bahamas	Great Abaco Bonefish Club	$1616[5]	For total cost add airfare from home airport to Marsh Harbour, plus gratuities.
Andros, Bahamas	Cargill Creek Lodge	$1,725	For total trip cost add airfare from your home airport to Andros Town, Bahamas, plus any gratuities.
Turneffe Islands, Belize	Turneffe Flats	$1,750[3]	For total trip cost add airfare from your home airport to Belize City, plus any gratuities.

TABLE 13.3 (*continued*)
TYPICAL COSTS FOR A WEEK OF BONEFISHING IN 1992

LOCATION	LODGE/RESORT/MOTEL	COST[1]	COMMENTS[2]
Andros, Bahamas	Andros Island Bonefish Club	$1,780	For total trip cost add airfare from your home airport to Andros Town, Bahamas, plus any gratuities.
Key Largo, Florida	Ocean Reef Club	$1,840–$3,769	For total trip cost add airfare from your home airport to Miami, plus any gratuities.
Yucatan peninsula, Mexico	Boca Paila	$1,900	For total trip cost add airfare from your home airport to Cancun, Mexico, plus any gratuities.
Christmas Island, Kiribati	Captain Cook Hotel	$1,995[4]	For total trip cost add airfare from your home airport to Honolulu, plus any gratuities.
Islamorada, Florida	Cheeca Lodge	$1,998–$4,490	For total trip cost add airfare from your home airport to Miami, plus any gratuities.
Grand Bahama Island, Bahamas	Deep Water Cay	$2,195	For total trip cost add airfare from your home airport to Deep Water Cay, Bahamas, plus any gratuities.
Ascension Bay, Mexico	Casa Blanca	$2,495	For total trip cost add airfare from your home airport to Cancun, Mexico, plus any gratuities.

[1] Cost is per person for 7 nights/6 days based on double occupancy and includes all costs but beverages, tips, and airfare from angler's home airport to commercial airport nearest destination. Room rates are based on 1992 published high season rates and include tax. Guide fee is based on full day fishing, going rates or $300 in Florida ($150/person). Meals in Florida are estimated at $20–$40 per person, economy; $25–$50, moderate; $50–$75, luxury and include tax. Meals are estimated at $25–$50 per person elsewhere. Local transportation costs from nearest commercial airport to resort are included; car rental in Florida is estimated at $150 ($75/person).

[2] Transportation costs from airport nearest angler's point of origin to airport nearest the destination, plus gratuities (resort and guide) should be added to obtain total cost for a week of bonefishing.

[3] 7 days / 7 nights

[4] 6 days / 6 nights   [5] 1993 Rates

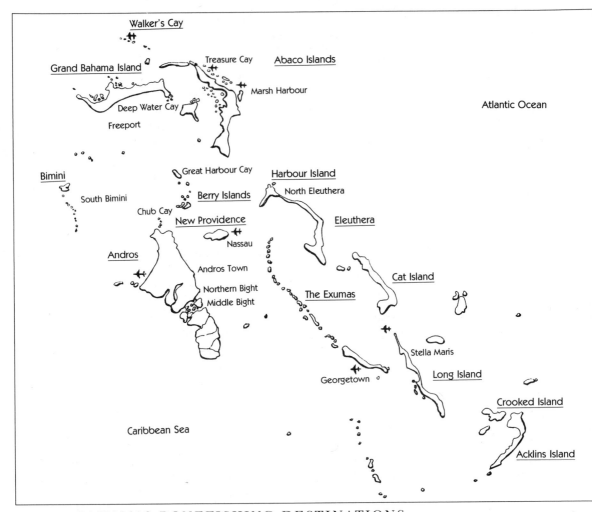

BAHAMAS BONEFISHING DESTINATIONS
The Bahamas, lying just east and south of Florida, offer the greatest number and variety of bonefishing destinations in the world, from Walker's Cay in the north to Crooked Island and Acklins Island in the south.

Guide experience is also unpredictable in many of the Bahamas locations. No association exists to organize and train guides. Some fishing lodges, such as the Andros Island Bonefish Club, Cargill Creek Lodge, Deep Water Cay Club, and Walker's Cay Hotel and Marina, train their guides. But otherwise, guiding is entrepreneurial. Sometimes you may end up fishing with a local bottom fisherman trying to pick up spare cash. Other times you may fish with guides like Joe Cleare of Harbour Island and Rudy Dames of Bimini—men who have spent their entire lives stalking bonefish.

Some destinations allow only wading for bonefish. Others like this one in the Bahamas are better fished from skiffs. Both types of fishing are available to anglers in a wide choice of accommodations — and costs.

Many Bahamian flats contain hard-packed sand with turtle grass. Many others behind cays, inside lagoons, and in sounds hold sediment too soft for wading. Poled boats dominate the fishing here and give anglers access to flats. Wading is popular on those with safe bottoms.

Although bonefish inhabit all of the Bahamas, only eight major areas currently offer sufficient guides, flats, and comfortable accommodations to qualify as popular destinations.

The Abaco Islands

The Abacos are a chain of large islands and small cays shaped like a 130-mile-long boomerang. They lie along the northern rim of the Bahamas on the very edge of the Atlantic. The Abacos have three main bonefishing areas: Walker's Cay in the far north, Treasure Cay above Marsh Harbour, and the newly opened Marls and Cherokee Sound area south of Marsh Harbour.

Fish at Walker's Cay average four to six pounds. The area typically holds good numbers of large fish in small pods or schools. Anglers rarely see large schools here. You can fish both by wading and poled boat. Guides at Walker's have above-average experience for the Bahamas. Flats, while not extensive, offer seclusion and solitary fishing. (Most guests who stay at Walker's Cay come for offshore fishing.)

Treasure Cay, on the east side of Great Abaco, also has bonefish that average four to six pounds. But Treasure Cay offers more expansive flats. Anglers find bottoms here a mix of hard-packed sand and turtle grass, and fishing is by both wading and poled skiff. You arrange for guides through the local hotels.

The largest of Abaco's flats, the Marls, consist of an immense mangrove wilderness on the west side of the island. Fish in the mid-size range occur in very large numbers here with some large fish hanging along the mouths of creeks and the edges of the deeper cuts that lace this sprawling marine wilderness. Occasionally permit in the 25- to 35-pound range appear.

Other Fishing

The big offshore fishing center at Walker's Cay has marlin, sailfish, tuna, wahoo, dolphin, and king mackerel, and holds many IGFA records.

Accommodations

Anglers can stay at the Walker's Cay Hotel and Marina in the northern Abacos. This full resort and offshore fishing destination features a 75-slip marina, swimming pools, and tennis courts. The hotel supplies Florida bonefishing guides and uses modern well-outfitted skiffs.

Treasure Cay Beach Hotel and Villas and the Green Turtle Yacht Club are located in the middle of the Abacos chain. You reach them through Treasure Cay Airport. The Great Abaco Bonefish Club, 30 minutes south of Marsh Harbour ferries daily expeditions into the 200 square-mile back country flats area known as the Marls. The GABC also fishes Cherokee Sound for ocean bones on the east coast. The lodge has a dozen guides with modern skiffs and is one of the better run fishing camps in the Bahamas.

Getting There

You reach Abaco resorts through three airports: Walker's Cay in the north; Treasure Cay in the middle; and Marsh Harbour (the largest) in the south. Flights arrive from Ft. Lauderdale at a private airstrip on Walker's Cay. Flights from Miami, West Palm Beach, and Nassau service Treasure Cay and Marsh Harbour.

Grand Bahama Island/Deep Water Cay

Deep Water Cay is about one hundred miles due east of Palm Beach. It lies just off the east end of Grand Bahama Island. This quiet, private fishing resort offers privacy and solitary fishing. The only town nearby is the small village of McLeans Town.

Fish at Deep Water Cay average four to six pounds, but larger fish are numerous. The club record stands at fourteen pounds, eight ounces, and fish over ten pounds are taken each year. Anglers fish from modern sixteen-foot poled skiffs. Most local guides here have a decade or more of experience.

Deep Water Cay offers anglers an extensive two hundred square miles of flats to fish, either by wading or by boat. The area has many cays and inlets to protect anglers from winds. Its long finger-like cays interlaced with creeks are rich in prey and attract many bonefish. Anglers will find fishable conditions for most tides or winds. Fishing pressure is low.

Other Fishing

Deep Water Cay also offers good permit fishing, with fish in the twenty-five to forty-five-pound range found nearby. A thirty-nine-pound, fourteen-ounce fish taken in October 1988 held the saltwater sixteen-pound line class IGFA record for three years.

Accommodations

Deep Water Cay Club, the only accommodation at this location, is one of the oldest and most established fishing lodges in the Caribbean. It offers an Orvis tackle shop, experienced guides, and modern skiffs. The club has a saltwater pool.

Getting There

Flights service Freeport from several Florida cities and Nassau. The club is a one-hour taxi ride. Charters are also available direct from Palm Beach to the club's private airstrip.

Bimini

Bimini forms the western edge of the Bahamas, only fifty miles east of Miami. It consists of a number of islands, islets, and cays. North Bimini, seven miles long and only three hundred yards from the Gulf Stream, serves as one of the largest big-game fishing centers in the world.

As in the Florida Keys, Bimini attracts bonefish anglers with its big fish and numerous world-record catches. Jim Orthwein set three of the five current IGFA saltwater fly-rod world records for bonefish here. One, a fifteen-pound fish taken on a four-pound tippet, is the largest recorded bonefish ever taken on a fly. Two IGFA saltwater line class records for bonefish were also set at Bimini, including a sixteen-pound fish taken on twelve-pound line in 1971.

Most anglers bonefish in the Bimini area in poled skiffs. A modest number of flats interspersed with keys and lagoons offer some protection from winds. Fishing pressure is moderate to heavy in season and the area experiences a considerable amount of boat traffic.

Other Fishing
Bimini offers some of the best offshore fishing in the world for blue and white marlin, king mackerel, bluefin tuna, wahoo, and dolphin.

Accommodations
Anglers stay at the Bimini Big Game Fishing Club, located on North Bimini, a large offshore angling center with a one hundred-slip marina, pool, and tennis courts. The club maintains working agreements with seven or eight good bonefishing guides. Many can capably guide fly-fishing anglers.

Getting There
Flights from Miami and Ft. Lauderdale arrive at the airport on South Bimini. Water taxis make the short ride to the club. Also, Chalk's flies pontoon planes to Bimini harbor from Nassau/Paradise Island, Miami/Watson Island, and Key West.

The Berry Islands

This fragile-looking, delicate, thirty-island chain lies in the middle of prime bonefish waters. It is just south of Grand Bahama Island and north of the Tongue-of-the-Ocean. Bonefish run large on the Berry Islands' flats, averaging as high as seven pounds at Ambergris Cay. Anglers consistently report large ten-pound-plus trophy bones at both Ambergris and Chub Cays. The Berries offer both wading and poled boat bonefishing on over twenty miles of flats stretching north from Chub Cay to Great Harbor and Great Stirrip Cays. Fishing pressure is extremely light.

Other Fishing
Anglers frequently report large schools of permit in this area, and some large individual fish. A forty-pound permit taken in 1987 established the IGFA record for eight-pound line (conventional tackle). Chub Cay functions as a big-game fish center for blue and white marlin, dolphin, and wahoo.

Accommodations
The Chub Cay Club, located in the southern end of the Berry Islands, accommodates big-game fishermen more than flats fishermen. But it can also arrange fishing with several local bonefishing guides. The club is semi-private but offers its dining room and some rental rooms to the general public. Great

Brad Babson, grandson of bonefishing author and pioneer Stanley Babson, stands in front of the family cottage in the small Bahamian out-island village of Dunmore Town after an afternoon fishing the flats off Eleuthera.

Harbour Cay Club, located on the northern end of the Berries, on Great Harbour Cay near Bullock's Harbour, offers an eighty-slip marina, two restaurants, and a nearby nine-hole golf course.

Getting There

Miami, Nassau, and Ft. Lauderdale flights arrive at Chub Cay and Great Harbour Cay. A short taxi ride from the airport takes you to either of the two resorts.

North Eleuthera / Harbour Island

Harbour Island and its picturesque, colorful village of Dunmore Town lie just off the northeast corner of North Eleuthera, one of the largest Bahamian islands. While the east side of Harbour Island faces the Atlantic with pristine pink beaches, the west side overlooks a channel and a modest but productive array of bonefish flats, mangrove stands, and marly creeks. Harbour Island functions as a water sports center for diving, snorkeling, boating, and sun-bathing. It is very popular as a family vacation destination.

Fish average five pounds on the North Eleuthera flats. When water temperature and tides are favorable, anglers often see larger fish up to twelve or thirteen pounds. Fishing pressure can be heavy in the high season of

February through April, however, and big fish here can be as sophisticated as those in the Florida Keys. Boating pressure and water sports can also be a problem.

Other Fishing

Marinas offer some limited offshore fishing. Bottom and reef fishing can also be arranged.

Accommodations

Three resorts on Harbour Island serve anglers. The most convenient is the Romora Bay Club, which overlooks the harbor and has a dock where guides can pick up guests. Dunmore Beach, a New England inn-type resort, and Runaway Hill, a small, intimate hideaway, are both on the ocean side of the island. You walk or taxi to the town fishing dock to meet guides.

Getting There

Miami, Ft. Lauderdale, and Nassau flights arrive at North Eleuthera airport. A short cab ride and water taxi ferry you to Harbour Island.

Andros Island

Andros sits smack in the middle of the Bahamas, about 150 miles southeast of Miami. This largest Bahamian island, forty miles wide and over a hundred miles long, is sparsely inhabited, with only 2400 people. Three east-west bights divide the island across its middle, rimmed by thousands of acres of flats. Sand flats also border the island's east and west coasts. Just east of the island, at the edge of Tongue-of-the-Ocean, the water plunges to a depth of six thousand feet — one of the deepest points in the world.

Andros' bonefish average five pounds. Anglers commonly see both large schools of small fish and many pods of threes and fours. Ten- to fifteen-pound fish are seen frequently. The abundance of remote flats requires anglers to use boats for most fishing. Andros has more fishable flats than any other island in the Caribbean and West Indies, with hundreds of miles of channels and cays lacing its large bights. Both the east and west sides of the island contain acres of firm-bottomed sand flats, which offer good wading and good visibility. The bights partially protect anglers from winds, but their softer bottoms require boats for most fishing.

Fishing pressure at Andros remains fairly low, but it may be increasing with this destination's growing popularity. Guides here are quite capable and some have Florida Keys training. Some Andros lodges now offer day trips to the southwestern tip of the island, which contains many fish in both large schools and small pods. Few anglers have fished here. Those who have report very large daily catches, calling it the Christmas Island of the Atlantic.

Other Fishing

You can see tarpon year-round at Andros, mainly in the creeks on the west coast. Anglers have landed fish in the thirty- to sixty-pound range. Permit average eight to twelve pounds, but anglers have taken them as big as forty. Reefs here hold snapper and grouper, and the Tongue-of-the-Ocean area produces marlin, dolphin, mackerel, tuna, and wahoo.

Accommodations

Most anglers stay at the Andros Island Bonefish Club, Cargill Creek Lodge, or Charlie's Haven, mid-way down the east coast near the North Bight. Both the Bonefish Club and Cargill offer experienced guides and equipment and are geared to serious fishermen. Charlie's Haven, one of the oldest bonefishing lodges in the Bahamas, has basic clean rooms and is run by Charlie Smith, after whom the Nasty Charlie was named. Cargill offers the best accommodations.

Getting There

Flights arrive daily at Andros Town from Nassau and Miami. You reach lodges by a thirty-minute taxi ride.

The Exumas

This spine-like, one hundred-mile long chain of islands and cays lies east and southeast of Andros. Largely uninhabited, even its capital, Georgetown, contains only eight hundred residents. Located in the middle of the Bahamas, the Exumas border Eleuthera, Cat Island, and Exuma Sound to the east, and the six-thousand-foot-deep Tongue-of-the-Ocean to the west.

Site of the annual Bahamas Bonefishing Tournament, the Exumas offer an abundance of bonefish flats. Fish are in the four- to six-pound range and anglers sometimes see larger fish. A thirteen-pound, twelve-ounce bonefish was caught here in 1956 on conventional gear, an IGFA record for the twenty-pound saltwater line class. Flats here allow both wading and poled-boat fishing.

Other Fishing

The Exumas offer good offshore fishing for a wide variety of fish, including blue and white marlin, king mackerel, bluefin tuna, wahoo, and dolphin.

Accommodations

The Peace and Plenty Hotel, located in Georgetown on Great Exuma, over-looks Elizabeth Harbor. Anglers reach flats and guides via a six-mile taxi ride. (The newer Peace and Plenty Beach Inn is on Bonefish Bay, about a mile away.) The Out Island Inn, Exuma's largest hotel, overlooks the harbor and has its own guides and skiffs.

Getting There

Flights arrive from Ft. Lauderdale and Nassau at Georgetown. Travelers reach hotels by a twenty-minute taxi ride.

Long Island

Long Island lies along the edge of the Atlantic Ocean. Sixty miles long and only three miles wide, it runs south and east of the Exumas toward the Acklins and Inagua Islands. Long Island's western shore borders the eastern edge of the Grand Bahama Bank. Its high eastern shore, with an elevation of over 175 feet, drops steeply to the Atlantic.

Long Island bonefish, typical of those of many Bahamas fisheries, average four to six pounds. Anglers fish by both poled boat and wading. Stella Maris, the island's one resort, has several nearby flats. Additional flats and creeks are located at the northern tip of the island at Cape Santa Maria, and require a twenty-mile taxi ride from Stella Maris. Fishing pressure is light.

Other Fishing

Anglers occasionally see permit on the flats. Extensive deep-sea fishing off-shore attracts many people.

Accommodations

The Stella Maris Inn on the northern part of Long Island maintains five guides and boats, limiting the number of poled-skiff bonefishermen to ten.

Getting There

Flights service Long Island from Miami and Nassau. Reaching Stella Maris requires a short taxi ride from the airport.

BISCAYNE BAY AND THE FLORIDA KEYS

The cradle of modern bonefishing offers the biggest fish and the most experi-enced guides. From Miami south through Key Biscayne to Islamorada, Mara-thon, and Key West, this area contains some of the best bonefishing in the

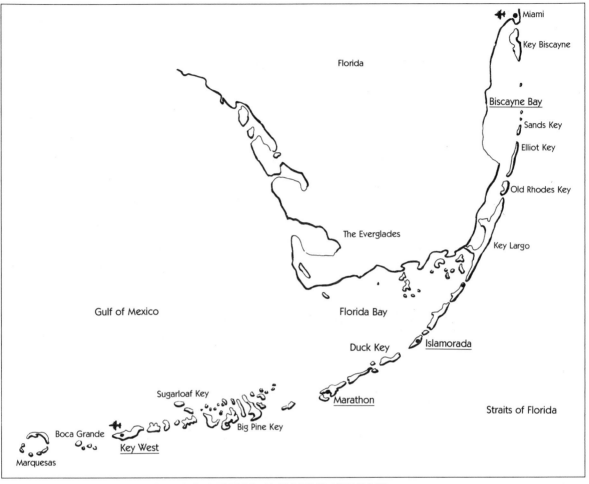

FLORIDA BONEFISHING DESTINATIONS
Bonefishing in Florida extends from Miami's Biscayne Bay, through Islamorada and Marathon, to Key West.

world. Yet, located at the northern limit of bonefishing, it experiences a shorter season than many tropical flats destinations. Boating, tourist, and fishing pressure are all high and the fishery is constantly threatened by pollution, netting, and civilization in general. But the Florida area offers anglers the biggest fish and the most experienced bonefishing guides in the world.

Biscayne Bay

The Biscayne Bay area, just south of Miami, serves as the northern border of bonefishing in the Atlantic. The flats begin at the Rickenbacker Causeway.

From there, they extend south in a string of shallows that stretch along the shores of Soldier Key, Ragged Key, Sands Key, Elliot Key, and Old Rhodes Key, ending at Key Largo. Many people live, work, and play in this area. Biscayne Bay bonefish see a lot of anglers and heavy boat traffic.

Most anglers fish this area by poled skiff. Fish run very large here and Biscayne Bay has accounted for a number of trophy bonefish over the years. Fish average an amazing six to eight pounds. April and May are peak months.

Other Fishing

IGFA saltwater line class records taken in the Biscayne Bay and Miami areas include horse-eye jack, king mackerel, Spanish mackerel, permit, Atlantic sailfish, hammerhead shark, cubera snapper, and skipjack tuna.

Accommodations

Anglers can choose from many budget to luxury accommodations in the Key Biscayne/greater Miami area. Most are within a twenty- to thirty-minute drive of major marinas. The Budgetel Inn, the Hampton Inn, and the Fairfield Inn-by Marriott, all located near the Miami International Airport, offer modern, clean accommodations for under $70 a night. The Silver Sands Motel has moderately expensive oceanfront accommodations on Key Biscayne proper. The Sonesta Beach Hotel and Tennis Club, also on Key Biscayne, is a full-scale luxury resort with health club, tennis, and numerous water-sports activities.

Getting There

You reach the Biscayne Bay area by a twenty-minute drive from the Miami International Airport.

Upper, Middle, and Lower Keys

The Florida Keys stretch roughly 110 miles off the southern tip of Florida, arcing to the southwest from Key Largo to Key West. A single highway, U.S. Route 1, runs down its spine, conveniently announcing distances with mile-marker signs throughout its length.

The Upper Keys extend from Key Largo at the bottom of Biscayne Bay south to the Matecumbes. They include the important bonefishing center of Islamorada. The Middle Keys edge south from Lower Matecumbe through Marathon, a second major bonefishing center. The Lower Keys consist of the rest of the keys and islets down to Key West. This is primarily a tarpon and permit center, but bonefishing is also popular.

Bonefishing in the Keys is productive on both the Atlantic Ocean side of the Keys and on the western Florida Bay side. As commonly occurs at other

The Florida Keys hold large, wary bonefish. Angler Ben Estes, guided by Captain Eddie Wightman, landed this 11-pounder off Shell Key using his rapid-epoxy fly pattern. (Photograph by Captain Eddie Wightman.)

bonefishing destinations, bonefish tend to follow the tide cycles as they feed. These Florida Keys waters, however, are intricate, varied, and difficult to read. Fish will favor one flat on one cycle of the tide and a different flat on another. Guides are indispensable in figuring out which is which.

Keys bonefish run very large here. Anglers have taken two of the five IGFA saltwater fly-rod world records at Islamorada, a thirteen-pound, four-ounce fish taken on an eight-pound tippet in 1973 and a fourteen-pound, six-ounce fish taken on a twelve-pound tippet in 1985. Of fourteen IGFA saltwater line class world records, eight were taken in the Keys, seven of them at Islamorada. The largest was a fourteen-pound, ten-ounce fish taken on eight-pound line in 1988.

Most Florida Keys bonefishing consists of poled-boat fishing. Anglers can wade on some of the firmer flats on the ocean side of the Keys and even in a few bay-side areas. But most anglers here prefer to fish from skiffs.

The Florida Keys offer the largest number of guides (and the most experienced) of any bonefishing destination in the world. Some guides specialize in spinning, others in fly fishing. Some also differentiate themselves among bonefish, tarpon, and permit. But many guide for all species. Most Keys guides work out of one of three areas: Islamorada, Marathon, or Key West. They normally use sixteen-foot or larger shallow-draft hulls with large outboard motors that let them cover the long distances to remote flats fast. Once at a flat, anglers are quietly poled into position to find and cast to feeding fish.

While the day rates for Florida's guides and boats approach the high end of the range among all destinations, a Keys guide can teach you a lot in a short time. They can also show you flats and fish you would never see at most other

"Outside" flats, unlike inside flats, are close to the ocean and more exposed to wave and tidal action. They hold rich stores of prey in their scattered grass beds and in their burrow-filled firm-sand bottoms. They are usually ideal for wading. Most flats on the east side of the Florida Keys are outside flats, as are those at the edges of atolls such as the Turneffe Islands.

destinations. If you wish, you can also rent a boat and fish on your own in the Keys. You can learn which flats are safe and productive for wading. Or you can split your time between wading and poled-boat fishing. You will learn much by both methods.

Day rates for a guide average $275 to $350 for a full day, with one or two anglers per boat. Guides can be arranged through most major marinas in the Keys, including the following:

- Ocean Reef Club, Key Largo-(305)367-2611
- Holiday Isle, Islamorada-(305)664-2321
- Whale Harbour Marina, Islamorada-(305)664-4511
- Bud-'N-Mary's Marina, Islamorada-(305)664-2461

- Islamorada Yacht Basin, Islamorada-(305)664-4338
- Hawk's Cay Marina, Marathon-(305)432-2242
- Garrison Bight, Key West-(305)294-3093
- Oceanside Marina, Key West-(305)294-4676
- Lands End Marina, Key West-(305)296-3838

Some local outfitters also book anglers with guides. Two headquartered in Islamorada are World Wide Sportsman (George Hommell) and World Class Outfitters (Randy Towe).

The prime time to fish for bonefish in the Keys is April, May, and early June, depending on the temperature. Mid-summer water temperatures are usually too warm to hold as many fish. But fall, apart from hurricanes, can sometimes see them return as heavily as the spring season. Rates are lower, too.

"Inside" flats — those that have barriers such as keys, peninsulas, and shorelines to protect them from direct scouring by the ocean — have soft bottoms that discourage wading. Found in locations such as the back country of the Florida Keys and the bights of Andros, these inner flats offer abundant prey, many bonefish, and sheltered fishing areas.

Other Fishing

Florida offers an astonishing abundance of fishing. Bonefishing anglers can fish for tarpon and permit in addition to their primary quarry. The entire 4,000 square miles of shallows in the Keys hold tarpon. Two of the six IGFA saltwater tarpon fly-rod world records were set in Marathon in 1985: a 127-pound tarpon taken on eight-pound tippet and a forty-two-pound, eight-ounce tarpon taken on four-pound tippet. Peak is April through June.

Also, Key West offers one of the best permit fisheries in the world. All five IGFA saltwater fly-rod records for permit were set here, two at Key West and three at nearby Sugarloaf Key. The largest of these was a forty-one-pound eight-ounce permit taken with eight-pound tippet in 1986 off Key West.

Accommodations

In the upper Keys, the Shoreline Motel and the Ocean View at Holiday Isle, both in Islamorada, offer compact, economical, but very well-kept rooms. Plantation Yacht Harbour, also in Islamorada, features moderately priced accommodations in a resort setting with tennis courts, pool, and marina. Cheeca Lodge in Islamorada and Ocean Reef Club in Key Largo are both luxurious, full-service resorts.

In the Middle Keys, the Coral Lagoon Resort and the Faro Blanco Resort, in Marathon, each offer attractive, well-maintained, and moderately priced rooms. Rainbow Bend, a small resort located on Grassy Key near Marathon, rents moderately priced units and caters to fishermen. Prices include daily use of Boston Whalers. Hawk's Cay, located on Duck Key north of Marathon, is a sixty-acre resort island with expensive accommodations and full-resort services.

In the Lower Keys, John Cole's Key West Angler's Club appeals to many fly fishermen. The Comfort Inn and the Blue Marlin Motel in Key West both offer modern, spacious, and moderately priced rooms. The Pier House and Pelican Landing function as expensive, full-service resorts with luxurious accommodations.

Getting There

Flights from Miami arrive at Key West daily. You can also drive the entire length of the Keys on U.S. Highway 1.

MEXICO'S YUCATAN PENINSULA

Mexico's Yucatan Peninsula extends along the 220-mile coastline of the Mexican state of Quintana Roo. It ranges from Cancun at its north border to Belize at its southern edge. The most productive bonefishing here is at Boca

Paila/Pez Maya and Ascension Bay. These two areas hold large schools of small to moderate-sized fish. They also offer anglers one of the best chances in the world for a grand slam of permit, tarpon, and bonefish. Boca Paila/Pez Maya destinations also have some advantages for anglers traveling with a non-fishing spouse, with nature trips, golf, and tours of Mayan ruins nearby.

Boca Paila/Pez Maya Area

Some outfitters say they book the Boca Paila/Pez Maya area, which natives call "the Rio," more frequently than any other bonefishing destination. East Coast and Midwest anglers like it because they can travel to it quickly and it offers them a chance at ten to twenty bonefish per day.

Bonefish flats here produce a large number of smaller fish, averaging two to four pounds, and anglers sometimes catch over one hundred fish in a week. Extensive flats, lagoons, and mangrove islands give anglers a variety of fishing environments, allowing them to find shelter from winds. Most fishing is done from skiffs, but wading is possible on some hard-bottomed flats.

South of the Rio lies the remote, less-populated flats of Ascension Bay. Anglers reach them from Boca Paila by a two-hour boat ride (see Ascension Bay Area, below).

Other Fishing

Small tarpon under twenty-five pounds, snook, and permit in the ten- to fifteen-pound range offer anglers alternatives to bonefishing.

Accommodations

Two resorts in the Rio area offer bonefishing and both have comparable accommodations, Boca Paila and Pez Maya. Both are comfortable, attractive, and suitable for non-fishing companions.

Getting There

Flights from most major U.S. cities arrive daily at Cancun. Travel to Boca Paila and Pez Maya requires a two-hour taxi ride south from Cancun.

Ascension Bay Area

The Ascension Bay flats lie inside an enormous bay located halfway down the coast of Mexico's Quintana Roo on the Yucatan Peninsula. They are about twenty-five miles south of the Boca Paila area.

The perimeter of Ascension Bay shelters its flats to a limited extent from weather and winds. Combined with its southerly location and temperate climate, Ascension Bay offers anglers a destination that is less sensitive to winter weather than many other bonefishing locations.

In the coldest months, the mangrove-studded cayes and islets of places like Mexico's Ascension Bay offer protection from winds and chilling temperatures.

Bonefish here average two to four pounds, but anglers will encounter some five-pound and larger fish as well. Ascension Bay contains mostly hard-bottomed flats and supports both wading and poled-skiff fishing. Boats from resorts reach most flats in a few minutes.

The area offers good variety, with many sand and grass flats as well as lagoons bordered by mangroves. Some easily reached, popular flats have been named (Laguna Santa Rosa, Esperanza, and Tres Mares), but most anglers find fishing pressure here extremely low. You seldom see another fisherman. Guides are moderately to highly experienced and all bonefishing is catch-and-release.

Ascension Bay's expansive flats stretch over six hundreds square miles. They may comprise the largest single complex of flats in the Atlantic after the Bahamas. Happily, they lie in the middle of a 1.2 million-acre nature preserve that should guarantee their future.

Other Fishing

Ascension Bay also holds permit in the ten-pound class, mostly in schools, with occasional larger fish seen. Small tarpon in the fifteen- to twenty-pound range also feed here occasionally, as well as jack crevalle, barracuda, and snapper.

Accommodations

The Ascension Bay Bonefish Club, on Punta Allen, sits on the northern end of Ascension Bay. Run by Jan Isley, a former Key West guide, this intimate lodge caters to only six anglers at a time. Casa Blanca stands on the tip of Isla Casa Blanca at the southern mouth of Ascension Bay. The comfortable lodge, opened in 1989, is remote and entirely self-contained. The lodge provides guides and skiffs.

Getting There

Flights travel from many U.S. cities to Cancun daily. A 2 1/2-hour taxi ride takes you to the Ascension Bay Bonefish Club. A forty-five-minute charter flies you from Cancun to Casa Blanca.

BELIZE

Belize, formerly British Honduras, lies just south of Mexico's Yucatan Peninsula. Located five hundred to six hundred miles farther south than the Bahamas and Florida, Belize has lush rain-forest jungles growing along its coastline. It offers a more tropical environment for hunting bonefish than northerly locations. Belize contains four bonefishing areas: the mainland coastal flats; the flats around Ambergris Caye at the northern end of its coastline; and two flats areas that lie inside offshore atolls.

Bonefishing in Belize varies considerably from one area to another and you should study them closely to see which matches your requirements. Some areas have mostly large schools of smaller fish, while others, like the Turneffe Islands, also hold large fish. Some places, such as Ambergris Caye, offer only poled-skiff fishing, while others can be both waded and fished by boat. Belize contains one of the most varied fisheries of any bonefish destination, with abundant permit, tarpon, snook, and barracuda. For non-fishing companions, it also offers diving and snorkeling along its great barrier reef, which is larger than any other in the world except Australia's.

Climate is sub-tropical, with temperatures of sixty-seven to eighty-eight degrees Fahrenheit year-round. From November through March easterly winds blow in from the Atlantic. Constant winds blow at Turneffe Island and Glover's Reef locations, as they do at other atoll-type flats like Christmas Island and Los Roques.

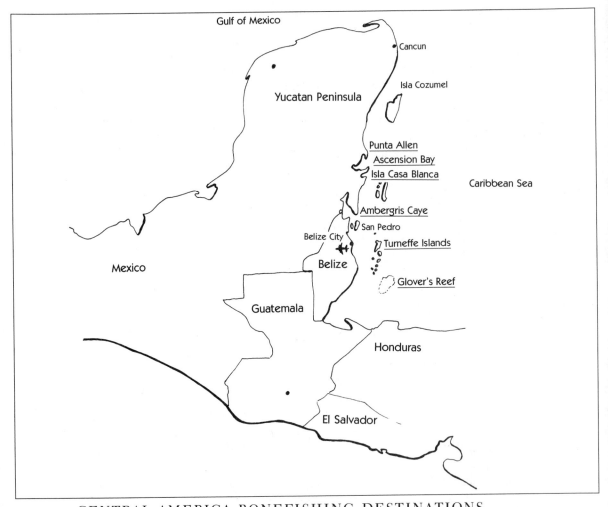

CENTRAL AMERICA BONEFISHING DESTINATIONS
Mexico's Ascension Bay and Rio areas offer large schools of bonefish. Belize features the most varied bonefishing, with mainland flats, Ambergris Caye, Turneffe Islands, and Glover's Reef.

Mainland Flats

Numerous flats and cayes lie off the mainland and are easily accessible by boat. Anglers who fish these flats, inland of the great barrier reefs, will find them somewhat silty, soft-bottomed, and unsuitable for wading. Constant wind and wave action, along with active feeding fish, turn these waters muddy daily. This limits most sight-fishing to hunting for easily spotted, tailing fish. Fish average two to four pounds. Schools of twenty-five to fifty or more fish are common.

Other Fishing

Other coastal fishing is primarily lagoon and river fishing for tarpon and snook. Tarpon average twenty pounds, but fish over one hundred pounds have been landed. Snook run about fifteen pounds.

Accommodations

Anglers fish the mainland flats from Belize River lodge, which is one mile from salt water on the western shore of the Belize River. The lodge also offers river and backcountry tarpon fishing and fifty-foot cruisers to offshore flats.

Getting There

Flights are available from U.S. cities to Belize City. Cabs take about ten minutes to reach the lodge from the airport.

Ambergris Caye Flats

Inside the barrier reef sits Ambergris Caye, which is the geological end of the Yucatan Peninsula. Located fifteen miles offshore of Belize's northernmost coast, the caye occupies an area about the size of the state of Vermont. It has its own small airport. Two lodges accommodate flats anglers.

Anglers in this area fish from poled skiffs to large schools of two- to four-pound fish. Some fish run larger. The area contains an abundance of shallow flats but their soft bottoms do not support wading. Lodges can arrange for local guides.

Other Fishing

Sight-fishing for permit and tarpon also attracts anglers to Ambergris Caye. Permit run larger than in the Yucatan, but smaller than in the Bahamas and Keys. Tarpon average twenty to one hundred pounds. Some bigger fish are found in crystal-clear, three- to five-foot-deep waters.

Accommodations

Two lodges are located on Ambergris Caye, the El Pescador Lodge, one of the most established in this area, and the newer Belizian, a deluxe, intimate hideaway. Both have docking facilities.

Getting There

Airlines fly daily from many U.S. cities to Belize City. From there you take a short flight to the San Pedro airport on Ambergris Caye, then taxi to the resorts.

Turneffe Islands and Glover's Reef

Belize offers anglers two offshore atoll bonefishing areas. The Turneffe Islands, Belize's largest and northern-most atoll, lie thirty miles off the coast. Typical of most atolls, the Turneffe area consists of a ring of reefs that rises abruptly from the ocean floor, surrounding a circular lagoon full of sand flats, cayes, mud, and mangrove stands. Farther south, Glover's Reef provides anglers a second, though smaller, atoll fishery.

The bonefish of the Turneffe Islands average three to five pounds, with large schools seen every day. As in the Bahamas, anglers see larger singles and doubles often and, on occasion, some trophy fish over ten pounds. Anglers find wading and visibility excellent on bottoms of hard sand and coral with scattered grass. Large fish often feed selectively here. They can become extremely nervous in the thin water of the atolls. Anglers sometimes stalk fish in water so shallow they can see the fish's eyes and backs bulge from the water.

Anglers can also fish deeper water in reef areas where fish hunt for churned-up prey. Reef bonefish are less skittish, but these large fish usually run across coral when hooked, destroying leaders and fly line. Drifting in poled boats is also available. The farthest flats are about thirty minutes away from the lodges.

Other Fishing

The Belize atolls offer anglers good permit fishing. Small tarpon also appear on the flats. Offshore anglers can pursue blue and white marlin, wahoo, tuna, and king mackerel, and anglers can fish the reefs for barracuda, snapper, and grouper.

Accommodations

The Turneffe Islands offer anglers two lodges. Turneffe Flats sits on the northeastern side of the islands, one thousand yards from the reef. Turneffe Island Lodge, located on Caye Bokel on the southern side of the islands, also offers diving.

Glover's Reef has one lodge — Manta Reef Resort — which is located on a remote, twelve-acre site and is limited to four anglers at a time. It offers diving for non-fishing guests.

Getting There

Airlines fly daily from many U.S. cities to Belize City. Both a taxi ride and a boat ride are required to reach the lodges, with two hours traveling necessary for the Turneffe Islands and over three hours for Glover's Reef.

LITTLE CAYMAN ISLAND

The Caymans contain small bonefish and few serious flats anglers fish here. The area, however, may offer an interesting alternative to certain anglers. Since the Caymans have some of the best diving in the world as well as an unusual landlocked tarpon fishery, travelers with multiple interests may find it a desirable destination.

Little Cayman, the smallest of the three-island Cayman chain in the British West Indies, lies south of Havana and east of the Yucatan's Boca Paila. It offers a somewhat more temperate climate than the more northerly flats of Florida and the Bahamas.

Cayman bonefish average two to three pounds and travel in large schools. Anglers use light tackle in the 5- to 7-weight range and practice strict catch-and-release. Lodges arrange for guides, and anglers can both wade and drift-fish. The flats, while not extensive, see little pressure, as fishing is limited by the small number of guests.

Other Fishing

Anglers can fish for landlocked baby tarpon in the two- to fifteen-pound class in a small inland lake nearby. Deep-sea fishing is offshore.

Accommodations

Anglers can stay at the Southern Cross Club, situated on a one thousand-foot-long white sandy beach on Little Cayman. The club provides fly-fishing equipment and flies.

Getting There

Flights from many U.S. cities land at Grand Cayman. You reach Little Caymen by a connecting flight on Cayman Airways, then a one-mile taxi ride from the airport.

VENEZUELA

The tidal flats of Los Roques sprawl across the inside of an oval-shaped atoll eighty miles north of the coast of Venezuela. The flats are dominated by El Gran Roque, a steep, rocky island inhabited by about five hundred lobster and conch fishermen. The rest of the area remains unpopulated, and Venezuela has made it a national park, restricting further development.

Los Roques bonefish grow larger than those of the Yucatan and Belize fisheries, but most are smaller than the fish of Bimini and Florida. They average about five pounds, with fish sighted in the eight- to twelve-pound range.

Anglers sometimes compare Los Roques to the Pacific Ocean's Christmas Island, because, like the Pacific atoll fishery, Los Roques fish are plentiful and come in many large schools.

Los Roques flats cover a seemingly endless one hundred fifty-square-mile area inside the atoll. Most flats contain firm bottoms and vary from white sand to turtle grass or coral. Several hundred cayes and islands provide variety and some shelter from daily winds. Boats ferry anglers to and from the flats, which anglers fish by wading. Outfitters recommend April to September as prime season; January through March can be windy and have tides and temperatures that make fishing unpredictable. Fishing pressure is low except for a couple of close-in flats near El Gran Roque. Guide experience is generally low.

Other Fishing
Los Roques offers fishing for jacks, mackerel, barracuda, snapper, and grouper at the edge of flats, with a major billfish population offshore. Five- to twenty-pound tarpon inhabit mangrove lagoons at Rio Chico and anglers fish for peacock bass at inland Guri Lake.

Accommodations
The Macabi Lodge, a small, colonial-style inn, provides accommodations to anglers on El Gran Roque and transports them in thirty-foot boats to fishable wading flats.

Getting There
Flights connect many U.S. cities with Caracas. An air charter carries you to the Gran Roque airport, then you cab to the inn.

CHRISTMAS ISLAND

Christmas Island, one of the largest coral atolls in the world, sprawls across the mid-Pacific Ocean 1200 miles south of Hawaii and about one hundred miles north of the equator. Part of the Gilbert Island chain, it is in the republic of Kiribati (pronounced Kir-uh-bas).

Christmas Island presents anglers with an enormous 640-square-mile patchwork of flats scattered across a huge lagoon area inside the atoll. Some flats are so small anglers can wade them in minutes. Others stretch for miles and take hours. Some flats offer shallow fishing, others feature deeper water as they slope to the blue water outside the atoll. Many deep channels lace across the flats, connecting one feeding area to another.

Most flats contain firm, sandy bottoms with good visibility. Anglers reach some flats in water taxis or punts, others by van over narrow unpaved roads.

In many ways Christmas Island ranks as the ideal bonefishing destination. It holds huge numbers of fish year-round. While fish average about five pounds, many fish in the six- to nine-pound range feed here and anglers see ten- to fifteen-pounders year-round. So many fish inhabit this huge atoll, anglers can often average one or two dozen fish a day and sometimes many more. A skilled angler will probably take more bonefish here than at any other known bonefishing destination except possibly the Yucatan, where fish run much smaller.

Several aspects of Christmas Island may compromise this destination for anglers, however. It takes longer for East-coast anglers to travel to Kiribati than to any other bonefishing destination. Once there, lengthy treks to the flats consume fishing time. While the area's bright sand flats offer some of the best wading in the world, anglers who have a strong preference for fishing from skiffs may find it disappointing. The abundance of coral can also be a problem, and anglers must take care to prevent damage to leaders and fly lines. Spring tides here present a special problem, because daily tides are unequal in height. During new and full moons when the low tides are at their lowest, flats are emptied of water. Bonefishing is limited primarily to the highest high tides, often only five hours a day.

But most anglers who have fished many destinations feel that Christmas Island is the best place in the world for beginners. You can catch large numbers of medium-sized bonefish and get more experience handling fish here than at most other places. Because of the fish density and excellent visibility, you will find it easier to fish here than at most Atlantic destinations. On balance, Christmas Island can be something of a bonefish heaven for many anglers.

Christmas Island's location on the equator gives it the most reliable year-round climate of all bonefishing destinations. Temperatures stay consistently in the mid-eighties or higher during the days and drop to about seventy-two degrees at night. The area does not experience the frequent cold fronts that can push fish off the flats in many Atlantic destinations. Except for wind, which blows hardest in winter, it is difficult to tell a day in August from one in January. Some wind occurs daily year-round, mostly from the east and ranges from ten to twenty miles per hour, which is common to most bonefishing destinations. Winds are calmest in June, July, and August.

Other Fishing

Anglers also fish here for one hundred-pound giant trevally, blue trevally to fifteen pounds, and striped trevally to twenty pounds. Offshore fishing offers marlin, sailfish, yellowfin, and wahoo.

Accommodations

The Captain Cook Hotel, run by the Kiribati government, provides the only accommodation on Christmas Island. The hotel offers anglers clean and comfortable, but not luxurious, facilities.

Getting There

U.S. airlines fly daily into Honolulu. From there, a once-a-week flight connects Christmas Island. Flight time is two hours, forty-five minutes.

SPECIALIZED TRAVEL SERVICES

Several travel companies and outfitters specialize in making arrangements for fly-fishing anglers. A few have considerable experience in saltwater flats destinations. Since many lodges (except those in the Florida Keys) only book reservations through these specialized travel agencies, the agent's services are virtually pre-paid. Anglers should take advantage of them. They will not only make the physical travel arrangements, they can also help with destination selection, tackle, and other gear required.

Most outfitters employ at least one or two individuals who travel to the major flats locations regularly and can answer questions on tides, fishing, seasonality, flies, arrangements for a non-fishing travel partner, or getting your tackle there intact.

Many of them are also exploring new bonefishing destinations that may well hold virgin fishing opportunities for the future. Some of the most interesting areas being investigated are the Bikini Islands, Fanning Island, the Cook Islands, and the Republic of Tonga in the South Pacific, and the north and south coasts of Cuba. Some of the more experienced outfitters specializing in bonefishing trips are included in Table 13.4.

TABLE 13.4
SPECIALIZED TRAVEL SERVICES

COMPANY	ADDRESS	TELEPHONE	CONTACT
Angler Adventures	P.O. Box 872 Old Lyme, CT 06371	(203) 434-9624 (800) 628-1447	Chip Bates Doug Schlink
Blue Ribbon Flies	P.O. Box 1037 West Yellowstone, MT 59758	(406) 646-7642	Craig Mathews Jackie Mathews
Club Pacific	790A 27th Ave. San Francisco, CA 94121	(415) 752-0192	Mel Krieger
Fishing International	P.O. Box 2132 Santa Rosa, CA 95405	(800) 950-4242	Bob Nauheim
The Fly Shop	4140 Churn Creek Rd. Redding, CA 96002	(916) 222-3555	Mike Michalak
Frontiers	P.O. Box 959 Wexford, PA 15090	(800) 245-1950	Mike Fitzgerald Susie Fitzgerald
Pan Angling Travel	180 N. Michigan Chicago, IL 60601	(312) 263-0328	Jim Chapralis
Pathways International	P.O. Box 3276 Spartanburg, SC 29304	(800) 628-5060	Will Hudson
The Saltwater Angler	219 Simonton St. Key West, FL 33040	(305) 296-7272	Jeffrey Cardenas
World Class Outfitters	P.O. Box 1571 Islamorada, FL 33036	(305) 852-3177	Randy Towe
World Wide Sportsman	P.O. Box 787 Islamorada, FL 33036	(305) 664-4615	George Hommell
Seasons International	P.O. Box 885 Exeter, NH 03833	(800) 788-4567 (603) 772-6600	Lynn Hendrickson

14

Advice from Some Veterans of the Flats

There are not many anglers with extensive experience in this sport of bonefishing with flies. I have known a few of them. I have come to know a few more while writing this book — gifted and generous fishermen who gave freely of their time and advice.

Most of these flats veterans share a few critical traits. They crave high-intensity angling. They are compulsive about their tackle and technique. And they share a compelling passion for this sport and this game fish — a passion you can almost feel in their words when they speak of it.

But each of these fishermen is different, too. Some fish a single place hundreds of days each year. Others have fished nearly every location in the world that bonefish inhabit. Some concentrate on presentation. Some focus on their fly choices. Others emphasize understanding the fish itself. But one thing they all share is a willingness to help others in the sport. They will freely pass along advice and insight they have learned the hard way. Their experiences are offered here that others might learn from them.

JIM ORTHWEIN

Jim Orthwein, a St. Louis investor, retired chairman of a major U.S. advertising firm, and owner of the New England Patriots, holds three bonefish fly-rod world records. All three fish were taken in Bimini, and all three succumbed to the same fly pattern — Jim's Golden Eye Shrimp.

Bonefishing techniques vary. Some work better at one location than another. Some suit one angler's style better than another. But wherever you fish and whatever your preferences, the experiences offered by the eleven veteran guides and flats anglers included in this chapter can broaden your perspective.

Casting and Stripping Strategy

Casting and stripping depend largely on three factors: the speed at which the fish are traveling; the depth of the water; and the size and sink rate of your fly. It is necessary to cast farther in front of fast-moving fish than in front of slow-moving fish and to cast still farther in front of fast-moving fish in deep water, so that your fly has time to sink before the fish get to it.

When fishing a shrimp imitation, I strip it steadily about a foot or slightly more at a time. If I am fishing a crab imitation, I first let it sink and then give it a few erratic jerks, then stop, let it sink again, and repeat.

I cast as close to tailing fish as possible, and when casting to pairs or more of cruising fish I try to get the fly between them, where two or more of them can see it at the same time. It is very important not to cast past the fish and best to present your fly in front of and on the near side of cruising fish. If you cast into a school of fish,

JIM ORTHWEIN

be sure only your fly and leader, and not your line, penetrate the school.

Drag Setting

I recommend a light to medium-light drag and I never tighten it during a run. At times it may be necessary to loosen it during a long run, but normally I set a light drag to begin with and don't fool with it. I do not use palming techniques except possibly when the fish is being netted. There is no way that palming techniques can equal a good, smooth disc drag.

Playing Fish and Line Management

More bonefish are lost getting the slack line from the bottom of the boat onto the reel than at any other time. Making a circle with your thumb and index finger and letting the line run loosely through it is a good way to accomplish this, as long as you remember not to pinch the line between your fingers.

On the initial runs at least, hold your rod as high above your head as possible to keep the line and the fish off the bottom. Keep your rod tip pointed at the fish. When the fish is tiring and fairly close to the boat, you can drop the rod tip and put pressure on the fish at a ninety-degree angle to his head, thus turning and tiring him further.

Length of Runs by Large Fish

I have had large bonefish run off over two hundred yards of backing at unbelievable speed. My fifteen-pound record bonefish made four of these long runs and then numerous ones of shorter and shorter distances, and finally came to the net after circling the boat for at least ten minutes in shorter and shorter circles. I have hooked two bonefish, which my guide Rudy Dames and I estimated at twenty pounds, that took all my backing and kept going, one on the first run and one on the second run—a disappointing experience but one that brings you back.

Sighting Fish

There are five methods of spotting bonefish: tailing, riffling, flashing, mudding, and finning. You can add to this trailing them on the bottom and hearing them. Bonefish make a unique sound when they are startled.

Jim has also found an interesting way to use cold fronts to his benefit. Taking advantage of the fact that smaller bonefish are more susceptible to cold, at least initially, he likes to fish the early parts of cold fronts. He finds that small fish are forced off the flats, letting him concentrate on large fish without the juveniles always trying to snap up his fly.

Jim uses Seamaster reels, two older anti-reverse models and a newer direct-drive model. He also likes the inexpensive Valentine reels. For rods, Jim uses 9 1/2-foot, 8- and 9-weight Sage rods rigged with Mastery green or gray fly lines. While he usually uses floating lines, he says there is also a place for intermediate lines on windy and wavy days. He uses nine- and twelve-foot leaders, which he connects loop-to-loop to a two-foot Climax forty-two-pound butt that is nail-knotted to his line.

CAPT. VIC GASPENY

Vic Gaspeny has been a Florida Keys guide since 1975. He holds the current saltwater fly-rod world record for the twelve-pound tippet class for a fourteen-pound, six-ounce fish he took in Islamorada in 1985. He caught his

CAPTAIN VIC
GASPENY

record fish on a guide's day off, while being poled by friend and Bud-'N-Mary's marina owner Richard Stanczyk.

Knowing When to Strike Bonefish

Many bonefish "takes" go unnoticed because the angler doesn't feel any pull on his line. Typically, when a bonefish is interested, it swings in behind the fly and swims toward the retrieving fisherman. Often, the fish will bite the fly while he's swimming faster than the angler is stripping his fly. It's just like pulling a truck on a rope. If someone is driving the truck toward you, you won't feel any pull at all.

A few strikes are actually *felt* — these are the easiest to hook up on. They occur when a fish takes the fly and turns away instantly. But most of them don't. And if you allow for some bow in the fly line from wind and current, the problem of sensing a strike is compounded even more.

The most successful bonefish anglers, such as Sandy Moret and Richard Stanczyk, read the fish's movement to tell them when to tighten and strike. With fish that are shallow "tailers," the dorsal fin and tail usually rise and twitch when the fish inhales the fly.

In deeper water, any fish that darts toward the fly usually has it. Skiff guide Rick Ruoff told me long ago that when a bonefish follows a fly, it almost always eats it. Thousands of casts later, I'm a believer.

Fish that pursue the fly but don't strike just seem to meander behind the fly. A master of this type of "read" is Capt. John Kipp. He suggests that on these tentative fish you should stop the fly for a moment. If the fish then stops on it, it's usually a take. Often you see the fly line "hop" a bit as the fish inhales.

Years ago, I was explaining this "body language" technique to a fellow guide while we were casting to a pod of large bonefish mudding in four feet of water. My friend cast to a bonefish and it darted toward his fly, then raced away. He insisted the fish didn't bite, until he brought in the fly. Its epoxy head was smashed by the bonefish's crushers.

The body language you should look for depends on the fish. Any of these can mean a strike: a tailing fish that raises and twitches its fins; a fish that darts to the fly (they sort of "quiver" toward it); or a fish that stops on the fly when it stops.

Water Temperature and Feeding Bonefish

I've caught bonefish in water as cold as 61.5 degrees, when the water temperature was warming up after a cold spell. When the temperature is going down, sixty-eight degrees is usually the cut-off point. It's funny that bonefish will quit at sixty-eight degrees when it's dropping and then start up again when it is so much lower. I guess they must adjust to the cold a little bit, and then it doesn't feel so bad at sixty-one degrees or so when it's warming up again.

On the high end, I've caught fish in water as high as 94.2 degrees, but I really have trouble with them over ninety-one degrees. Fly, bait, or otherwise, you can still find a few but you just have trouble getting them to eat.

Flies, Sink Rates, and Water Levels

One of the most important things is getting the fly to the level of the fish. You shouldn't use the same fly for a tailing fish that you use for fishing in four to five feet of water. I usually prefer to change weight on a fly rather than change patterns. You can use lead strips or dress a fly thinner so it is less water-resistant and goes down faster. When I fish in deep water, I like a fly that's big enough to get their attention and make a little push as you move it through the water. These are much more aggressive fish. I may also use a fast sink-tip fly line to get it there quickly. Many's a time, a fly is floating over the fish's head when they are swimming by and the angler thinks he's got it right in them.

His Record Fish

My friend Richard Stanczyk fishes the fly tournaments each spring and I pole him around every year before the competitions. It's how he gets himself tuned up. After the tournament's over he takes me out and poles me around so I get a chance to fish.

So in 1985 he took me out right after the fall tournament was over and I just wanted to catch any fish we could find. I had been guiding so much I hadn't caught any fish myself in months. I told him I just wanted to go anywhere we could find some small fish, so I'd be sure to get one.

But Richard said he knew where there were some big ones, and sure enough he did. He took us to this flat and up comes this one fish—he was so dark and his dorsal fin was folded back, he looked just like a shark.

Richard got the boat in the right position and just waited him out. He deserves half the credit for that fish; he put the boat exactly right. These big fish can hear you pushing the boat if you get too close. But we waited until the fish came to us. He swam toward us at the perfect angle. Then I threw out and got him. He just grabbed up that fly and ran. I could feel him shake his head at the end of the run. He kept trying to rub the hook out of his jaw. Once we saw his size, we ran down to the World Wide Sportsman where George Hommell is an IGFA representative. It turned out that fish was the biggest bonefish ever taken in the twelve-pound tippet category. In fact, it was the second biggest fish ever taken on a fly, period. And I got it on my day off. It was right comical.

Vic likes nine-foot Sage and Loomis rods in 8- to 11-weights, depending on winds and depths. He also likes Abel, Pate, and Fin-Nor reels. He says just about every experienced angler he fishes with uses the direct-drive models. For lines, he feels most of the Cortland and Scientific Anglers weight-forward models work fine. He likes a sinking tip for water more than four or five feet deep, because it gives anglers a more direct connection for hook-ups. Vic uses long leaders —usually 14 feet, tapered with thirty-pound, twenty-pound, and ten-pound clear Stren. He makes sure that his last segment of tippet is always four to six feet long to keep the knot out of the fish's field of vision.

BEN ESTES

Ben Estes, an Augusta, Georgia neurosurgeon, first learned to fly cast and tie flies from Capt. Jimmie Albright. Later in life, Lefty Kreh helped him polish his casting technique. Ben caught his first bonefish on a fly while being poled by his Aunt Frankee, who along with sisters Bonnie and Beulah were three of the Florida Keys' foremost bonefishing guides in the 1940's and 1950's. Today Ben fishes for bonefish regularly in Florida, Christmas Island, Mexico, and the Bahamas. He is also an avid tarpon and permit angler.

Stripping Technique

I learned this stripping technique from noted Keys guide Capt. Eddie Wightman, who I have fished with for many years.

First of all, you need to cast close enough in front of the bonefish for him to see the fly, but not to spook. This is usually three to four feet for tailing fish. Try to have the fly land when the fish is tailing, and try to put it close enough so he can hear a gentle "plop."

For a swimming fish in deeper water cast farther away so the fly will sink to his level. And also so he can intercept it in a natural fashion. The fly should not move toward the fish when it is stripped. The distance to lead the fish can vary from six to twelve feet or more, depending on the depth and speed he is swimming.

What you must do is watch the fish. First make sure he sees the fly. If you are fishing in turtle grass, give a long slow strip to lift the fly up out of the grass. If the bonefish does not seem to see the fly, gently pick it up and cast again. As soon as he sees the fly or turns on it, begin stripping with six-inch strips. If the fish follows and shows excitement by making little quick nervous actions, then speed up the six-inch strips several times, drop the fly, and pause. Then watch the fish.

In shallow water you may see him tail on the fly. Most of the time the fish will eat the fly if he has aggressively followed it, and if you have allowed it to sink quickly to the bottom.

The pause should be about two seconds. Then do a firm two-foot

BEN ESTES

strip-strike with the stripping hand. If you feel him, set the hook with the butt of the rod. Set it firmly, but not too hard. If he misses the fly do several more fairly quick six-inch strips, drop the fly, pause about two seconds, and again strip-strike. This often causes the bonefish to take the fly aggressively. The strip-strike is used so that the fly will not be taken out of play if there is no hook-up.

If you cannot see the fish well, count off the seconds anyway and start the strip-strike — softer at the beginning, then firmly if you feel him. If not, start stripping again, varying a pattern of three to eight six-inch strips. Pause for two seconds after each series of strips, and allow the fly to drop to the bottom. Then repeat the strip-strike.

This method is often effective in deeper water, in "muds," or in any setting where it is difficult to see fish take the fly.

On non-grassy bottoms with good visibility, start stripping right away. Start slowly at first in order not to scare the fish. When the bonefish chases the fly, briefly pick up the pace, drop the fly, pause for about two seconds, and strip-strike. If you are fishing on sand, start to strip very slowly like a crab or shrimp trying to sneak away. Allow the fly to kick up small puffs of sand or "muds" during the strip.

The reason for the pause is that most of a bonefish's food sources do not try to outrun him, as this would be difficult to do. This is a fact of nature. Bonefish prey try to hide in cover such as sand or grass when they are chased. And bonefish are equipped with a mouth design that allows them to root the prey from their hiding places. There are exceptions, but for the most part bonefish are bottom feeders.

Watching the fish react to the fly and timing the length of the drop are most important. The two-second pause is not absolute, and it depends on how far above the bottom the fly is traveling. But if you wait much longer than two seconds, and the fish does have your fly, he is likely to spit it out. If you do *not* pause about two seconds, you are likely to take the fly away before he can eat it.

Drag Setting and Turning Fish

I use just enough drag to keep the reel from overrunning. On the first run, I let him go unless he is headed for an obstruction. Later I use the rim control and put pressure on, but just enough to get him in before he runs himself out.

If he's getting too much line out, sometimes you have to either go after him or put light palm pressure on him, but I almost never change the drag setting. If you have to, you can turn fish by putting your rod tip low in the direction opposite to where they are going, but most of the time they come around by themselves.

Best Destinations

If you want to catch a lot of fish, go to Mexico and Ascension Bay. These are mostly one- and two-pounders, but you'll catch more fish than you can count. Christmas Island is good but it's so hard to get there. It's a good place for someone to learn, though, and you can catch lots of four- and five-pound fish.

The Mecca is the Florida Keys, but the fish are hard. Most places the bonefish will react to the fly one way or the other — they either take it or they spook from it. But in Islamorada they give you what we call the "sophisticated spook." They know you are there and they see your fly. But they just ignore it and go on eating.

Ben likes Abels and STH reels and Sage nine-foot three- and four-piece travel rods. He builds leaders out of Trilene, Ande, and Climax, and uses Umpqua, Climax, and Orvis ten- and eight-pound tippet material. He rigs the end of his fly line by nail-knotting a one- to two-foot butt extension of forty-pound Climax or fifty-pound J-line and attaches leaders with a loop-to-loop connection.

CRAIG MATHEWS

Expert Montana fly fisherman, fly tier, and owner of West Yellowstone-based Blue Ribbon Flies, Craig applies his clear-headed trout hunter approach to the big shallow-flats bonefish in Belize. He has come up with some innovative new approaches.

Aiming the Fly in Different Water Conditions

I try almost always to lead big cruising fish by at least six feet and sometimes by as much as twelve feet. Belize flats are thin — sometimes you see the fish's eyes literally bulge out of the water. Getting to the bottom takes no time at all. But in water that skinny the fish spook real easy. I find even with the smallest flies I throw, I have to drop them that far from the fish. Once in a while, if the big singles and doubles aren't around, we'll throw at the school fish tailing in the reefs. You can drop a fly right on top of them.

Fly Presentation Strategy

In shallow, six-inch to ten-inch water, I like to lead the fish by six to twelve feet. I start with a single, slow six-inch strip, then two slow six-inch strips, followed by a twelve-inch strip — or sometimes no strip at all. I cast beyond and to the far side of fish so it is looking away from me when it sees the fly. When the fish approaches the fly I try to watch both the fish and my fly line, then use a strip-strike to set the hook.

Fly Color for Different Conditions

Bonefish eat crabs, mollusks, marine worms, shrimp, sea-lice, squid, and sea urchins. In bright sun, on coral bottom, and in shallow water, I use subtle natural colors like tan, olive, and gold. But brighter colors like pink, white, and chartreuse work better on cloudy days, in deep muds, and during spring tides and high-pressure weather systems.

CRAIG MATHEWS

Drag, and Playing Fish Around Hazards

I set my drag at minimum — very light — and never palm the reel or alter the drag during runs. For turning large fish, I take *all* pressure off them and they seem to begin to circle or return to the spot where they were hooked. The more pressure you put on them, the more line they try to rip off and then they use the coral to defeat you. If I hook a fish around coral, conch, or any obstruction, I back off completely on the drag until the fish stops. Then I walk to the hang-up, free the line, and hit him again.

Casting to Spooked Fish

I have had good luck with one technique I use on fish that are halfway spooked and cruising fast. I'll throw a pink Bitters or an orange Bitters — something with a lot of color. Or I'll try a Sea Lice, because I think they kick up a lot of sea lice when they're moving like that. I'll just peg it right in amongst them and give it a couple of short sharp jerks and I've had fish just swing out and nail it. Just pound it out to them and let it slap the water. When they're running scared like that, it takes a lot to get them to stop.

Pops (guide Winston "Pops" Cabral) taught me that one. He said, "Try it," and I said to myself, "Oh, sure." Then it worked the first time I tried it. Only thing is, when they pick it up in a hurry like that, they turn and run with it so fast, it's easy to break them off. But that technique probably stops fish two or three times out of every ten you try it. And these are fish you would never get otherwise.

Craig uses a four-piece nine-foot Sage RPL-X 8-weight rod and a two-piece Orvis nine-foot HLS 8-weight. He has two Abel reels and uses Mastery floating bonefish taper lines with Orvis leaders that he lengthens at the tippet end to twelve to sixteen feet. For knots, he uses nail, double surgeon's, and improved clinch or Duncan loops.

JOE CLEARE

Joe has guided anglers in the Bahamian out-islands for over forty years. He was for many years both guide and fishing partner of the late author Stanley Babson. He guides exclusively for bonefish, and can almost always find fish for anglers. Joe works the flats nearly year-round. He has probably spent more hours in pursuit of *Albula vulpes* than any man alive.

Seeing Fish in Different Conditions

Fishermen who haven't bonefished much think the fish look the same all the time. But bonefish have as many as thirty to forty different looks depending on the color of the bottom and the brightness of the sun. Fish on grass can be so gray-green you can hardly see them. On white sand, sometimes they turn pure white—the only part you can see is their eye. Other times you see only their shadows.

You have to look for all these different disguises, not just one. And once you see a fish, you must never look away—because just when you do, they will change. And when you look back to see them again, you won't be able to find them.

Finding Bonefish

Many fishermen think the best time to find fish is on the early rising tide. Rising tides are good. But you can find fish on any tide.

JOE CLEARE

Bonefish feed all the time. You just have to figure out which flats they like — which ones have the right amount of food and water — and then go look for them. It's not hard. You let them tell you where they are by their signs. You look for signs of fresh feeding. Once you find where fish have been digging, you know the fish are near. Look for the muds. You'll find the fish.

Also, sometimes the fish will come in fresh on the tide. But many times they come in even when the tide is falling. Some flats have deep holes and the fish feel safer there than if they were off the flats. They can eat there too. Also some fish, especially big fish, will feed right through the tides. They wait inside and outside cuts, where the current brings them food without them having to work too hard. You should always look closely around cuts.

Keeping Fish from Breaking Off

The harder you pull, the harder a bonefish will pull back. If you get a fish that runs into mangroves or around bottom coral and tangles your fly line all around, just take all the drag off. Walk toward the fish and untangle the line as you wind it onto the reel. If the fish goes in the mangroves, you can usually lead him back out if you don't pull too hard or fast. Once you have the line clear, he may run again. But then you can play him normally again.

Shiny Flies

Some flies that have a lot of shine are very good early or late in the day. But when the sun is bright and the water is clear, shiny flies are so bright sometimes, they don't look right to the fish. The fish may not spook — it's not like when you snag or make too much noise. They just turn away and ignore it. When this happens with a shiny fly that has been working, try a fly with the same size and color but without any shine in it. Many times the bonefish will start to take the fly again.

Spawning Fish

When bonefish get ready to spawn, they get together in these big swarms on top of the water. They become very aggressive and you can fish right in close to them. They will even take surface flies sometimes and you can just cast over and over again right into these huge schools of rolling fish.

BOB NAUHEIM

Creator of the Crazy Charlie fly pattern and owner of Fishing International, a California-based fishing travel business, Bob has fly-fished for over forty-five years. He took the first organized group of anglers into Christmas Island when it was opening up in 1983, and he has probably fished every known bonefishing destination in the world. He is always exploring new areas, like the Republic of Tonga in the South Pacific.

Habitats and How to Fish Them

Mangrove flats, like grass flats, are full of feed and hold bonefish well. They are often soft and must be waded carefully around the periphery or fished from a boat. Bonefish will follow the shallow channels in the mangroves, spreading out to tail and feed among the stick-ups. Fishing mangrove flats is not easy. An angler must be

BOB NAUHEIM

a good caster, able to measure the wind, to fish them well. Otherwise he will have his cast line wrapped around a mangrove or two and his presentation wrecked.

Once the bonefish is hooked, hold the rod high and try to keep him clear of the stick-ups. Most bonefish hooked among the mangroves don't make it to the boat. Heavier tippets will improve numbers of landed fish.

Bonefish often use the channels through the mangroves to enter and exit certain flats. Once you learn these spots they are wonderful places to stake out at the beginning of the incoming tide, or as the tide is dropping out. There are times this can be like a turkey shoot.

Grass flats are excellent bonefish habitat. Even if you spook the school off the grass with a hooked fish, they'll often come right back. Under these circumstances an angler can station himself in position to intercept fish and have marvelous fishing without moving but a few paces. Check out grass patches thoroughly. Watch the perimeter for fish moving on or off the grass. Eyed flies such as the Crazy Charlie are less effective here. I tie my Charlies blind (without the bead-chain eyes) when fishing over grass or heavy coral. Without the eyes the fly sinks more slowly and can more easily be controlled and kept from hanging up.

Line Treatment

Fly lines pick up grime during the day from the bottom of the boat and from the water. Also the line picks up twists from roll casting and just casting in the wind. If your fly line doesn't lie flat on the floor of the boat, it is only because it has twists in it, and a line that doesn't lie flat is a disaster waiting to happen. To eliminate this and clean your line at the same time, remove the fly at the end of the fishing day and troll the fly line behind the boat for a minute or two. While the line is out, I then clip a silicon line cleaner onto the line above the tip top and then reel the line back in. The line is cleaned and straightened in one fell swoop.

Casting Accurately in Crosswinds

When casting crosswind, always gauge the speed of the wind and how it will affect you. Rifle shooters call this "windage." If you cast directly toward the fish you have spotted, the crosswind will carry the line away from them. It is best to first lay out a cast well short of the fish to see how the wind carries it. This one short cast will instantly give you the angle you'll want to use to point successive casts to cover the fish.

Aiming the Fly at Schooling and Mudding Fish

Unless it is very high light and I can see all the fish in the school, I am very cautious with the cast when approaching a school of tailing bonefish. I make my first throw much shorter than the clearly visible tailers. If there is no take, the next cast is extended farther. That's because there are invariably fish in the school closer to me that are not tailing, and a long cast to the visible tailing fish over those unseen fish will spook the entire school. I spooked a great many schools to learn this lesson!

When fishing shallow muds, examine them carefully before casting. If the fish are all in the mud you have no choice but to cast blindly into it. But if you see fish on the edge of the mud, work to the visible fish. Remember that bonefish usually feed across the current, so if you can't see fish, they will be on either end of the top edge of the mud and not the down-tide edge. Mudding bones are pretty eager takers.

Reading Water

All fish displace water as they swim. This displacement can be more easily observed in the shallow waters of the flats. There are two types of displacements: "nervous water" and "pushes." Nervous water appears as a slightly agitated chop in the surface film that is different from the water surrounding it. It usually indicates a school of happy fish moving and feeding slowly across the tide. Pushes look like wind-spears on the water surface, only fatter. You'll get a good idea of what a push looks like the first time you spook a school of bonefish. Pushes indicate fish that are moving from one place to another; these fish can be happy as well.

Planning a Trip with Tides in Your Favor

Remember, you want as many incoming tides and top of the tides as you can get. Let's say your first day of fishing is on Sunday. Ideally you should have a low tide that day at around 4:00 A.M. For ease in illustrating this example, let's assume that all tides are of seven hours duration and advance them an hour each day. This means that the high tide will be at 11:00 A.M. during your first day of fishing. Get out early and fish over the top of the tide. Now follow me:

Monday's tides: low 5:00 A.M. to high 12:00 noon
Tuesday's tides: low 6:00 A.M. to high 1:00 P.M.
Wednesday's tides: low 7:00 A.M. to high 2:00 P.M.
Thursday's tides: low 8:00 A.M. to high 3:00 P.M.
Friday's tides: low 9:00 A.M. to high 4:00 P.M.
Saturday's tides: low 10:00 P.M. to high 5:00 P.M.

You've just completed a perfect week with the tide right every day during the high sun period! There is more variation than this simple chart indicates, but you get the drift. Not all areas have tide charts available, unfortunately, but use them whenever you can to plan a trip.

Bob prefers reels with right-hand wind and direct-drive. He owns a Mark II Seamaster and a couple of direct-drive Fin-Nors. He also often uses a wide-spool, rim-controlled, disc-drag model 71SS Martin his company keeps as a loaner. For rods, Bob prefers nine-foot 8-weight graphite, and likes Sage,

Orvis HLS, Scott, and Powell. For lines, Bob uses weight-forward floating designs and finds Scientific Anglers best. He says the line's irregular surface creates less friction through the guides, allowing it to be shot easily, although it is a bit noisier than some other models.

JACK GARTSIDE

Former Boston school teacher and cab driver Jack Gartside is today one of the most innovative fly tiers in the sport. He has also developed a lifestyle that combines Montana trout with Florida and Mexican bonefish into a mix envied by anglers everywhere. Jack does most of his solo bonefishing by wading. He is not afraid to try new methods, explore fly designs, and to fish at unorthodox times.

Water Temperatures to Fish

I look at water temperature from the point of view of what the bonefish eats—what is comfortable for the food that they are feeding on. When the water is fairly hot, crabs are not all that active. Neither are shrimp. They burrow down into the mud and are scarce.

Small creatures are much more susceptible to temperature changes than the bigger predatory fish. So when it's cold, the food tends to disappear. If the foods that the fish eat were active at higher and lower temperatures, then the bonefish would be very active in the higher or lower ranges, too. But when the prey disappears, the fish disappear. Everything depends on the food, I think. The fish are out there for only one reason, the food. They are not there to play tennis.

Presentation and Water Depth

Presentation depends on water depth. If the water is very thin, then I'll be a bit more delicate. But if it's deeper, I tend to be more aggressive—very aggressive—in my casting. In fact, I sometimes slap that fly down with cruising fish. I try to lead it, but I make a commotion to get its attention. The deeper the water, the more aggressive I would be and the more likely I would be to create a "sound sensation," let's say.

If fish are coming toward me and I have a lot of time, I might

JACK GARTSIDE

just cast it out ahead and let it sink to the bottom. Then, as the fish start to move up on it, I'll move it.

But if they are moving away, I'm right on their noses. Don't give them a chance to think about it. Try to get them to make just a quick reaction. Or try to get the lead fish to do it, anyway.

They are much more secure as they get farther away from the surface of the water. In deeper water I tend to give the fly lots of action; in shallower water I tend to be a little less active. In deeper water you cannot move a fly fast enough for a bonefish.

Fishing in Deep Water

I also do a lot of so-called "blind fishing." I find that long, quick hauls with significant pauses are the best way to get their interest. I've caught as many bonefish this way — just under the surface with a five-inch-long white bucktail fly — as probably any other way. I can't see them because I'm fishing water that's too deep. But I am fishing where I know they hold. And they do hold a lot in places. Bonefish are not always on the move. They have definite lies — places they go where the tide will bring food to them. They can be very lazy and opportunistic. They can't be on the move all the time.

I'll fish these places just as I would a trout stream, picking them for certain qualities. In places where the water is two to three feet deep, they will come right up from the bottom and grab it. I love it. I started fishing this way for barracuda, but I was getting more bonefish than barracuda. They just "wang" it—it's an exciting way to fish. It's not for everybody because you're not seeing anything until it happens. And that's not why a lot of people go bonefishing. But sometimes when other fishing is slow, I'll use this blind method. I like to catch fish, and there's nothing wrong with being surprised.

Bonefish Feeding Habits and Ambushing

Bonefish are opportunistic feeders. They eat eels, shrimp, crabs, worms, isopods, and urchins. They'll feed on a falling tide until it is almost too late to get out of shoreline holes and tidepools. If you want to know where to look for them, go to a flat at low tide. Look for signs of their food like crab holes, shrimp holes, and sponges where many of the small creatures like isopods live. Then get a ladder or a lawn chair and camp out by the food so you can ambush them as they come in to feed. Some of the best times to fish are low light, either early or late in the day. Many anglers never see this because they only fish with guides during the normal work day.

CHARLIE NEYMOUR

Now head guide at Cargill Creek Lodge in Andros, Charlie cut his teeth guiding at age nine under Andros' other "Charlie" (Smith), for whom the Crazy Charlie was named. He fishes the flats in the Florida Keys now and then to keep himself tuned and up-to-date on new techniques.

Pulling Big Bonefish from Mixed Schools

Big bonefish sometimes hang around schools of smaller fish and use them like body guards. The small fish run and grab anything new that comes along and test it for the bigger fish. If they spook, the whole school spooks. This happens often in Andros and we have a technique for it. First you cast to the mixed school and let the small fish come to your fly. Then you retrieve the fly slowly enough to interest the small fish, but fast enough so they can't catch it. You

CHARLIE NEYMOUR

use it to draw them away from the large fish. Then you recast to the large fish and just twitch the fly.

Fishing Mangroves

Bonefish feed wildly in mangroves on high tides. You can hear them popping the snails and crabs off the mangrove roots and splashing their tails as they feed and move from one mangrove bush to the next. You can use this to intercept the fish on the right tides. The best time to get them is before they go into the mangroves, when they are still hungry. Station yourself in front of the mangrove stands facing the deep-water channels about halfway through a rising tide, and you will see plenty of taking fish coming in. You can also catch them coming out of the mangroves on a falling tide, although they are generally full of food and harder to take.

Flies for Andros' Big Deep-Water Bonefish

Flies like the Clouser Deep Minnow, with heavy eyes, are important not only to get the fly down fast, but also because they bounce on the bottom and kick up puffs of mud like shrimp do. This gets them noticed by the fish better.

Barbless Hooks

No one should ever fish for bonefish with barbed hooks. We crimp down the barbs here all the time and hardly ever lose fish. We also probably hook more because the hook penetrates more easily. But even if it didn't, the fish are too important to take the chance of injuring them by too much handling removing barbed hooks.

JIM O'NEILL

A former Pacific Northwest mountaineering guide, Jim O'Neill is a professor of history at Wyoming's Casper College. An angler for thirty years, he fishes one hundred or more days a year for nearly all species of salmonids, as well as bonefish. His bonefishing has taken him to Andros, Los Roques, Belize, Exuma, and Islamorada.

Striking Strategies

I always use a strip-strike, once I feel resistance from the fish, followed immediately by raising the rod tip. For trout fishermen there is a natural tendency to strike bonefish with the rod tip, especially if you can see the fish take the fly. I have found that this often results in a premature strike that rips the fly out of the fish's mouth. I think the strike should be slow and deliberate. Bonefish, unlike the salmonids, will not usually spit out the fly immediately if they feel something hard, largely due, I am sure, to their regular diet.

Bonefish Runs

Anything's possible. To give one example, in Belize I hooked a large fish in the middle of a big flat, and it promptly ran out about 150 yards of backing—with me gradually tightening the drag all along. At that point, there was major commotion in the water, a radical change in direction, and the fish promptly ran off another one hundred yards of backing. I had 275 yards of backing on my reel

JIM O'NEILL

and could see the spool. I did ultimately land the fish, which measured twenty-nine inches on the tape, only to find that a small bite had been taken out just behind the anal fin. Apparently a barracuda had gone after him, and he was still able to evade that predator, even with the drag! One of the main reasons I continue to fish for bonefish is simply because their runs are more spectacular than anything I have ever caught on a fly rod.

Casting and Aiming Strategies

This clearly depends on the speed and behavior of the fish and the type of bottom encountered. Tailing and mudding fish require very close casts, almost hitting them with the fly. Cruising fish have to be led enough so that they don't spook, but not so far that they miss the fly. This can be quite a bit in front on light-colored flats, closer on grass. Fly patterns obviously play a role, too. Ideally, for cruising fish, I want my cast to be far enough in front to give the fly time to settle to the fish's level and positioned so that one or two quick, short strips bring it across his nose.

Hooks

Hooks should be kept extremely sharp. The angler has to be vigilant, especially when fishing coral flats, and a file is my most frequently used tool, over snips and forceps.

I think barbless hooks and pinched barbs give a better and more penetrating strike. They also make releasing fish easier. But given the structure of a bonefish's mouth and their regular diet, I am not convinced that a barbed hook does serious damage.

Controlling Runs

I normally set the drag at medium to light-heavy tension, and frequently increase it gradually during a run. I like to be able to palm an exposed spool as well for added control. Big fish can (sometimes) be turned by "leading" them with the rod tip and a very tight line. If that doesn't work, and it often doesn't, hope for the best — hope there's no coral or mangroves in the direction the fish is heading.

For rods, Jim's favorite is a nine-foot Orvis boron graphite Shooting Star for a 9-weight line. He also likes the Sage RPL-X line. He has used mostly direct-drive reels but now uses a Billy Pate anti-reverse model. For lines he likes the older Scientific Anglers Ultra II bonefish tapers best and he ties his own nine- to twelve-foot leaders out of Mason, with tippets of Maxima for smaller flies.

CAPT. JEFFREY CARDENAS

Key West tarpon, bonefish, and permit guide Jeffrey Cardenas is owner of the Saltwater Angler and was *Fly Rod & Reel's* 1989 Guide of the Year. He is highly respected by both clients and colleagues for his excellence in boatsmanship, fish-finding ability, and angling expertise. He is also a conscientious environmentalist, active in protecting the fish and habitats of the saltwater flats. Jeffrey has long been guide and friend to John Cole in his quests for tarpon.

Getting the Fly to the Fish

Lower Keys fish are very well fed in their natural habitat. They are not going to spend much time searching for a hidden fly or waiting for flies to get to them. When I cast a fly I want it to go to his dinner table right now. It is critical to sink bonefish flies to the proper depth. A selection of different weights of eyes allows the versatility of fishing tailing bones in as shallow as eight inches or to cruising bones four feet deep.

CAPTAIN JEFFREY CARDENAS

For tailing fish, I try to put the fly right on their head. Bonefish flies are stripped with very little action. Just a twitch and watch the fish. Get his attention and let it sit. When he takes the fly, strip-strike, gently raise the rod, and lean into it.

Flies That Work

Like bonefish everywhere, matching the hatch exactly is not critical. Some of the most beautifully tied shrimp flies don't catch fish. Bonefish want something that looks like it is alive, something that is not going to attack them, and something that is presented at the proper depth in their eating zone. No other material — with the exception of marabou — has the life of rabbit fur under water. Bonefish like to eat a fly right after the drop when it is on the bottom. When the rabbit undulates as it sits on the bottom, it's like ringing a dinner bell for the bones.

Hooks

I like #4 Partridge Sea Prince stainless hooks. There is no reason why carbon steel should ever be used in the construction of bonefish or permit flies because very few flies are ever left in the fish. I like the Partridge hooks for their strength and the downward point on the O' Shaughnessy bend. That point finds a place to catch in the fish's mouth. Stainless bead eyes and a stainless hook insure that the fly won't be corroded before you ever get the chance to use it.

Jeffrey says he likes direct-drive reels with cork disc drags and nine-foot 6- to 12-weight rods, depending on the size of fish. He feels travel rods are improving but still don't cast as smoothly as two-piece rods do. He likes Mastery floating lines in light colors, and finds that dark lines disappear in the air but are visible in the water. He does not use sinking-tip or intermediates for bonefish. For leaders he likes Mason hard nylon with Maxima clear tippets, nine to sixteen feet long.

LEFTY KREH

The grand master of saltwater fly fishing, Lefty has fished for bonefish everywhere they are found and considers them his favorite game fish. Lefty has also helped more anglers pursue saltwater species through his articles, books, personal appearances, and videos than any other angler since Joe Brooks.

Casting in the Wind

There are several problems when you try to deliver a fly to a bonefish with the wind blowing toward you.

One is that you have to get the fly line and leader to turn over properly. If you are wading you will generally be casting at short ranges, since visibility on windy days will only let you see fish at close range. Even if you are in a boat, if you are casting no more than twenty feet of line (plus the leader), you should use a line one size heavier than the rod calls for. When using the properly matched line and only twenty feet or less outside the guides, it is very difficult to get the rod to load well enough to develop the line speed to make the cast. The heavier line permits the rod to load faster. Of course, on calm days a heavier line will often spook fish because of the heavy splashdown, and should be avoided.

LEFTY KREH

Secondly, most casts on light, breezy days should be aimed slightly above the water. This results in expending most of the forward energy of the cast, permitting the fly to fall softly to the surface. But if you follow this procedure on windy days, the leader will be blown back as it falls. Casting into the wind is one of the few times you should aim the fly *at* the surface. This allows you to straighten out the leader, but the fly is placed immediately in the water as soon as it is straight and the fly doesn't blow back.

Splashdown and Wind

On windy days you can drop a fly with a little more splash than on calm ones without frightening a wily bonefish. On windy days I favor flies like the Crazy Charlie or Clouser Deep Minnow, which are armed with either bead-chain or lead eyes. If the angler develops good line speed, these weighted flies will turn over very well into the teeth of a stiff breeze. Fluffy flies, like the Bonefish Special, Snapping Shrimp, etc., offer resistance to the wind and frequently are blown back toward the angler.

Choosing Flies to Match Backgrounds

One of the fundamental techniques when you are seeking *bottom-feeding* fish is that most of the time you should use flies that match the color of the background. If you are after bonefish in the Bahamas, for example, where the flats are almost always very light in color, cream, white, yellow, and pale tan flies should be a first choice. If you fish the Florida Keys and are working over olive-colored turtle-grass flats, then a darker fly would be recommended.

However, if I try several light flies over a light bottom, and feel the presentations were good, and get only refusals, I switch to a darker fly.

The only exception I can think of to this basic rule is at Christmas Island. These are very white flats — and *most* of the time a light-colored fly is best. But there is a black crab with a red claw that over the eons has managed to survive on those flats — most exceptional in nature. There are times when a small black chenille body and a little wing of red calftail dressed on a 6 or 4 hook will be the most effective fly at Christmas Island.

Bibliography

FISHING

BABSON, STANLEY M. *Bonefishing*. New York: Winchester Press, 1965.

BROOKS, JOSEPH W. *Salt Water Fly Fishing*. New York: G.P. Putnam's Sons, 1950.

——*Salt Water Game Fishing*. New York: Harper & Row, 1968.

HEILNER, VAN CAMPEN. *Salt Water Fishing*. Philadelphia: Penn Publishing Company, 1937.

INTERNATIONAL GAME FISH ASSOCIATION. *World Record Game Fishes*. Pompano Beach, Florida: IGFA, 1992.

KAUFMANN, RANDALL. *Bonefishing with a Fly*. Portland, Ore.: Western Fisherman's Press, 1992.

KREH, BERNARD "LEFTY." *Fly Fishing in Salt Water*. New York: Lyons & Burford, Publishers, 1984.

——*Salt Water Fly Patterns*. Fullerton, Calif.: MARAL, n.d.

LEISER, ERIC. *The Book of Fly Patterns*. New York: Alfred A. Knopf, 1987.

MCCLANE, A.J. (Editor). *New Standard Fishing Encyclopedia*. New York: Henry Holt and Company, 1965.

REIGER, GEORGE. *Profiles in Saltwater Angling*. New York: Prentice-Hall, 1973.

SAMSON, JACK. *Saltwater Fly Fishing*. Harrisburg, Penn.: Stackpole, 1991.

SAND, GEORGE. *Salt-Water Fly Fishing*. New York: Alfred A. Knopf, 1970.

SCHULLERY, PAUL. *American Fly Fishing: A History*. New York: Lyons & Burford, Publishers, 1987.

SOSIN, MARK, and LEFTY KREH. *Fishing the Flats*. New York: Lyons & Burford, Publishers, 1983.

——*Practical Fishing Knots II*. New York: Lyons & Burford, Publishers, 1991.

STEWART, DICK, and FARROW ALLEN. *Flies for Saltwater*. North Conway, NH: Mountain Pond Publishing, 1992; distributed by Lyons & Burford.

UNDERWOOD, JOHN, and TED WILLIAMS. *Fishing "The Big Three."* New York: Simon & Schuster, 1982.

WATERMAN, CHARLES F. *Modern Fresh & Salt Water Fly Fishing*. New York: Winchester, 1972.

WENTINK, FRANK. *Saltwater Fly Tying*. New York: Lyons & Burford, Publishers, 1991.

BONEFISH

ALEXANDER, ELIZABETH CORWIN. "A Contribution to the Life History, Biology, and Geographical Distribution of the Bonefish, *Albula vulpes* (Linnaeus)." Master's Thesis, University of Miami, Coral Gables, 1958, 1–137.

BIGELOW, HENRY B., et al. *Fishes of the Western North Atlantic*. New Haven: Yale University Press, 1963.

BOHLKE, JAMES E., and CHARLES C. G. CHAPLIN. *Fishes of the Bahamas and Adjacent Tropical Waters*. Wynnewood, Penn.: Livingston Publishing Company, 1968.

BRUGER, GERARD E. "Age, Growth, Food Habits, and Reproduction of Bonefish, *Albula vulpes*, in South Florida Waters." *Florida Marine Research Publications* no. 3 (1974): 1–20.

COLTON, DOUGLAS E., "Patterns of Reproductive Maturation in the Bonefish (*Albula vulpes*) in Bahamian Waters." Photocopy of original from author. (n.d.), 1–9.

COLTON, DOUGLAS E., and WILLIAM S. ALEVIZON. "Feeding Ecology of Bonefish in Bahamian Waters." *Transactions of the American Fisheries Society* 112 (1983): 178–184.

COLTON, DOUGLAS E., and WILLIAM S. ALEVIZON. "Movement Patterns of Bonefish, *Albula vulpes*, in Bahamian Waters." *Fishery Bulletin* 81, no. 1 (1983): 148–154.

ELDRED, BONNIE. "Larval Bonefish, *Albula vulpes* (Linnaeus, 1758), (Albulidae) in Florida and Adjacent Waters." *Florida Board of Conservation Marine Laboratory Leaflet Series* 4, pt. 1 (Pisces), no. 3 (1967): 1–4.

ERDMAN, DONALD S. "Bonefish, *Albula vulpes* (Linnaeus), from Puerto Rico and the Virgin Islands: Habitat, Food, Spawning Season, and Leptocephali." Photocopy from author, 1975, 1–13.

— "Notes on the Biology of the Bonefish and its Sports Fishery in Puerto Rico." Paper presented at the Fifth International Game Fish Conference, 1960, 1–11.

FISH, MARIE POLAND, and WILLIAM H. MOWBRAY. *Sounds of Western North Atlantic Fishes*. Baltimore: The Johns Hopkins University Press, 1970.

FITCH, JOHN E. "Life History Notes and the Early Development of the Bonefish *Albula vulpes* (Linnaeus)." *California Fish and Game* 36, no. 1 (1950): 3–6.

FOREY, PETER L. "A Revision of the Elopiform Fishes, Fossil and Recent." *Bulletin of the British Museum (Natural History) Geology* Supplement 10 (1973): 1–222.

GREENWOOD, PETER HUMPHREY. "Notes on the Anatomy and Classification of Elopomorph Fishes." *Bulletin of the British Museum of Natural History (Zoology)* 32, no. 4 (1977): 65–102.

HOAR, W.S., and D.J. RANDALL. *Fish Physiology*. New York: Academic Press, 1971.

JOHANNES, R. E. *Words of the Lagoon, Fishing and Marine Lore in the Palau District of Micronesia.* Berkeley: University of California Press, 1981.

JONES, PHILIP W., et al. "Development of Fishes of the Mid-Atlantic Bight." *Fish and Wildlife Service FWS/OBS-78/12* 1 (1978): 66–72.

LAGLER, KARL F., et al. *Ichthyology.* New York: John Wiley, 1977.

McEWAN, MARY RUTH. "Comparison of the Retina of the Mormyrids with That of Various Other Teleosts." *Acta Zoologica* 19 (1938): 427–465.

MOYLE, PETER B., and JOSEPH J. CECH. *Fishes: An Introduction to Ichthyology.* Englewood Cliffs, New Jersey: Prentice-Hall, 1982.

NICOL, J.A.C. *The Eyes of Fishes.* Oxford: Clarendon Press, 1989.

SHAKLEE, JAMES B., and CLYDE S. TAMARU. "Biochemical and Morphological Evolution of Hawaiian Bonefishes (*Albula*)." Systematic Zoology 30, no. 2 (1981): 125–146.

TAMURA, TAMOTSU, and WARREN J. WISBY. "The Visual Sense of Pelagic Fishes, Especially the Visual Axis and Accommodation." *Bulletin of Marine Science of the Gulf and Caribbean* 13, no. 3 (1963): 433–448.

TAVOLGA, WILLIAM N. "Sensory Parameters in Comunicating Among Coral Reef Fishes." *Mt. Sinai Journal of Medicine* 41 (1974): 324–340.

—*Sound Reception in Fishes.* Stroudsburg, Penn.: Dowden, Hutchinson & Ross, 1976.

WEBB, PAUL W., and DANIEL WEIHS. "Optimization of Locomotion." In *Fish Biomechanics*, edited by Paul W. Webb. New York: Praeger Publishers, 1983.

WHITEHEAD, P.J.P. The Synonymy of *Albula vulpes* (Linnaeus, 1758)." Cybium 10, no. 3 (1986): 211–230.

BONEFISH PREY

BARNES, ROBERT D. *Invertebrate Zoology.* New York: Holt, Rinehart and Winston, 1980.

BROOK, IVER M. "Comparative Macrofaunal Abundance in Turtlegrass (*Thalassia testudinum*) Communities in South Florida Characterized by High Blade Density." *Bulletin of Marine Science* 28, no. 1 (1978): 212–217.

CALDWELL, ROYL., and HUGH DINGLE. "Stomatopods." *Scientific American*, January 1976, 81–89.

ENGSTROM, N. A. "Depth Limitation of a Tropical Intertidal Crab, *Cataleptodius floridanus*: Role of Predation by Bonefish." *American Zoologist* 22, no. 4 (1982): 376.

FARFANTE, ISABEL PEREZ. "Western Atlantic Shrimps of the *Genus Penaeus*." *Fishery Bulletin* 67, no. 3 (1969): 499–590.

FAUCHALD, KRISTIAN. *The Polychaete Worms: Definitions and Keys to the Orders, Families and Genera.* Los Angeles: Natural History Museum of Los Angeles County, 1977.

GOSNER, KENNETH L. *A Field Guide to the Atlantic Seashore.* The Peterson Field Guide Series. Boston: Houghton Mifflin Company, 1979.

KAPLAN, EUGENE H. *A Field Guide to Southeastern and Caribbean Seashores.* The Peterson Field Guide Series. Boston: Houghton Mifflin Company, 1988.

MANNING, RAYMOND B. *Stomatopod Crustacea of the West Atlantic*. Coral Gables: University of Miami Press, 1969.

MCCLANE, A. J. "What the Bonefish Eats." *Fishing World*, March/April 1981, 60–71.

MCNULTY, J. KNEELAND et al. "Some Relationships Between the Infauna of the Level Bottom and the Sediment in South Florida." *Bulletin of Marine Science of the Gulf and Caribbean* 12, no. 3 (1962): 322–332.

MEINKOTH, NORMAN A. *The Audubon Society Field Guide to North American Seashore Creatures*. New York: Alfred A. Knopf, 1981.

MINER, ROY WALDO. *Field Book of Seashore Life*. New York: G.P. Putnam's Sons, 1950.

MORRIS, PERCY A. *A Field Guide to Shells of the Atlantic and Gulf Coasts and the West Indies*. The Peterson Field Guide Series. Boston: Houghton Mifflin Company, 1975.

O'GOWER, A. K., and J. W. WACASEY. "Animal Communities Associated with *Thalassia diplantheria*, and Sand Beds in Biscayne Bay." *Bulletin of Marine Science* 17, no. 1 (1967): 175–210.

PURCHON, R.D. *The Biology of the Mollusca*. Oxford: Pergamon Press, 1968.

RUPPERT, EDWARD, and RICHARD FOX. *Seashore Animals of the Southeast*. Columbia: University of South Carolina Press, 1988.

SALOMAN, CARL. H., et al. "Distribution of Three Species of Shrimp (Genus *Penaeus*) in Waters Contiguous to Southern Florida." *Bulletin of Marine Science* 18, no. 2 (1968): 343–350.

TABB, DURBIN, and RAYMOND B. MANNING. "A Checklist of the Flora and Fauna of Northern Florida Bay and Adjacent Brackish Waters of the Florida Mainland." *Bulletin of Marine Science of the Gulf and Caribbean* 11, no. 4 (1961): 552–664.

VOSS, GILBERT L. *Seashore Life of Florida and the Caribbean*. Miami: Banyan Books, 1976.

WARMKE, GERMAINE L. *Caribbean Seashells: A Guide to the Mollusks of Puerto Rico and other West Indian Islands, Bermuda and the Lower Florida Keys*. Narberth, Penn.: Livingston Publishing Company, 1961.

WARMKE, GERMAINE L., and DONALD S. ERDMAN. "Records of Marine Mollusks Eaten by Bonefish in Puerto Rican Waters." *The Nautilus* 76, no. 4 (1963): 115–120.

WILLIAMS, AUSTIN B. *Shrimps, Lobsters, and Crabs of the Atlantic Coast of the Eastern United States, Maine to Florida*. Washington, D.C.: Smithsonian Institution Press, 1984.

GENERAL

CARSON, RACHEL. *The Edge of the Sea*. Boston: Houghton Mifflin Company, 1955.

COULOMBE, DEBORAH A. *The Seaside Naturalist: A Guide to Nature Study at the Seashore*. Engelwood, New Jersey: Prentice-Hall, 1984.

MCCLANE, A.J., and KEITH GARDNER. *McClane's Game Fish of North America*. New York: Times Books, 1984.

RICCIUTI, EDWARD R. *The Beachwalker's Guide: The Seashore from Maine to Florida*. Garden City, New York: Doubleday & Company, 1982.

ROBINS, C. RICHARD, and G. CARLETON RAY. *A Field Guide to Atlantic Coast Fishes of North America.* The Peterson Field Guide Series. Boston: Houghton Mifflin Company, 1986.

U.S. DEPARTMENT OF COMMERCE. NATIONAL OCEANIC AND ATMOSPHERIC ADMINISTRATION. *Monthly Climatic Data for the World*, Washington, D. C. 44 nos. 1–12 (January–December 1991).

U.S. DEPARTMENT OF COMMERCE. NATIONAL OCEANIC AND ATMOSPHERIC ADMINISTRATION. *Tide Tables 1992: Central and Western Pacific Ocean and Indian Ocean.* Washington, D.C.: Government Printing Office, 1991.

U.S. DEPARTMENT OF COMMERCE. NATIONAL OCEANIC AND ATMOSPHERIC ADMINISTRATION. *Tide Tables 1992: East Coast of North and South America.* Washington, D.C.: Government Printing Office, 1991.

WALKER, ERNEST P., et al. *Mammals of the World.* Baltimore: The Johns Hopkins University Press, 1975.

WEYL, PETER K. *Oceanography: An Introduction to the Marine Environment.* New York: John Wiley & Sons, 1970.

Index

(Entries in boldface denote fly patterns; entries in italics denote species classifications. Genus or family names appear in conventional roman typeface)